Doing Right by Kids

Doing Right by Kids

Leveraging Social Capital and Innovation to Increase Opportunity

Edited by Scott Winship,
Yuval Levin, and Ryan Streeter

AEI PRESS

Publisher for the American Enterprise Institute
WASHINGTON, DC

Library of Congress Cataloging-in-Publication Data

Names: Winship, Scott Robert, editor. | Levin, Yuval, editor. | Streeter, Ryan, 1969- editor.
Title: Doing right by kids : leveraging social capital and innovation to increase opportunity / edited by Scott Winship, Yuval Levin, and Ryan Streeter.
Description: Washington, DC : AEI Press, [2024] | Includes bibliographical references.
Identifiers: LCCN 2024031496 | ISBN 9780844750767 (paperback) | ISBN 9780844750774 (ebook)
Subjects: LCSH: Poor children—Government policy—United States. | Poor children—Services for—United States. | Social mobility—United States.
Classification: LCC HV741 .D635 2024 | DDC 362.70973—dc23/eng/20240801
LC record available at https://lccn.loc.gov/2024031496

AEI PRESS

Publisher for the American Enterprise Institute
for Public Policy Research
1789 Massachusetts Avenue, NW
Washington, DC 20036
www.aei.org

Printed in the United States of America

Contents

Introduction

SCOTT WINSHIP, YUVAL LEVIN, AND RYAN STREETER

L et's start with the good news: Material hardship among American children has fallen dramatically over the past 60 years. The best measure available indicates that in 2022, 13 percent of children were poor, down from 62 percent in 1963.[1] At the end of the 1990s boom, child poverty stood at 19.5 percent, so it has fallen by one-third just since 2001. Even in families headed by a single mother, the likelihood of a child being poor has dropped by 75 percent since 1993.[2]

Unfortunately, declining poverty has not expanded opportunity, to judge by some of the most meaningful ways of measuring it. On the economic side, children of the poorest parents still tend to rank low on the income ladder themselves. Nearly half of children raised by parents in the bottom fifth of family income end up in the bottom fifth themselves as adults.[3] Nor has this tendency toward intergenerational immobility diminished over the years when poverty has fallen. Child poverty fell by 36 percent from 1963 to 1982; however, looking at poor children born in those two years, the likelihood of rising out of the bottom fourth by adulthood rose only modestly among men and fell among women.[4]

Opportunity also has a social component—the ability to surround oneself with supportive and caring family members, neighbors, friends, and institutions. This social aspect of opportunity has fared much worse than the economic dimension. Social capital (the value inhering in our relationships) and associational life (the sum of what we do together) have deteriorated over the past 50 years.[5] Marriage has declined, divorce has become more common, and single parenthood has risen. Men have become more disconnected from the world of work. Crime and incarceration have increased. Churchgoing and group membership have become rarer. Trust and happiness have diminished. These declines have been widespread but more pronounced among those lower down the socio-economic ladder.[6]

The decline in poverty has a number of sources. Economic growth played the biggest role. Increased educational attainment raised skill levels, productivity, and earnings. Lower taxes increased disposable income, as did the expansion of the safety net.

But that ever-growing safety net, while reducing immediate hardship, has also encouraged behaviors that lower income in the longer term, reduce intergenerational mobility, and weaken family and associational life. Perverse incentives embodied in many safety-net programs discourage work, marriage, saving, human capital investment, and deferred gratification.[7] That is to say, far from simply failing to increase upward mobility or reverse social capital declines, welfare policy actually has contributed to the deterioration of opportunity.

Welfare reforms and other policy changes over the past three decades have increasingly oriented the safety net toward work, further reducing poverty.[8] The reforms may even have helped arrest the decades-long increase in the nonmarital birth rate.[9]

Yet more and more, the left's answers to the problems of poverty and limited opportunity involve increasing the amount of no-strings-attached money given to poor—and even middle-class—families, whether in the form of a universal basic income, child allowances, free tuition, or student loan forgiveness. Progressives believe that increased federal spending on child investments—such as for public preschool—will by definition translate into greater upward mobility. This assumption ignores the unfortunate fact that the vast majority of federal programs attempting to change individual behavior are unsuccessful.[10] Progressives believe that the federal government is always the source of solutions to problems of limited opportunity, and they disregard the growth-sapping effects that a ballooning federal debt will ultimately have.

Given the left's indifference to unintended consequences, rigorous evaluation, and fiscal responsibility and its inflexible faith in federal policy, conservatives must lead the way in developing a 21st-century opportunity agenda that increases upward mobility and renews associational life. However, since the 2016 election, most of the right's energy has been directed toward a populism that has too little faith in the potential for upward mobility in America and shares too many of the left's presumptions.

What is needed is a conservatism that appreciates the economy's strengths but seeks to help more Americans take advantage of those strengths. Such an agenda would, to be sure, emphasize the importance of economic growth, dynamism, work, family, and individual responsibility. It would call for a reinvigoration of civil society and oppose the backsliding of safety-net policy. It would be clear that the federal government's role in expanding opportunity must be limited.

But an effective opportunity agenda also would require that conservatives take more seriously than we have the problems of entrenched poverty. These problems often highlight long-standing inequalities between African Americans and white Americans.

For example, 12 percent of children spend at least half their childhood below the official poverty line.[11] But while that is true of just 5.5 percent of white children, 40 percent of black children experience this extent of poverty. Not only are black children much more likely to experience poverty, but they are much less likely to escape it as adults. While 28 percent of white men raised in the bottom fifth of family income end up stuck in the bottom fifth as adults, 50 percent of black men raised poor remain so.[12] Among white and black women, those rates of immobility are 33 percent and 62 percent. Entrenched poverty also has a geographic component. Across childhood, 6 percent of white children experience an average neighborhood poverty rate of 20 percent or higher. That is true of 66 percent of black children.[13]

In addition to a greater focus on intergenerational mobility and neighborhoods, an effective conservative opportunity agenda would require more attention to early childhood inequalities. Children from disadvantaged backgrounds begin kindergarten far behind socioeconomically advantaged kids in math and reading skills and school readiness generally. By the time they graduate, those gaps have shrunk, but they remain vast.[14]

These early childhood gaps will not be narrowed without greater prioritization from conservatives. Unlike their liberal counterparts, conservatives rightly start from the hardheaded position that most of what the federal government has tried in this area has failed. In part, that is because it is so difficult to overcome the disadvantages of family disruption and dysfunction. But an effective opportunity agenda must be softhearted as well, seeking to find successful, scalable models that rely on local administration with a federal role in funding experimentation and disseminating knowledge about what does and does not work.

The present volume is an initial attempt to fill in the details of what a modern conservative opportunity agenda should look like. It focuses on children, particularly poor children. Sharing a distinctive emphasis on policy innovation and the importance of social capital, the seven contributions in these pages by leading policy analysts model a way of approaching the problem of limited upward mobility.

Their common emphasis on social capital is no coincidence. It is the function of a shared conviction that there is more to opportunity than money. Social networks—composed of family, friends, neighbors, teachers, and others with whom children interact—can expand or constrict opportunities in dozens of ways, including by influencing children's values, providing role models, connecting kids to people with resources (knowledge, money, and personal connections), offering emotional support, and imparting skills and cultural norms. Social capital also inheres in kids' connections to institutions—the more or less recognizable organizations and collections of people interacting in patterned ways to achieve ends together. A family is an institution, as is a neighborhood, a school, a religious congregation, a labor union, a corporation, and a government, to name just a few. The decline of social capital and associational life has worked against expanding opportunity even as child poverty has fallen.

The volume begins with three chapters examining policy related to educational institutions. Education policy is the most direct way government attempts to affect child opportunity. It focuses primarily, though by no means exclusively, on imparting knowledge and academic skills that generally pay off in the labor market in adulthood. Schools also influence what students value and their aspirations, social and emotional skills, civic-mindedness, and cultural capital—that is, their familiarity with cultural referents that can mark them as refined and worldly or unsophisticated and provincial. This volume's contributors address in varying ways these responsibilities of our educational institutions. One chapter each is devoted to early childhood education, primary and secondary education, and higher education.

Following these initial chapters, the volume turns to the central institution of the family, the greatest influence on child opportunity, for better or worse. After a chapter on shoring up family stability, the focus shifts to the safety net—perhaps the most important way government affects parental behavior that can help or hinder child success.

The final chapters are about the importance of neighborhoods for child opportunity. The first considers how to improve opportunity-impeding communities and how to expand access to opportunity-promoting places. The volume closes with a look at one important way neighborhoods affect children: through the presence or absence of community violence.

Innovation is another theme spanning the chapters. It reflects the conservative insight that much of what government currently does produces disappointing results. This calls for approaching the problem of limited opportunity with a degree of epistemological humility; we have limited knowledge of how policy could most effectively increase upward mobility. But we must not stop trying to find policies that work well and can scale up.

The chapters call for experimentation, evaluation, and accountability; putting more choice in the hands of parents and young adults; and offering parents and young adults more choices and information to aid in decision-making. The chapters recognize the importance of policy signals and seek to craft approaches that avoid perverse incentives while nudging parents to make decisions that are likely to improve child opportunity.

We offer a brief overview of the chapters to follow before offering some concluding thoughts.

Early Childhood Education

Compared with primary, secondary, and postsecondary education, early childhood education is not centrally organized around well-established institutions dominated by state provision of services. But given the large gaps in skills and knowledge that kindergartners bring with them upon arriving at school, it is incumbent on those who care about expanding opportunity to address inequities at this life stage.

In his chapter on early childhood education, Chester E. Finn Jr. sensibly delimits the role of policy in this area—to prepare children for kindergarten who otherwise would be unprepared. This group is something like one-quarter of all preschoolers. It might be said that Finn would be a fan of universal pre-K, except for it being "needless," "unnecessary," and "wasteful" for the majority of prepared children and "sorely inadequate" for unprepared children.

Rejecting the view that if government doesn't pay for the enrichment of school-ready children and the childcare of middle-class parents, then voters will oppose investing in those who need help, Finn argues for targeting assistance to the truly disadvantaged. And he distinguishes assistance aimed at "child development" generally (including health and socialization) from that aimed narrowly at cognitive and academic readiness for school. Head Start may have important benefits in the former domain, targeted to disadvantaged children. But in its current design, it cannot effectively supply the knowledge and cognitive skills needed for kindergarten.

Finn's solution primarily involves reorienting federal early childhood programs to promote kindergarten readiness. These programs include Head Start but also the Preschool Development Grant program, some Title I educational funding, and the Maternal, Infant, and Early Childhood Home Visiting Program. Finn also wants to subsidize spending by low-income parents on the cognitive and academic needs of their preschoolers. That could take the form of vouchers, refundable tax credits, or education savings accounts (ESAs). And Finn recommends a national assessment of school-age children during kindergarten, via the program that currently tests a subset of fourth, eighth, and 12th graders.

Primary and Secondary Education

Turning to K–12 schooling, Michael Q. McShane notes how the COVID-19 pandemic affected parents' interest in alternative educational arrangements for their children. Rates of homeschooling temporarily jumped during the pandemic, as did innovative responses such as microschools and hybrid homeschools. Microschools involve small numbers of students (think of "pandemic pods") meeting in nontraditional settings, while hybrid homeschools combine part-time in-school attendance with at-home education.

McShane would build on the pandemic responses that grew out of necessity by promoting further innovation in primary and secondary schooling. He favors charter schools and an expansion of ESAs, which provide public dollars to eligible parents who may use the funds for children's educational expenses. Charter schools are public schools that operate independently of school districts and can therefore offer specialized education. ESA dollars can go toward private school tuition, tutoring, support services for special needs, and other educational expenses.

ESAs have grown popular in recent years; as we write this, 13 states have them (with seven having universal programs).[15] As American Enterprise Institute scholar Frederick M. Hess has noted, in their current forms, ESAs tend to support primarily private school tuition, often tying use of the accounts to a requirement that students not be enrolled in public school.[16] In many states, ESAs are available only to students with special needs. We would offer that future ESA programs would do more to help low-income families if they not only gave priority to poor children when funds are limited (as some do today) but also provided them more generous funding than they do other kids. Today, that is the case only in North Carolina.[17]

McShane prefers enough state policy flexibility that ESAs can be used for new institutions such as microschools and that charter schools can serve nontraditional students such as those in hybrid homeschools. He argues for the deregulation of educational institutions to promote innovation. Questioning what he sees as an outsized focus on solutions that scale up, McShane also urges funders and policymakers to value smaller local innovation, citing the VELA Education Fund as an exemplar. Finally, he emphasizes the need for schools to operate more efficiently—in terms of money and time use.

Higher Education and Postsecondary Training

Beth Akers and Preston Cooper, in their chapter on higher education, also zero in on educational efficiency and accountability. The value of a typical college degree for lifetime earnings endures. But Akers and Cooper emphasize that the return on investment varies markedly across schools and college majors (and, undoubtedly, students). Cooper's analyses indicate that a fifth of bachelor's degrees generate a return of a half million dollars, but nearly three in 10 are literally not worth the paper on which the diploma is printed. Different majors result in similarly unequal payoffs.

Akers and Cooper argue that federal policy should not subsidize degrees that leave students economically worse off. Current accreditation policies place a heavy emphasis on educational inputs instead of outputs. Akers and Cooper propose denying federal Pell Grant and loan funding to any degree programs without a positive return on investment. This reform would force colleges and universities to either increase the earnings of degree program graduates or lower the tuition for programs with low earnings potential.

Recognizing that such a change could discourage institutions of higher education from enrolling disadvantaged students who might have poor outcomes, Akers and Cooper propose tuition assistance for such students that would make education more affordable to them and lower the cost bar that institutions would have to exceed to provide the student a positive return on investment.

We note that it is straightforward to modify this approach to federal education assistance so that it incorporates schools' and programs' dropout rates or dynamically scales federal funding available to students depending on degree program outcomes. That is, rather than being disqualified from federal aid, a program's students might see their funding reduced by a given percentage from the maximum amount for top-performing programs.

Akers and Cooper round out their chapter with proposals for encouraging innovation in the form of coding boot camps, apprenticeships, and other alternatives to traditional higher education. They would rely on private investment until institutions establish a track record by which return on investment may be assessed. Effective institutions could then repay investors with retroactive federal aid. In the meantime, students could be protected from underperforming institutions through degree insurance and income-share agreements that shift risk to the institutions themselves or outside investors.

Stable Families

Educational institutions clearly play an important role in expanding opportunity. But as Finn notes, they cannot be expected to negate the impact of disadvantages children bring with them from outside the school. The next chapters in the book focus on how kids' social surroundings affect their opportunity. Most obviously, children are influenced, for good or ill, by their parents. The contribution by Brad Wilcox and Robert Lerman addresses the most important aspect of family environment—whether children grow up with both their biological parents.

As Wilcox and Lerman document, the vast majority of the most advantaged children continue to grow up with two married parents. But over the past 50 years, middle- and working-class children and poor kids have become much more likely to live without their father or mother. They are more likely than socially and economically advantaged children to be born to an unmarried mother and more likely to experience their parents' divorce.

Wilcox and Lerman review a variety of explanations for these trends. Men's earnings and employment advantages over women have diminished, making marriage less appealing to mothers. (As one of us—Scott Winship—has argued, rather than men doing worse in absolute terms over time, their gains have been much smaller than those of women. If men have become less "marriageable," it is because women's standards for men have risen with their own economic status.)[18] Education and workforce development policy has failed to help noncollege men as the economy has evolved. Marriage disincentives in safety-net programs prevent couples from tying the knot. And cultural acceptance of nonmarital child-rearing has grown.

To confront these worrisome trends, Wilcox and Lerman offer five proposals. First, they favor a sizable increase in federal funding for apprenticeships. These apprenticeships are likely to be valued in trades that disproportionately appeal to men, and they might thereby improve male marriageability. Next, the authors propose expanding the child tax credit. Because a child allowance, available whether or not parents work, would tend to incentivize single parenthood, Wilcox and Lerman argue that the credit should retain an earnings requirement, as is the case for current policy.

Wilcox and Lerman also advocate a reduction in marriage penalties in means-tested safety-net programs and refundable tax credits. They propose that many more married parents with young children be deemed eligible for safety-net benefits, pushing out to higher incomes the marriage penalties entailed in the programs. One possible side effect relevant to themes of the next chapter might be that more families become dependent on government benefits, but such a policy, while expensive, would make it easier for many low-income couples to get or remain married.

Rounding out their proposals, ESAs are featured again, as a way to help families enroll in private schools (including religious schools) that might do a better job conveying the values, knowledge, and skills needed to promote stable marriage in adulthood. Finally, Wilcox and Lerman wish to see a public and private campaign around the "success sequence"—the following of ordered steps, from high school graduation and full-time employment to marital childbearing—that promote economic success and family strength.

The Safety Net

Building on Wilcox and Lerman's focus on the family, Angela Rachidi and Matt Weidinger consider reforms to the safety net. Such reforms may be justified from various perspectives and motivated by any number of objectives, but this chapter maintains an emphasis on encouraging children's upward mobility. While antipoverty programs reduce short-term hardship, their design may discourage parents from getting or staying married and getting or keeping a job.

Rachidi and Weidinger review a daunting literature on the effects of reforms to cash welfare, food stamps, the earned income tax credit, and child support enforcement on a variety of parent and child outcomes. While the evidence is often mixed, a majority of studies find that reforms that promote or discourage work, marriage, or fertility have at least a small effect in the expected direction. Policies that are generous without requiring employment discourage work and marriage and encourage nonmarital fertility. Policies that make it more difficult to receive benefits without working or provide larger benefits with additional work tend to encourage work and marriage and discourage nonmarital fertility.

The evidence as to how safety-net programs and reforms affect children is similarly complex. Rachidi and Weidinger note an array of studies that find benefits to children both from participation in safety-net programs and exposure to work-promoting reforms to these programs. They rightly lament the lack of research on longer-term outcomes.

Poorly designed safety-net programs may have short-term benefits for children even as their parental incentives discourage children's opportunity in the long run. We note that dozens of local guaranteed income experiments, which provide unconditional cash to families for a short duration, are ongoing around the country. The emphasis on immediate outcomes in the evaluations of these programs misses the possibility that a policy of *permanent* unconditional cash transfers might counteract these initial improvements by changing behavior over time.

Rachidi and Weidinger would reform the safety net to better promote work and independence, focus on the long term rather than just immediate impacts, and operate more efficiently and with more accountability, more fiscal responsibility, and a limited federal role. They propose replacing the earned income tax credit, child tax credit, and head-of-household filing status with a working family credit. The working family credit would encourage work as well as existing tax policy does. It would also mitigate the marriage penalties faced by couples whose combined earnings are high enough that their earned income tax credit is reduced from the maximum amount available.

Rachidi and Weidinger's second reform would allow states to run opportunity demonstration projects that would combine up to six large safety-net funding streams. These pilots would focus on mitigating work and marriage disincentives and improving job training—all in service of promoting the upward mobility of poor children. The authors hope these pilots eventually would inform national reforms drawing on the most successful approaches.

Rachidi and Weidinger advocate new tax-favored flexible savings accounts—with family savings partly matched by the federal government. And they favor greater residential options and relocation assistance for recipients of housing subsidies. To help pay for these proposals, the authors propose to shift some program costs to states while giving them financial incentives to successfully move beneficiaries into work.

The Importance of Place

Rachidi and Weidinger's brief mention of residential mobility nicely tees up the next chapter, by John W. Lettieri. Lettieri describes the importance of neighborhood influences for child outcomes. Each additional year children spend in a high-poverty neighborhood worsens their prospects for upward mobility. Neighborhoods matter, in part, because they immerse children in social settings that can promote or impede opportunity.

More than one in four children live in a neighborhood where at least one in five residents is in poverty. Despite rising incomes and declining poverty nationally, the number of high-poverty areas—and the share of people living in them—has jumped since 1980. Once poor, neighborhoods rarely become better off. The problem is exacerbated by the geographic concentration of economic growth in recent years in a small number of metropolitan areas. Finally, residential mobility has declined over the past 15–20 years, and disadvantaged people who do move tend not to end up in high-opportunity areas. Because of land-use and zoning restrictions, it has become more difficult to move to opportunity. Economic segregation has worsened as a result.

Lettieri urges policymakers to both invest in poor neighborhoods and help parents choose more advantageous neighborhoods in which to raise their children. He wants states and municipalities to deregulate land use and zoning to promote more affordable housing, noting that federal policy might offer them incentives to do so. Lettieri also supports tax incentives for investment in low-income communities, as exemplified by the recent Opportunity Zones experiment. And he would reform the federal housing voucher program to offer more generous subsidies to families with young children and for moves to high-opportunity areas.

In addition to better targeting of federal funds already intended for low-income areas, Lettieri calls for federal and state pilot projects to uncover effective place-based strategies. Finally, to reduce concentrated joblessness, he would like to see a wage subsidy or geographically triggered boost to the earned income tax credit. Such a policy would make employment more attractive to potential workers and allow employers to consider employees whom they could not have justified hiring at a higher wage. It could also make it affordable to move to high-cost cities that provide more opportunity.

Community Violence

One of the most tragic ways kids' neighborhoods can affect them is through the impact of community violence. While violent crime is down from its peak over 30 years ago, it remains as high as it was at the end of the 1960s, after doubling during that decade. Homicide is comparatively rare, but it increased sharply in 2020 and has remained elevated since. What's more, violent crime is highly concentrated in a small number of neighborhoods. Research finds that high community violence translates into lower upward mobility out of poverty.

Joshua Crawford, in the volume's final chapter, emphasizes that when public order breaks down, the safety that we take for granted in our day-to-day lives is in doubt, affecting everyone in the community. Most importantly and most directly affected are the children who become victims of violent crime. Then there are the opportunities destroyed when youth are pulled into street gangs—recruited as early as age 5 and often seeking personal protection.

But far more children and young adults must live with the *indirect* effects of community violence. These include the anxiety and isolation caused by feeling unsafe and the fallout from neighborhood neglect and deterioration. Living amid community violence increases aggressive behavior in children and worsens academic outcomes. Moreover, as danger grows, economic investment and property values decline, hurting wealth accumulation, employment, and school quality. The flight of relatively stable families creates a dearth of valuable social capital.

Contrary to calls in some quarters to "defund the police," Crawford cites evidence that increased police funding reduces violent crime. He points to the Community Oriented Policing Services hiring program, which provides federal funding toward hiring new state and local police, as an effective federal effort to help communities. He describes the success in reducing gang violence that "focused deterrence policing" has seen in many cities. This strategy involves outreach to the most violent offenders, promising resources to those who are amenable to change and swift, predictable consequences for those who continue to offend. Federal grants to law enforcement agencies could incentivize such strategies.

Crawford also highlights the importance of accountability for criminal offenders, arguing for sentence enhancements for explicitly defined gang-motivated crimes. Incarceration keeps offenders off the streets and deters would-be offenders. He proposes reducing physical disorder that leads to crime, by enforcing city codes related to abandoned property, tearing down abandoned property, maintaining vacant lots, and increasing effective street lighting. Finally, Crawford encourages expanding the availability of victim services in police departments.

Conclusion: Doing Right by Kids

The American economy is a miracle of wealth creation that has lifted middle-class incomes to all-time highs and reduced poverty to all-time lows. Yet populists on both the left and the right today mistakenly believe it to be fundamentally broken. Economic policy and politics have increasingly revolved around debates that presume we have entered "late-stage capitalism." This risks not only counterproductive government intervention that will threaten our society's capacity to flourish economically but also continued neglect of the primary economic problem facing all rich nations—the problem of unequal opportunity.

Children do not pick their parents, the neighborhoods where they are raised, or the influences to which they are exposed. They lack a fully developed mental capacity to behave rationally and responsibly, with an eye toward the long run. Inequality in child environments starts to produce opportunity gaps even before birth, and from day one, it exerts its effects unremittingly. As a result, too many Americans enter adulthood lacking the habits, values, skills, knowledge, and confidence to benefit from the great wealth-producing American economy.

The result is not only social injustice and a costly system of government redistribution; it is also diminished economic growth and fulfillment of human potential and a loss of faith in the meritocratic system that undergirds the American economy's success.

Conservatives cannot cede the issue of expanding opportunity to the left. Progressive approaches, preferences, and assumptions have brought the nation where it is today, for better but also for worse. Free cash and universal public provision of services will not move the needle on opportunity—economic or social. Or rather, they are likely to make matters worse.

The creative and thoughtful ideas that follow offer a model for how a hardheaded, softhearted conservatism can bring its insights to bear on policymaking to expand opportunity. It is our hope that they will inspire policymakers to give priority to a new conservatism of opportunity and find creative ways for limited government to increase the upward mobility of poor children. We owe them nothing less.

Notes

1. Jeehoon Han, Bruce D. Meyer, and James X. Sullivan, "Annual Report on U.S. Consumption Poverty: 2022," University of Notre Dame, December 6, 2023, Table 1, https://sites.nd.edu/james-sullivan/files/2023/12/2022-Consumption-Poverty-Report_12_12_2023.pdf. These estimates are after taxes and cash and noncash transfers and use a poverty threshold anchored to the official 2015 level.

2. Scott Winship, *Poverty After Welfare Reform*, Manhattan Institute, August 2016, https://media4.manhattan-institute.org/sites/default/files/R-SW-0816.pdf. These estimates are also after taxes and cash and noncash transfers and use a poverty threshold anchored to the official 1996 level. The reported estimates run to 2012, but the official poverty measure indicates that poverty fell by 31 percent from 2012 to 2022. We apply that decline to the 2012 estimate in Scott Winship's report. See US Census Bureau, "Historical Poverty Tables: People and Families—1959 to 2022," Table 4, https://www.census.gov/data/tables/time-series/demo/income-poverty/historical-poverty-people.html.

3. Scott Winship, *Economic Mobility: A State-of-the-Art Primer; Contemporary Levels of Mobility*, Archbridge Institute, March 2017, 18, Figure 3, https://www.archbridgeinstitute.org/wp-content/uploads/2017/04/Contemporary-levels-of-mobility-digital-version_Winship.pdf.

4. Scott Winship, "Economic Mobility in America: A State-of-the-Art Primer, Part 3: Trends in the United States," Archbridge Institute, 17, 25, Figures 6 and 13,

November 2021, https://www.archbridgeinstitute.org/wp-content/uploads/2022/02/Economic-Mobility-in-America_Part-3_Scott-Winship-1.pdf. See also the studies reviewed in the report.

5. US Congress, Joint Economic Committee, *What We Do Together: The State of Associational Life in America*, May 2017, https://www.lee.senate.gov/public/_cache/files/b5f224ce-98f7-40f6-a814-8602696714d8/what-we-do-together.pdf.

6. Charles Murray, *Coming Apart: The State of White America, 1960–2010* (New York: Forum Books, 2012).

7. Charles Murray, *Losing Ground: American Social Policy, 1950–1980* (New York: Basic Books, 1984).

8. Scott Winship, "Yes, the '96 Welfare Reform Helped Reduce Child Poverty," *National Review*, September 7, 2016, https://www.nationalreview.com/2016/09/welfare-reform-child-poverty-reduced-1996-prwora.

9. Scott Winship, "Will Welfare Reform Increase Upward Mobility?," *Forbes*, March 26, 2015, https://www.forbes.com/sites/scottwinship/2015/03/26/will-welfare-reform-increase-upward-mobility; Robert Rector, *Marriage, Abortion, and Welfare*, Heritage Foundation, May 22, 2023, https://www.heritage.org/sites/default/files/2023-05/SR271_0.pdf; and Scott Winship, "A Half-Century Decline in Marriage . . . That Ended 30 Years Ago for Disadvantaged Kids," American Enterprise Institute, April 21, 2022, https://www.aei.org/research-products/report/a-half-century-decline-in-marriage-that-ended-30-years-ago-for-disadvantaged-kids.

10. David B. Muhlhausen, *Do Federal Social Programs Work?* (Westport, CT: Praeger, 2013).

11. Caroline Ratcliffe and Emma Kalish, *Escaping Poverty: Predictors of Persistently Poor Children's Economic Success*, US Partnership on Mobility from Poverty, May 2017, 3, Figure 1, https://www.urban.org/sites/default/files/publication/90321/escaping-poverty_0.pdf.

12. Scott Winship, Richard V. Reeves, and Katherine Guyot, "The Inheritance of Black Poverty: It's All About the Men," Brookings Institution, March 22, 2018, https://web.archive.org/web/20180401121005/https:/www.brookings.edu/research/the-inheritance-of-black-poverty-its-all-about-the-men.

13. Patrick Sharkey, *Neighborhoods and the Black-White Mobility Gap*, Pew Charitable Trusts, Economic Mobility Project, July 2009, https://www.pewtrusts.org/~/media/legacy/uploadedfiles/wwwpewtrustsorg/reports/economic_mobility/pewsharkeyv12pdf. See also the chapter by John W. Lettieri in the present volume.

14. In the mid-2000s, the math and reading gaps between kindergartners whose mothers lacked a high school diploma and those with college-graduate mothers were between 15 and 17 points, scored on the same scale as a conventional IQ test. Fast-forward to the 2019 graduating class of high school seniors, and the math and reading disparities between students with parents at those schooling levels were still two-thirds the size of the initial gaps. (They would have been larger still, but some students had already dropped out and were not assessed.) Julia B. Isaacs and Katherine A. Magnuson, "Income and Education as Predictors of Children's School Readiness," Brookings Institution, December 14, 2011, https://www.brookings.edu/research/income-and-

education-as-predictors-of-childrens-school-readiness; and National Assessment of Educational Progress, "NAEP Data Explorer," https://www.nationsreportcard.gov/ndecore/landing.

15. Policy Circle, "Education Savings Accounts," https://www.thepolicycircle.org/minibrief/education-savings-accounts.

16. Frederick M. Hess, "What Is an Education Savings Account, and Why Does It Matter?," *Education Next*, May 11, 2023, https://www.educationnext.org/what-is-an-education-savings-account-and-why-does-it-matter.

17. Mark Leblond and Ed Tarnowski, "Educational Freedom and Choice Hits Escape Velocity: End-of-Session Wrap-Up," EdChoice, December 2023, https://www.edchoice.org/engage/educational-freedom-and-choice-hits-escape-velocity-end-of-session-wrap; EdChoice, School Choice in America Dashboard, April 17, 2023, https://www.edchoice.org/school-choice-in-america-dashboard-scia; and H. B. 259, 2023–24 Gen. Assemb. (N.C. 2023), https://dashboard.ncleg.gov/api/Services/BillSummary/2023/H259-SMBE-123(sl)-v-2.

18. Scott Winship, *Bringing Home the Bacon: Have Trends in Men's Pay Weakened the Traditional Family?*, American Enterprise Institute, December 14, 2022, https://www.aei.org/research-products/report/bringing-home-the-bacon-have-trends-in-mens-pay-weakened-the-traditional-family.

1

Promoting Upward Mobility from the Starting Gate

CHESTER E. FINN JR.

O ne of the best and most important things a civilized society and advanced economy can do is equip its children with a solid start in education. If we know anything for sure about education, it is that kids who still struggle with the basics of reading, writing, and arithmetic when they reach third grade almost never succeed in middle school, high school, and the subsequent worlds of work, college, and citizenship.[1]

But early childhood education ought to be simpler than it is. Properly understood, its job is to get kids ready to succeed in kindergarten and beyond. As a societal or governmental activity, its job is to do that for the kids who otherwise would not be ready, for many children are clearly ready without the government doing anything new or different for them.

Other children are not so lucky, and what is doubly unfortunate is that they come disproportionately from disadvantaged families—mostly low income, often black or brown, frequently without two parents at home. These girls and boys enter school without the knowledge, skills, habits, and behaviors that we associate with "kindergarten readiness." They then depend primarily on the school to both make up for what they did not bring with them and carry them forward at full speed. That is a far bigger assignment than most schools can manage.

Rather than pursuing the straightforward (if daunting) objective of getting kids ready for school who otherwise would not be, early childhood education policy has become complicated, politicized, frequently confused or commingled with other policy realms, and full of both good and bad ideas, based on mixed and troublesome evidence as to its efficacy.[2] Reaching a common understanding of early childhood education's purpose and the federal government's role in administering it will chart a path forward for legislators and a path upward for disadvantaged children.

The Policy Challenge

There are no national data on kindergarten readiness, but a number of states assess it. In Maryland, where I served a term not long ago on the state board of education, the excellent Kindergarten Readiness Assessment system reported that in fall 2021, "the majority of kindergarteners (60%) do not demonstrate the knowledge, skills, and behavior to actively engage in the kindergarten curriculum."[3] The figure was still 58 percent in fall 2022, a tiny recovery from the worst pandemic setbacks.[4] Yet the situation was deeply worrisome before the plague struck: In fall 2019, 53 percent of young Marylanders had been ill prepared. Texas reported in 2019 that 47 percent of its kindergartners were similarly unready for kindergarten success.[5] The previous autumn (2018), Ohio's number was 59 percent.[6]

Such data are obviously cause for alarm, but let us also note that half or nearly half of entering kindergartners in these states have been found adequately prepared according to the states' own measures. Let us note, too, that roughly half of those in the unprepared category were "approaching" readiness, meaning that roughly one-quarter—admittedly a crude estimate—of America's entering kindergartners are far from ready to succeed in school.[7] Another quarter could do with some help. But half or close to half seem to be getting what they need already. So as we consider what is to be done, let us not roll every 5-year-old into the same category. Existing pre-K arrangements seem to be meeting the needs of millions of young children.

The preparedness situation is considerably worse, however, for minority youngsters. In Maryland, just 33 percent of African American and 19 percent of Hispanic kindergartners were well prepared in 2019 to engage successfully with the curriculum, compared with 53 percent of Asian and 54 percent of white students.

We have long expected our K–12 schools to solve the unpreparedness problem by raising almost every child's boat to sea level—well, grade level—and keeping them there as they proceed through the elementary, middle, and high school years. Yet we know from experience that reality often dashes that expectation. With happy exceptions, often in the private and charter school sectors, American schools are not powerful enough to accomplish this dual mission for many of the children who need it.

"Compensatory" education works badly: For the most part, kids who start behind stay behind, as grade-level work baffles those who did not master the work in previous grades. And the further behind they start, the further behind they stay. This is true whether their gaps are academic, behavioral, or what today is fashionably termed "social and emotional."[8]

These gaps emerge early. Children's minds are little sponges, and they are learning from birth. But how much, how well, and what they learn depend on how they are raised and the experiences they have. Successful early reading, for example—which we typically associate with first grade but increasingly commences in kindergarten—generally assumes that children already recognize the letters of the alphabet and can say the "names" of those letters. This calls for prior exposure to the alphabet and, even earlier, some acquaintance with distinguishing among various shapes, sizes, and sequences.

Successful early reading also requires a degree of prior vocabulary. The more vocabulary children have the better, as it is one thing to "sound out" a word that one then recognizes and knows the meaning of and quite another thing to sound out a word that rings no bells. Yet decades of research have shown the chasm between the vocabulary experiences of small children from advantaged and disadvantaged households.

To sum up: Ensuring that children are prepared to succeed in kindergarten and beyond is the foremost task—arguably the only essential task—of early childhood education. And that is where public policy should focus: on those children who are not otherwise satisfactorily prepared.

Misguided Universalism

Misguided universalism is a big challenge all by itself. Yet instead of focusing on the pitfalls of universalism, the early childhood policy debate gets complicated and unfocused. I see two main reasons.

First, much of the advocacy in this realm, including that from President Joe Biden—as recently as his 2024 State of the Union address—as well as private foundations, think tankers, and animated teachers unions, seeks, in the name of "universal pre-K," to add another grade to public education so that it begins at age 4 instead of 5. Sometimes, as in Biden's version, it goes down to age 3. (In some states, private operators are also included, and their advocates and lobbyists push hard for inclusion in the education delivery system, though of course the public school interests would prefer to keep them out. The presence of thousands of "faith-based" education providers adds further complexity.) This "universal pre-K" strategy is meant to sweep all kids, whether or not they would be kindergarten ready without it, into a uniform, government-funded public education program. In my view and those of other critics, this is a needless windfall, unnecessary intervention, and wasteful public expense for a great many children and families, even as it is sorely inadequate in terms of meeting the pre-K needs of deeply disadvantaged youngsters.

Either this discordant plan is a front for public school expansionism, bent on adding another grade or two to its current 13, along with the staff (and dues-paying union members) that would accompany such growth, or it is a familiar but cynical political calculation: Only by appealing to the middle-class desire for taxpayers to underwrite the routine childcare needs of working parents and subsidize the preschool preferences of middle-class families will any movement occur on the pre-K front. The heck with the truly disadvantaged youngsters who need more than that strategy will yield. On balance, it appears to me that proponents of this approach are subordinating the interests of poor kids to the politics of getting something enacted.

Some say nothing will be done if it is only for the poor, but that is nonsense. America is awash in enormous, well-funded programs that target the poor. Medicaid, Pell Grants, and food stamps leap instantly to mind. And in the early childhood field, of course, there are already Head Start (discussed below) and chunks of the big Title I program that pays for pre-K education. Surely advocates know this.

They also understand that universal pre-K is an expensive proposition. Even Biden's multitrillion-dollar Build Back Better plan offered federal pre-K funding in declining amounts through 2027—with states entirely on their own thereafter to sustain the expanded program. And the many rules associated with the federal funding would hike the cost per student of preschool far higher than current spending levels in many places.

Unfocused Aims

The second confusion in this policy (and budgetary) realm is the tendency to conflate early childhood education with childcare for working parents and with an antipoverty strategy that, since the 1960s, has flown the flag of "child development."

Working parents need somewhere safe and salubrious to leave their young children while they are out. Sensitive to this need, many employers provide day care or childcare centers for their workers, and any number of government programs seek to provide (or subsidize) this for other parents, especially those who cannot readily afford it on their own. One can have education without childcare—for example, tutors who visit homes while parents are there—and one can and often does have childcare that meets children's essential needs without teaching them much of anything. Moreover, working parents in need of childcare often need it while their children are still babies, and they typically need it during their working hours, which often do not align with a standard school schedule.

The concept of child "development" within this policy realm is even more confusing, because of course it ought to include education as a key element. Here is how the Centers for Disease Control and Prevention describes "healthy development" for young children:

> Healthy development means that children of all abilities, including those with special health care needs, are able to grow up where their social, emotional and educational needs are met. Having a safe and loving home and spending time with family—playing, singing, reading, and talking—are very important. Proper nutrition, exercise, and sleep also can make a big difference.[9]

By far the largest government-supported child development program, dating back to President Lyndon Johnson's War on Poverty, is Head Start, which is operated and funded through the US Department of Health and Human Services—conspicuously not through the Department of Education. Congress annually appropriates more than $10 billion to pay for Head Start, and it enrolls more than one million children each year, most of them age 3 and 4.[10] The program targets low-income children, precisely those for whom kindergarten readiness is often a problem.

The problem with Head Start (and many other "child development" programs) is that, despite its present-day assertion that it "promotes school readiness,"[11] in reality it is not an education program. It does not employ qualified teachers in most of its highly decentralized centers, it does not have a curriculum, and to my knowledge, its providers are barely held to account for the cognitive gains of the children they serve.

This largely explains why, over the decades, evaluation after evaluation of the Head Start program has found that either it has minimal effect on those children's cognitive outcomes or whatever effect it has dissipates during the early years of schooling.[12] To be sure, such slippage is also due to elementary schools' failure to capitalize on and sustain whatever initial gains the Head Start alumni arrived with. But the fact is that, despite modern-day tweaks, Head Start has never been much about actual kindergarten readiness on the cognitive or academic side. It has been more about the health and welfare—nutrition, dentition, and socialization—of deeply disadvantaged children. These are all good things to target, but this is not a formula for securing essential domains of school readiness.[13]

Head Start is loved by many, however. It employs more than a quarter million adults, and over half a century, it seems to have become a permanent piece of the federal government's social safety net.[14] It is not going away. It is also stubbornly resistant—and structurally ill-suited—to conversion into a full-fledged kindergarten-readiness program.

Many efforts to do exactly that over the years have come to grief over the objections of the Head Start lobby and the many people (often lacking college degrees) whose jobs depend on keeping the program pretty much the way it was. For example, when President George W.

Bush proposed in 2003 to refocus Head Start on reading and math skill development aimed at school readiness, the Children's Defense Fund's longtime leader, Marian Wright Edelman, protested that this would "break the sacred covenant between people and their federal government." "If it ain't broke," she declared, "don't fix it. More importantly, if it ain't broke, don't break it."[15]

Although Head Start has been resistant to fundamental changes, we must not leave the topic without reiterating that it costs $10 billion in federal funds per annum that, if successfully redirected to school readiness, could do needy kids quite a lot of lasting good.

Reforming Early Childhood Education Policy

Going forward, what should policy leaders do on the preschool front? They should start by acknowledging that K–12 education is a constitutional obligation of the 50 states and that the federal government has but a limited role in it. Mostly what Uncle Sam does in this realm is engage in research, data gathering, and assessment; enforce civil rights; and provide funds to supplement the education of children who are disabled, disadvantaged, or both. Yes, that is an oversimplification—the Department of Education alone operates dozens of programs—but that is the gist of it.

Pre-K education, too, is very much a state matter, and the states have approached it in different ways. Some operate extensive programs for 4-year-olds (and sometimes 3-year-olds) at state expense, while others leave preschool almost entirely to local decision, parental initiative, and the private sector.[16] This is largely why every effort to engage the federal government more forcefully in preschool, including President Biden's Build Back Better initiative, has bumped into the highly varying topography of state philosophies, policies, programming, and, not least of all, politics.[17]

Before getting into future programs and services, let us pause on the well-established federal role in data gathering. At present, the National Assessment of Educational Progress does not kick in until the spring of fourth grade. My colleague Michael Petrilli has suggested that it should instead start with kindergarten.[18] Were that to be done, we would move beyond spotty state-specific data and hugely increase our understanding of how prepared children are (and which children and where), at least as they near the end of kindergarten and head toward first grade. More, too, could be done on the data front via the several waves of the big, government-sponsored Early Childhood Longitudinal Study.

On the programmatic side, at the federal level we should consider a four-part approach (the first part of which is not actually about school readiness).

1. Washington should continue to subsidize the childcare needs of low- and moderate-income working parents. There are multiple mechanisms for this, including the child and dependent care tax credit and the Temporary Assistance for Needy Families program. But we ought not to confuse these forms of help with early childhood education.

2. Congress should convert Head Start to a bona fide kindergarten-readiness program while continuing to target it toward disadvantaged 3- and 4-year-olds. As noted above, previous efforts to effect such a transformation have run into opposition, but that ought not to stop us from trying again.

3. Policy leaders should review a slew of other extant federal programs that bear on the pre-K realm, whether operated by the Health and Human Services or Education Departments, to determine the feasibility of recasting them with a more explicit focus on school readiness. These include the Preschool Development Grant program; Early Head Start; the Maternal, Infant, and Early Childhood Home Visiting Program; elements of the Title I funding stream; and several early childhood or preschool programs associated with special education.[19]

4. Whether through refundable tax credits, vouchers, or education savings accounts, Washington should supply resources to low-income parents with which to purchase educational services and programs

for their preschoolers, as well as specialized instruction for themselves on how best to advance the school readiness of their own young children.

This is a demand-based strategy, very different from subsidizing an expanded supply of preschool education. Structurally, it could resemble the child tax credit, but it should be targeted laser-like toward low-income families with children under age 6. And the funds it makes available should be used for those children's education—admittedly a more restrictive approach than is found in, say, Sen. Mitt Romney's (R-UT) proposed Family Security Act 2.0.[20]

Such services might be "center based," in which case the funds would function much like income-based preschool vouchers. Or they might be home based, including online offerings, which might be designed for the children themselves or for their parents or other caregivers. But school readiness is the point throughout, and the "educational services and programs" for which these funds may be used must be designed for that mission.

The challenge is how to assure this in fact happens. Recognizing that money is fungible and there is no foolproof way to prevent parents from using such funds for unrelated purposes, it is worth trying to keep them focused. This likely means some form of regulation and quality control regarding eligible service providers. Much as Pell Grants can be used to attend only accredited colleges, here sound policy would require that these funds be usable to obtain education services only from effective providers. Ideally, such providers would use research-proven curricula and instructional methods and submit to before-and-after evaluations of the effectiveness of the services they provide, with eligibility terminated for providers that repeatedly produce unsatisfactory "value-added" results.

It is unrealistic to expect the IRS to manage this or maintain some sort of giant federal registry of approved providers. So eligibility review should be either delegated to states or outsourced to accrediting bodies. But, to repeat, the chief criterion for approval should be demonstrated effectiveness, which is different from the inputs-driven metrics commonly used in the early childhood education realm to designate "quality" pre-K operators.

Such a four-part policy agenda, plus better assessments and data gathering, could go a long way in preparing more American preschoolers for success in kindergarten and beyond. By targeting the school readiness of the children who are most behind, disproportionately found in the most disadvantaged families, this agenda would steadfastly focus on the goal of increased upward mobility.

Notes

1. Leila Fiester, *Early Warning! Why Reading by the End of Third Grade Matters*, Annie E. Casey Foundation, 2010, https://www.ccf.ny.gov/files/9013/8262/2751/AECFReporReadingGrade3.pdf.

2. Frederick M. Hess, "The Not-So-Certain Science of Pre-K," *Education Week*, May 24, 2022, https://www.edweek.org/teaching-learning/opinion-the-not-so-certain-science-of-pre-k/2022/05.

3. Robin L. Hopkins, *Coming Back Stronger: Resilience and Opportunity*, Ready at Five and Maryland State Department of Education, 2022, 2, https://earlychildhood.marylandpublicschools.org/system/files/filedepot/4/readinessmatters2021-2022_accessible.pdf.

4. Robin L. Hopkins, *Readiness Matters*, Ready at Five and Maryland State Department of Education, 2023, https://marylandpublicschools.org/Documents/reports/MSDE_ReadyAtFive_ReadinessMatters2023.pdf.

5. Texas Public Education Information Resource, "Texas Public Prekindergarten Assessment Results for 4-Year-Olds," https://www.texaseducationinfo.org.

6. Ohio Department of Education, Office of Early Learning and School Readiness, *Annual Report on the Kindergarten Readiness Assessment: Fall 2018 Administration*, September 2019, https://education.ohio.gov/getattachment/Topics/Early-Learning/Kindergarten/Ohios-Kindergarten-Readiness-Assessment/KRA-Annual-Report-2018-2019-1.pdf.

7. Hopkins, *Coming Back Stronger*; Hopkins, *Readiness Matters*; and Ohio Department of Education, Office of Early Learning and School Readiness, *Annual Report on the Kindergarten Readiness Assessment*.

8. Johns Hopkins University, Hub, "Kindergarten Readiness a Barometer for Long-Term Success, Study Finds," March 25, 2016, https://hub.jhu.edu/2016/03/25/jhu-nursing-study-kindergarten-readiness.

9. US Department of Health and Human Services, Centers for Disease Control and Prevention, National Center on Birth Defects and Developmental Disabilities, "Child Development Basics," September 23, 2021, https://www.cdc.gov/ncbddd/childdevelopment/facts.html.

10. US Department of Health and Human Services, Administration for Children and Families, Early Childhood Learning & Knowledge Center, "Head Start Program Facts: Fiscal Year 2019," May 13, 2022, https://eclkc.ohs.acf.hhs.gov/about-us/article/head-start-program-facts-fiscal-year-2019.

11. US Department of Health and Human Services, Administration for Children and Families, Early Childhood Learning & Knowledge Center, "Head Start Approach to School Readiness—Overview," January 20, 2022, https://eclkc.ohs.acf.hhs.gov/school-readiness/article/head-start-approach-school-readiness-overview.

12. Remy J.-C. Pages et al., "Elusive Longer-Run Impacts of Head Start: Replications Within and Across Cohorts" (working paper, Brown University, Annenberg Institute, Providence, RI, May 2019), https://www.edworkingpapers.com/sites/default/files/ai19-27.pdf.

13. Lauren Bauer, "Does Head Start Work? The Debate over the Head Start Impact Study, Explained," Brookings Institution, June 14, 2019, https://www.brookings.edu/blog/brown-center-chalkboard/2019/06/14/does-head-start-work-the-debate-over-the-head-start-impact-study-explained.

14. US Department of Health and Human Services, "Head Start Program Facts: Fiscal Year 2021," https://eclkc.ohs.acf.hhs.gov/about-us/article/head-start-program-facts-fiscal-year-2021.

15. Ron Hutcheson and Knight Ridder Newspapers, "Bush's Reform Plan Would Trip Up Head Start, Critics Say," *Orlando Sentinel*, July 8, 2003, https://www.orlandosentinel.com/news/os-xpm-2003-07-08-0307080087-story.html.

16. Allison H. Friedman-Krauss et al., *The State Preschool Yearbook 2020*, Rutgers Graduate School of Education, National Institute for Early Education Research, 2021, https://nieer.org/state-preschool-yearbooks/yearbook2020.

17. Katie Lobosco, "Biden's Universal Pre-K Plan Could Mean a Need for at Least 40,000 New Teachers," CNN, December 5, 2021, https://www.cnn.com/2021/12/05/politics/universal-pre-k-biden-hiring-teachers-build-back-better/index.html; and Yeganeh Torbati and Jeff Stein, "GOP Resistance to Preschool Plan Could Imperil Key Biden Proposal in Many States," *Washington Post*, November 30, 2021, https://www.washingtonpost.com/business/2021/11/30/biden-universal-prek-gop.

18. Michael J. Petrilli, "The Case for Starting NAEP in Kindergarten," Thomas B. Fordham Institute, January 20, 2022, https://fordhaminstitute.org/national/commentary/case-starting-naep-kindergarten.

19. US Department of Education, Office of Elementary and Secondary Education, "Preschool Development Grant—Birth Through Five," April 29, 2021, https://oese.ed.gov/offices/office-of-discretionary-grants-support-services/innovation-early-learning/preschool-development-grants; US Department of Health and Human Services, Administration for Children and Families, Early Childhood Learning & Knowledge Center, "Early Head Start Programs," March 30, 2020, https://eclkc.ohs.acf.hhs.gov/programs/article/early-head-start-programs; Health Resources and Services Administration, Maternal and Child Health, "Maternal, Infant, and Early Childhood Home Visiting (MIECHV) Program," December 2021, https://mchb.hrsa.gov/programs-impact/programs/home-visiting/maternal-infant-early-childhood-home-visiting-miechv-program; and Hannah Matthews and Danielle Ewen, "FAQ: Using Title I of

ESEA for Early Education," CLASP, January 2010, https://www.clasp.org/sites/default/files/public/resources-and-publications/publication-1/titleifaq-1.pdf.

20. Office of Mitt Romney, "Romney Family Security Act 2.0: 'One of the Most Important Efforts to Support the Family in Nearly Thirty Years,'" press release, June 21, 2022, https://www.romney.senate.gov/romney-family-security-act-2-0-one-of-the-most-important-efforts-to-support-the-family-in-nearly-thirty-years.

2

Promoting Innovation in American K–12 Education

MICHAEL Q. MCSHANE

In writing about the failed Easter Rising of 1916, Irish poet William Butler Yeats said, "All changed, changed utterly: A terrible beauty is born."[1] The coronavirus pandemic changed American education and changed it utterly. But born out of the suffering of millions of families is an invigoration of interest in new ways of educating children and organizing schools.

Nascent efforts that were puttering along before the pandemic subsequently had nitrous oxide injected into their engines. Public opinion swung to favor policies that support such new models. And families started to vote with their feet.

It is an incredible time to be working in education. We are on the precipice of massive changes that can make schools better for children, families, communities, and educators. Families and school leaders are rethinking what school can look like and how it should operate. There is an opportunity to create new, different, and better schools. But for that to happen, we have to support policies and practices that promote innovation, allow outside entities to get involved in education, and empower parents to find the educational environment that best meets their children's needs.

The State of Play

During such a disorienting time, it is important to take stock of where we are before we look to the future. Almost immediately, we can see the recent changes.

The first set of data comes from the US Census Bureau. While past surveys showed growth in homeschooling, the total population of home-schoolers in America had held steady at around 3 percent of American households from 2012 to 2020.[2] At the outset of the pandemic, the Census Bureau instituted a new instrument called the Household Pulse Survey to measure the impact of COVID-19 on American households. It included a question about homeschooling. The results from the first iteration of the survey, in the field from late April to early May 2020, found that the percentage of homeschooling households had grown to 5 percent.[3]

By the fall administration, in the field from late September to early October, that number had jumped to 11 percent.[4] As Census Bureau analysts put it, "It's clear that in an unprecedented environment, families are seeking solutions that will reliably meet their health and safety needs, their childcare needs and the learning and socio-emotional needs of their children."[5]

If that increase is not jaw-dropping enough, the Census Bureau broke down responses by race and geography, discovering a number of surprising findings. The racial or ethnic group that saw the largest growth in homeschooling and, by fall 2020, represented the largest collection of homeschoolers per capita was black families. While in spring 2020 only 3 percent of black families homeschooled, by the fall, 16 percent did. Hispanic families were next, with 12 percent homeschooling by fall 2020, followed by white families at 10 percent and Asian families at 9 percent.

When broken down by geography, a number of states saw gains of 10 percentage points or more in their homeschooling population. Florida's, for example, grew from 5 percent to 18 percent. Alaska's grew from 10 percent to an incredible 28 percent. But the growth didn't happen just in red states. Homeschooling families in deep-blue Massachusetts grew from 2 percent to 12 percent.[6]

These numbers have fallen from their pandemic highs (to 4 percent during the 2022–23 school year).[7] However, the pandemic seems to have made parents more interested in homeschooling. Polling from my colleagues at EdChoice, in partnership with Morning Consult Intelligence, a public opinion research firm, found the favorability of homeschooling grew throughout the pandemic. When asked in March 2020, 55 percent of parents polled said they had a more favorable view of homeschooling because of the pandemic. Support for homeschooling remained relatively stable throughout the pandemic, with 58 percent of parents reporting in May 2022 that the pandemic made them have a more favorable view of homeschooling.[8]

The top four demographic groups in terms of the percentage who said their view was "much more" favorable toward homeschooling because of the pandemic were, in descending order, those already homeschooling, those with children in private schools, parents of children in special education or with special needs, and parents in labor unions. All four demographic groups had more than one-third of respondents say their view was "much more" favorable. Hispanic, American Indian, and black families were more likely to say their view was much more favorable due to the pandemic than white or Asian parents were, and both liberals and Democrats said their view was much more favorable at higher rates than did conservatives, Republicans, and moderates.[9]

Survey data also show that parents using private schools and homeschooling were happier with their children's progress during the coronavirus pandemic than were those relying on public schools. In spring 2021, 55 percent of private school parents and 48 percent of homeschool parents thought the past year had gone "very well" for their children's academic learning, compared to only 30 percent of traditional public school parents.

The pattern held for emotional development: 47 percent of private school parents and 48 percent of homeschool parents thought their children were progressing very well, compared to only 26 percent of traditional public school parents. On social development, 50 percent of private school parents and 38 percent of homeschool parents thought the year had gone very well, compared to only 25 percent of public school parents.[10]

Families are also open to organizing school differently. When asked in February 2024 about their preferred schedule post-pandemic, 39 percent of parents stated they would prefer some kind of part-time schooling, mixing days at home with days at school. Only 51 percent wanted to go back to full-time five-days-per-week schooling.[11]

In addition, policies that support alternative educational options are popular with parents. EdChoice's Schooling in America Survey polls four policies—education savings accounts (ESAs), tax-credit scholarships, vouchers, and charter schools. In spring 2023, three in four respondents (75 percent) supported ESAs, 66 percent supported tax-credit scholarships, 67 percent supported vouchers, and 65 percent supported charter schools.[12]

In what was the largest expansion of school choice in American history, seven states enacted new choice programs in 2023, and 10 states expanded ones already in operation, making 10 states with universal or near-universal private school choice programs. Those states are Arizona, Arkansas, Florida, Indiana, Iowa, North Carolina, Ohio, Oklahoma, Utah, and West Virginia.

This is the foundation on which educational innovation can build. Parents and the broader public are open to rethinking education. And increasingly, funds are available for families to attend cutting-edge schools.

But what might these new developments look like? It is worth popping the hood on a couple of school models to see what they might be able to tell us about promoting innovation.

In This Corner, Your Challengers!

It is all well and good to talk about innovation, and nothing gets a group of education policy wonks more excited than discussing "the future of education" or "what schools could look like." The problem, of course, is all the picayune details that stymie new enterprises. Blue-sky thinking is great, but at some point, hopes clash with reality.

That is why it might be more helpful to look at actual innovative schools. There are not a lot of these kinds of schools, but they do have the advantage of existence. They have learned lessons, cleared hurdles, and surmounted barriers that could have stopped their growth or inhibited them from fully doing what they wanted to do. While there could be an entire book of case studies of these different schools, I just want to briefly highlight two types: microschools and hybrid homeschools.

Microschools. Microschools are small schools, usually limited to 15 students or fewer, that meet in nontraditional spaces. They often meet in homes or public libraries but can operate anywhere it is safe to house children for the day.

During the pandemic, a version of microschools, *pandemic pods*, temporarily became a household term as families worked to cope with schools that were closed to in-person instruction. Many of these families hired tutors to teach their children and the children of their friends or neighbors, while others simply rotated watching the children as they worked through their school's remote-learning work.

A couple of more formal arrangements are worth exploring in depth. The Southern Nevada Urban Micro Academy (SNUMA) was founded in North Las Vegas initially for the families of essential workers who had nowhere to send their children when Clark County Schools closed. The program was the brainchild of City Councilwoman Pamela Goynes-Brown, who taught in the Clark County district for more than 35 years. Under her leadership, the city partnered with a local group of education advocates to set up a series of small learning environments, compliant with COVID-19 restrictions, in libraries and recreation centers. Students worked through personalized math and literacy programs that were aligned with state curriculum standards for part of the day and then did enrichment classes such as yoga and foreign languages for the rest of the day. Not only were parents overwhelmingly satisfied with SNUMA, but internal assessments built into the learning software showed serious growth in math and English language arts proficiency.

SchoolHouse was another microschool provider. It matched families with each other and then with a vetted educator in their area to create a microschool. It pitched small class sizes and a rich learning environment to parents and flexibility around curriculum, scheduling, and learning methods to teachers. Because it had so little overhead, teachers could actually earn 10–20 percent more teaching for SchoolHouse than they did in traditional schools, even though they were teaching fewer students and doing so in ways that they had far more control over. By spring 2021, SchoolHouse enrolled around 250 students in 50 locations across 10 states.[13]

There is perhaps no bigger name in microschooling than Prenda. Former tech entrepreneur Kelly Smith started Prenda in his own home in Mesa, Arizona, after volunteering to run an after-school coding club for several years. Smith could not understand why kids who were so excited about the work they were doing in coding club were so bored and disengaged with their schoolwork. He believes that a mix of meaningful, challenging work and opportunities for collaboration is what gets kids interested and keeps them engaged.

Prenda schools, which are usually capped at 12 students, have a three-part school day facilitated by what they call a "guide." During the Conquer module, students work on math, reading, and English language arts material via personalized learning software on Chromebooks. This software can target lessons, quizzes, and practice to the students' ability levels, allowing them to operate at different grade levels in different subjects at the same time and keeping them constantly working at the edge of their abilities.

After Conquer, which usually takes between 90 minutes and two hours, the rest of the day is spent in Create, which is focused on arts, and Collaborate, which is project-based learning in social studies, science, and other academic subjects. In both Create and Collaborate, students work individually and in groups on projects curated by Prenda, and students have the opportunity to create their own projects for themselves and their classmates. Prenda was growing rapidly before the pandemic, but the coronavirus supercharged its growth.

The Whitney M. Young Academy, a microschool operated by the Central Florida Urban League, provides a great example of how microschools can serve disadvantaged students in particular. Students at the school divide their time between personalized online learning software and small-group coaching, as with Prenda and SNUMA, but the school also offers "two-generation" supports for parents, such as job training, parent education, and community events. Students can take advantage of the state's private school choice programs to cover the cost of their attendance.[14]

Hybrid Homeschools. During the pandemic, "hybrid" learning practically became a four-letter word. To comply with social-distancing guidelines, schools across the country alternated cohorts of students through school buildings, having students learn at home for part of the week and in school for the other parts of the week.

This approach seemed to satisfy no one. Those who wanted school open fully or who were under pressure as they tried to manage work and remote learning were underwhelmed with the support of schools. Those who thought schools were not safe and that children should stay at home did not think that exposing them to risk for two days per week was any better than exposing them to risk for five days a week. Pile on a lot of terrible communication, opaque decision-making, and last-minute shifts, and you have a recipe for Sturm und Drang.

Yet, as noted above, more than a third of parents appear to want some kind of hybrid schedule going forward after the pandemic. How can all of this be true?

Perhaps the best place to look for an answer is at hybrid homeschools that operated before the pandemic even started. Hybrid homeschooling is not new; in fact, blends of home and school were arguably the predominant form of education for much of recorded history. But even more recently, schools that have students attend part-time—be they traditional public schools, public charter schools, or private schools—have operated across the country for decades.

Colorado is home to an exceptionally large number of public hybrid homeschools, owing to the state's strong tradition of homeschooling and to educators and legislators who worked together to build connections between the traditional and homeschooling communities. Colorado has a part-time funding law that provides half funding for part-time students, giving schools an incentive to create programs that cater to homeschoolers.

In Westminster, Colorado, the Summit Academy homeschool program has students come to class for one day a week and work from home the other four. On the days they are in school, students participate in enrichment courses such as sign language, coding, robotics, and support classes for students with special needs. The program is free for students to attend and has created a strong link between the local homeschooling community and the charter school community.

Turning to the private sector, the University-Model network of schools originated in the Dallas–Fort Worth metroplex in the early 1990s and has now spread across the country. These private Christian schools have students attend classes for two to three days at home and two to three days at school (generally with younger students spending more time at home and older students spending more time in school).

The schools are founded on the idea that parents are the primary educators of children and that the school is there to walk alongside parents and support them in areas where parents cannot provide for themselves. University-Model schools are fully accredited and operate as private schools. From one school, Grace Prep in Arlington, Texas, the network has now grown to 97 schools.[15] The network also helps families and educators that are looking to start a new school, offering workshops, conferences, and resources that inform them as to what is involved in starting a hybrid homeschool and that make it easier to manage the administration of a new school.

When talking to families who participate in hybrid homeschooling, several themes emerge. First, families frequently use the phrase "the gift of time." These are parents who want to spend more time with their children. They are sad at back-to-school time. For many of them, the rhythms of school days, weeks, and years are out of sync with the rhythms of their family life. Students traipse zombie-like through their school day and after-school activities, slam down dinner, and spend the rest of their evening doing homework before going to sleep for too short a time. Then the day repeats.

Hybrid schools, on the other hand, operate on a more relaxed schedule that offers two to three unstructured days per week that families can use for quality time and removes the need for nightly homework, since at-home work occurs during the day. Many families argue this is healthier for their children, who feel under less pressure and have more time to blow off steam and talk to their parents and the other caring adults in their lives.

But hybrid homeschools are also fascinating, vibrant communities. Another phrase that is commonly heard among hybrid homeschooling families is that they are "doing life together." It takes a certain type of family with a certain philosophy about child-rearing to want to teach their children in a hybrid environment. Those families can feel like weirdos in traditional schools, where other parents might say that they cannot wait to get kids out of the house or that they want the kids to participate in as many extracurricular activities as possible to keep them out of their hair.

Hybrid homeschools allow families to find one another and build purposeful communities organized around accomplishing a common goal, enriching all of their lives, and creating a dense web of support for the children and adults of the community.

The Changes We Need

Both of these new school models can tell us important things about how innovation works in education. In turn, that can help us understand the policies and practices needed to promote it.

First, there is a life cycle to the adoption of educational innovations. This idea is not new. Everett Rodgers first postulated such a life cycle in his book *Diffusion of Innovations* in the 1960s.[16] It is also a key concept in the international bestseller *Crossing the Chasm* by Geoffrey Moore.[17]

Put simply, different types of people adopt innovations at different stages. Some people love new things, are comfortable taking risks, and do not mind the bugs and teething pains that come with trying something new. But, as one might imagine, these people are a minority. Most people want more certainty, fewer bugs, and confidence that innovations will be worth the price or hassle.

Educational innovations attract limited participation, but the pandemic might have helped them "cross the chasm" into the mainstream. Folks who started pandemic pods or enrolled their children in microschools during the pandemic did so when the other options available to them were not great. The bar for innovation was low. But with the pandemic in the past, the bar has risen, and innovative schools will have to prove their worth.

Similarly, most families do not have the bandwidth (financial, temporal, or emotional) to experiment with new school models; they have the capacity only to enroll their students in proven schools. The families that did experiment are outliers, and what makes them happy might not appeal to other families.

That said, what many of these schools have going for them is a laser-like focus on a small number of intense problems that parents have. The traditional public school system has accreted, over the past 150 years or so, the wants, desires, philosophies, fads, and fixations of generations of educators, policymakers, and families. It is difficult for traditional schools to coalesce around a clearly defined mission because a central authority, the school district, assigns students and teachers to them. Therefore, educators and administrators find themselves putting out hundreds of little fires to try to satisfy all the people sent their way, even though accommodating one group might anger another.

These innovative schools are much clearer about the populations they serve and the problems those populations have, and they have a shared understanding of how they want to fix them. Parents and teachers alike join the organization because they share that vision and agree that they want to work together on the same efforts to solve the problem.

For example, families that think the school schedule is alienating them from their children and harming their children's mental health have a serious problem on their hands. There is not a lot of tinkering around the edges that can fix that. A total rethinking of the schedule is required, and so schools have emerged that will do that. That is more likely to help and, in turn, engage families in the shared work of education, as their major problems are being solved.

To promote more innovation in the American K–12 system, policy needs to change. But while policy change is necessary, this alone is not sufficient. We as parents, taxpayers, voters, and educators also need to rethink how we approach the education system and how we formulate a method for changing it.

Two Policy Changes. New, innovative educational models need two things: money and freedom. Luckily, policy changes can give them both.

When it comes to money, the best way to support innovative models is to put resources in the hands of parents to find the educational option that best meets their children's needs. Innovation cannot be centrally managed; it bubbles up organically and iterates and refines itself at a small scale before growing. Parents are in the best position to judge how well a new school model is working because their children are actually in the school every day, and thus, they can gather the kind of details that more blunt instruments, like state accountability data systems, cannot.

The most promising movement to provide this funding has already been mentioned: ESAs. Modeled on health savings accounts, ESAs put education funding into a flexible spending account that parents can then use to pay tuition or purchase educational resources. The state maintains a list of approved providers, and the money can go only to appropriate uses.

ESAs have been incredibly popular among families of children with special needs. The unfortunate reality of the contemporary education system is that even though there are supposed to be legal safeguards at the state and federal levels to provide an appropriate education for students with special needs, parents are routinely dissatisfied with what is available to their children. Not only that, families must frequently sit through contentious meetings with school staff (often outnumbered at the meeting by teachers, specialists, and administrators) to develop educational plans for their children and, if they have the means, must frequently go to outside providers to round out the education their child receives.

ESAs allow families to find the best set of providers for their children, special needs or no special needs. If they find a single private school that they think is meeting their children's needs, like Prenda, they can spend their entire account balance there. If not, they can spend some money on tuition and some on tutoring, some on speech therapy and some on online resources. The key idea is that parents are in control, not bureaucrats.

Charter school policy can promote innovation as well, as it also empowers parents to find the right school for their children. Charter schools are autonomously operated public schools that are free for students to attend and that receive a "charter" from a state-approved oversight body. That charter spells out what the school is going to provide students and the metrics that should be used to judge whether it is meeting its goals. The charter sector has seen tremendous growth in the past three decades, starting from zero schools in the early 1990s and increasing to more than 7,500 schools today.[18]

However, to promote innovation, the charter authorizing process has to be open to it. Unfortunately, in too many places around the country, authorizers have become complacent and biased toward familiar, proven models. They are less likely to take a chance on someone who wants to do something new.

Part of that skepticism is entirely reasonable; authorizers are controlling millions of taxpayer dollars and the education of hundreds of children. But the whole idea behind granting charter schools more autonomy was to give them the freedom to experiment. And because they are schools of choice, families that enroll know what they are getting into. It is not like when a school with residentially assigned students tries something new; charter school parents can vote with their feet at any time.

If we specifically think about microschools and hybrid homeschools, access to public funding will determine who can participate. In places like Arizona, which has an ESA program that students can use to attend Prenda, and Colorado, which has charter authorizers that have approved hybrid homeschool programs, a wider swath of children can attend those schools. In places that do not have such supports, these options will be open only to families that can afford them. Access to public funding is the key, and there are flexible ways to achieve that.

The second necessary policy change is deregulation. Deregulation gives new entrants the freedom to try new and different things.

It is wildly underappreciated just how many rules and regulations public and private schools and—depending on where you live—homeschools must follow. Federal, state, and local authorities place requirements on everything, including the length of the school day and year, what subjects must be covered and how, how many students can be in a classroom, how long they must sit for given subjects, what textbooks can be used, and on and on.

In isolation, almost all the regulations are sensible and justifiable. Chances are someone at some point in the past did something dumb or harmful, and a regulation was written to prevent that from happening again. However, over the years, these rules and requirements have grown in number and strength and place increasing rigidity on schools and educators.

Innovative educational models frequently run into antiquated regulations. Many states, for example, measure student progress by seat time. That is, students have passed the fourth grade if they have sat in a fourth-grade classroom for a set number of instructional hours. For schools that are trying to take a more personalized approach, this can be a problem.

Perhaps a student is spending some of their time working on math at a fifth-grade level, reading at a third-grade level, and studying language arts at a fourth-grade level. How do they fit in? What hours of their schooling are spent in fourth grade, and what are spent in other grades? And this is to say nothing of a hybrid school model, in which children are only in "class" for half the usual amount of time. How do those students get credit?

Deregulation is an area where states and the federal government can play a positive role. Both the federal government and every state in the union should periodically convene panels of educators to comb through the education code and excise regulations that are not helping schools provide a better education to children. Innovative school leaders should be consulted about what regulations are standing in their way, and those regulations should be repealed. When that is not possible, state education agencies should create exemptions or alternative pathways for innovative schools so that needless regulations do not hold them back.

Two Attitude Changes. The policy debates around school choice are well-worn territory at this point. The proposition is simple: If we want people to have access to new and better schools, we have to give them financial support. There really is no other way. Most people understand the idea of deregulation as well.

But if we want to see innovation happen in the American K–12 education system, two changes in *attitude* need to take place. First, we need to rethink how we talk about educational productivity, and second, we need to get comfortable with smallness.

Let us start with productivity. Typically, when we talk about productivity in education, we are talking about the return on our financial investment. America spends an incredibly large amount of money on K–12 education. According to the National Center for Educational Statistics, the $14,400 per student we spent in 2018 was 34 percent higher than the Organisation for Economic Co-operation and Development average, putting us fifth in the world, behind only Luxembourg, Norway, Austria, and Iceland.[19] When we look at the results of international assessments, we do not finish fifth.

What is more, inflation-adjusted per-pupil educational expenditure has doubled in the past 40 years, yet it is hard to say that our system is twice as effective as it was in the early 1980s.[20]

But again, this is well-worn territory. I would argue that even more than wasting money, the American education system wastes *time*. Children spend a lot of time in school. On average, they will walk into a school for 180 days each year between age 5 and 18 for seven or so hours per day. That is some 2,340 days—or 16,380 hours—of school. The question we have to ask ourselves is: Are we getting the most out of that time? I would argue that we are not.

Schools waste a lot of time. Schools get bogged down with completing administrative tasks, shuffling students around, settling students down at the start of class, managing disruptive behavior, attempting to differentiate for students of varying abilities in the same classroom, and more. Students are also asked to do homework outside class after a day when their time was wasted and often after extracurriculars or other after-school activities that have tired them out. They slog through it but do not learn much from it.

What if schools, and the state and federal agencies that oversee them, really took time seriously? What if instead of trying to fill out the day, schools tried to squeeze the most out of every minute they had with children?

Both hybrid homeschools and microschools show what maximizing time looks like. Whether it is schools like Prenda using personalized learning software to deliver academic content as quickly and efficiently as possible to free up time for collaborative work or hybrid homeschools condensing in-person class to a fraction of that of traditional schools, entrepreneurial educators are creating more productive schools.

SNUMA, for example, took a population of students who all scored at least a year below grade level in math and got 87 percent of them at or above grade level within a year.[21] Those who care about maximizing limited resources should try to learn from these providers.

The second attitude shift that needs to occur to promote more innovation in the K–12 education system regards scale. For more than a decade now, scale has been the lodestar of education reform. "Can it scale?" has been asked about every promising effort. Even if the program is going gangbusters for a small number of students, if it cannot be scaled up to a network, a district, or a state, it is seen as inadequate. State policymakers, philanthropists, and advocates look at the scale of the problems of the

American education system and want to support schools and policies at that same scale.

The problem, of course, is that educational change is hard enough on a small scale. Anyone who has worked in a school can tell you it is not easy to ensure that every child in the building is getting a great education. Educators are pulled in numerous directions on any given day, and students bring a diverse set of needs, desires, and talents, even within a single classroom or grade. Schools struggle to staff themselves with uniformly great teachers and have higher and lower performers, just like anywhere else.

But even schools or programs that work well on a small scale can struggle to grow. Often a new initiative has the backing of administrators, teachers, families, and students and is developed and tinkered with over time in an environment that wants to see it succeed. This is doubly true for philanthropy-funded projects that often have great fanfare and hope when they get underway. That vigor and desire diminishes when an initiative becomes the policy of a district or a state. The new schools that are told to adopt an innovation by the school board or the superintendent do not have the same sense of ownership, and programs are rolled out with much less fanfare.

We have seen this happen repeatedly. Whether it is a new math curriculum, a new educational technology, or a new pedagogical practice, initial small-scale versions are smashing successes, only to flounder when an entire district tries to roll them out.

So what can be done? We can start to support smallness. Yes, the challenges are large. Yes, millions of children do not get the education they deserve. Yes, this has serious negative consequences for them and our society as a whole. All of this is true. But, paradoxically, our fervor to fix it all at once impedes progress. If, instead, we realized that problems in education emerge over a long time and are deeply context dependent, we would understand that our one big solution must actually be thousands and thousands of small solutions.

In practice, this looks like the VELA Education Fund.[22] Started as an offshoot of the education efforts of the Walton Family Foundation[23] and the Koch network of philanthropies, the VELA Education Fund provides small infusions of capital to enterprising educators. The fund provides micro-grants of up to $25,000 to parents and teachers who are trying to start something new.

VELA's application process is simple and straightforward and does not have the pages and pages of information and piles of red tape that grant applications usually require. The fund also offers larger "seed" grants of up to $250,000 for entrepreneurs as they grow. But primarily, VELA is looking to provide that small bit of startup capital to get things going.

One group VELA funded is the Zucchinis Homeschool Co-op in Atlanta, Georgia. Started by Mikala Streeter and Khabral Muhammad during the COVID-19 pandemic, it provides a nurturing educational environment for 4- to 10-year-olds from predominately low-income and minority backgrounds. It provides what it calls "a play-based, culturally relevant community."[24]

Students take care of a small urban farm, planting vegetables and feeding bunnies. They spend their mornings on more traditional academic content and then have the afternoon to do group projects and individual projects based on their interests. It is a place, Streeter says, where "they can all be nerds together."[25]

Many other small-scale solutions are emerging out of the disruption that the pandemic caused. Philanthropists can shift their strategies to support them. Because they are sending less money out the door, they can take a lighter touch with the application process and design it so that normal people can apply and win grants. They can develop a pipeline of investments that might start with $1,000 or $5,000 but can grow to $25,000 to $250,000 if the entrepreneur is successful. While it can seem daunting, making lots of small bets and following up with the ones that pay off maximizes the opportunity for success.

The Looming Threat

On July 23, 2020, the Mesa Unified School District in Mesa, Arizona, held a special meeting to discuss a potential partnership with Prenda. The plan was to enroll 100 students in a microschool pilot program. The students would still have a Mesa Unified teacher as their "teacher of record," but

Prenda would handle the children's education. The superintendent was on board. Many families were interested.

The partnership failed. Perhaps the best perspective on the opposition came from the left-wing website Truthout. The article about the meeting stated that "Organizers with Save Our Schools Arizona and the Mesa Education Association successfully beat back" the proposal "by flooding school board members with 76 public comments in opposition to the proposal" in the lead-up to the meeting.[26]

Numerous board members harangued Smith, accusing him of trying to segregate students by race and painting a picture of guilt by association because of his participation in a New Orleans–based workshop for educational entrepreneurs. And, seemingly to tick the final box of a bingo card, the president of the Mesa Education Association said, "In my mind, part of the reason they're having this problem is because Betsy DeVos is pushing this model."[27]

There is massive, well-funded, institutional opposition to educational innovation. It comes from the alphabet soup of professional organizations of teachers, administrators, school board members, and associated staff. It comes from colleges of education that have vested interests in continuing to define teacher and administrator job roles in the ways they have always been defined. And it comes from the politicians who rely on these groups for contributions, organization, and votes.

Conservatives need to confront this challenge head-on. They have both the morally correct and politically popular side of the argument. Would-be reformers on the left of the spectrum frequently do not have the space, freedom, or flexibility to challenge these established interests. They need the donations, the paycheck, or tenure. Conservatives are less often encumbered in these ways and should use that freedom to make a bold case for doing right by kids.

Notes

1. William Butler Yeats, "Easter, 1916," September 25, 1916, https://www.poetryfoundation.org/poems/43289/easter-1916.

2. US Department of Education, Institute of Education Sciences, National Center for Education Statistics, "School Choice in the United States: 2019," https://nces.ed.gov/programs/schoolchoice/ind_05.asp.

3. Casey Eggleston and Jason Fields, "Census Bureau's Household Pulse Survey Shows Significant Increase in Homeschooling Rates in Fall 2020," US Census Bureau, March 22, 2021, https://www.census.gov/library/stories/2021/03/homeschooling-on-the-rise-during-covid-19-pandemic.html.

4. Eggleston and Fields, "Census Bureau's Household Pulse Survey Shows Significant Increase in Homeschooling Rates in Fall 2020."

5. Eggleston and Fields, "Census Bureau's Household Pulse Survey Shows Significant Increase in Homeschooling Rates in Fall 2020."

6. Eggleston and Fields, "Census Bureau's Household Pulse Survey Shows Significant Increase in Homeschooling Rates in Fall 2020."

7. US Census Bureau, "Week 61 Household Pulse Survey: August 23–September 4," September 20, 2023, https://www.census.gov/data/tables/2023/demo/hhp/hhp61.html.

8. Morning Consult and EdChoice, "The Public, Parents, and K–12 Education: A National Polling Report" (PowerPoint presentation, May 2022), https://edchoice.morningconsultintelligence.com/assets/167575.pdf.

9. Michael Q. McShane, "Public Opinion Tracker Deep Dive: Let's Zoom In on Homeschooling Opinion," EdChoice, March 17, 2021, https://www.edchoice.org/engage/public-opinion-tracker-deep-dive-lets-zoom-in-on-homeschooling-opinion; and Morning Consult, *National Tracking Poll #2111039*, November 6–12, 2021, Table EC26, https://edchoice.morningconsultintelligence.com/assets/201397.pdf.

10. Morning Consult and EdChoice, "Gen Pop National Polling Presentation" (PowerPoint presentation, March 2021), https://edchoice.morningconsultintelligence.com/assets/116294.pdf.

11. Morning Consult and EdChoice, "The Public, Parents, and K–12 Education: A National Polling Report" (PowerPoint presentation, February 2024), https://edchoice.morningconsultintelligence.com/assets/277700.pdf.

12. EdChoice and Braun Research, "2023 Schooling in America Survey Questionnaire and Topline Results," 2023, https://www.edchoice.org/wp-content/uploads/2023/07/Questionnaire-SIA-ONLINE-2023-Final2-1a-marked-up-POSTED-with-HEADERS-2.pdf.

13. Sophia Kunthara, "SchoolHouse Raises $8.1M to Take Microschools Nationwide," Crunchbase News, April 8, 2021, https://news.crunchbase.com/venture/schoolhouse-microschools-startup-funding.

14. Juli Kim and Sharon Kebschull Barrett, "Pods in Action: The Central Florida Urban League," Center on Reinventing Public Education, May 2022, https://crpe.org/pods-in-action-the-central-florida-urban-league.

15. NAUMS, "The UMSI Network of Schools," https://naumsinc.org/find-a-um-school.

16. Everett M. Rogers, *Diffusion of Innovations* (Free Press of Glencoe, 1962).

17. Geoffrey A. Moore, *Crossing the Chasm: Marketing and Selling Disruptive Products to Mainstream Customers* (New York: Harper Business, 2014).

18. Jamison White, "How Many Charter Schools and Students Are There?," National Alliance for Public Charter Schools, December 6, 2022, https://data.publiccharters.org/digest/charter-school-data-digest/how-many-charter-schools-and-students-are-there.

19. US Department of Education, Institute of Education Sciences, National Center for Education Statistics, "Education Expenditures by Country," May 2022, https://nces.ed.gov/programs/coe/indicator/cmd/education-expenditures-by-country.

20. US Department of Education, Institute of Education Sciences, National Center for Education Statistics, "Table 236.55. Total and Current Expenditures per Pupil in Public Elementary and Secondary Schools: Selected School Years, 1919–20 Through 2020–21," https://nces.ed.gov/programs/digest/d23/tables/dt23_236.55.asp.

21. Paola Gilliam and Sharon Kebschull Barrett, "Pods in Action: Southern Nevada Urban Micro Academy," Center on Reinventing Public Education, March 2022, https://crpe.org/pods-in-action-southern-nevada-urban-micro-academy.

22. The VELA Education Fund has provided funding for my research in the past.

23. The Walton Family Foundation provided funding for the production of this book.

24. Life School, "Zucchinis Program," https://www.thelifeschool.co/k-8th-grade.

25. VELA Education Fund, "This One-of-a-Kind Homeschool Pod Grew Out of Necessity | VELA: Meet the Moment," YouTube, January 11, 2021, https://www.youtube.com/watch?v=dA68ohT5ZOc.

26. Candice Bernd, "COVID-19 'Microschools' Are Betsy DeVos's Latest Privatization Scheme," Truthout, August 3, 2020, https://truthout.org/articles/covid-19-microschools-are-betsy-devoss-latest-privatization-scheme.

27. Bernd, "COVID-19 'Microschools' Are Betsy DeVos's Latest Privatization Scheme."

3

Educational Pathways to Economic Opportunity

BETH AKERS AND PRESTON COOPER

Education, and especially education after high school, plays an important role in our society. Yet if you ask a dozen people what that role is, you are likely to receive a dozen different answers. Although we can all agree that education is important, or even crucial, to the economic and social well-being of our nation, we often disagree on what education should be and how best to get it there.

In *A Time to Build: From Family and Community to Congress and the Campus, How Recommitting to Our Institutions Can Revive the American Dream*, Yuval Levin aptly describes this tension. He posits that universities

> are expected to be training grounds for future professionals, gateways to economic mobility, sanctuaries for moral and philosophical exploration, havens for basic scientific inquiry, nurseries of expertise in every field of endeavor, fonts of public spiritedness and civic learning, hothouses of political engagement, and even providers of food, housing, entertainment, and leisure—all in conditions of safety, freedom, and order.[1]

In effect, the US system of higher education serves all those purposes. In this chapter, however, we focus on a particular role for our system of education after high school: being an engine for economic mobility. We do not dismiss the importance of the other rewards of higher education but do contend that its effectiveness in delivering economic opportunity is fundamental to our society's ability to reap fully the other, sometimes less tangible, rewards that education can deliver.

In this chapter, we describe the extent to which our existing system of higher education is effectively delivering economic opportunity, suggest opportunities for policy to better support this objective, and discuss the potential for innovation to reach this goal.

Evidence on the Returns to Higher Education

Our collective rhetoric about higher education implies the universal belief that education is "worth it." The enormous investments in institutions and financial aid programs at both the federal and state levels convey the message that education after high school returns a huge dividend to society, in one form or another. Likewise, the message to young people and their parents, as well as those further along in life and looking to better themselves, is that spending on education is worthwhile. Parents and guidance counselors tell students that, despite its steep cost, higher education pays.

Young people have taken this message to heart. Nearly two-thirds enroll in college immediately after graduating high school.[2] Their main motivations are financial: 84 percent of college freshmen report that a primary reason for attending college is "to get a better job."[3]

Decades of public policy have built a system that encourages individuals to spend on college. Direct financial aid, as provided in the federal Pell Grant and state grant programs, defrays the cost of tuition. The tax code offers numerous credits and deductions to encourage people to get educated. When grants and tax benefits run out, the federal government operates student loan programs—some without effective limits—to facilitate more spending on higher education.

Government's encouragement of individuals to pursue higher education is grounded in some empirical realities. Individuals who stop at a four-year college degree earn 68 percent more than those with only a high school degree, on average, and people with an advanced degree earn more than twice as much.[4] Unfortunately, that does not mean that sending everyone to college would increase their income by 68 percent.

It does not take a PhD in economics to appreciate the problem here. Those who choose to pursue education after high school are likely different from those who do not. College-going students may be more motivated, or their families may have more resources. Those differences likely have something to do with how much they will be able to earn.

Consider a typical high school graduate who does not pursue further education. In a parallel universe where he or she does attend college, that student would probably earn less later than the average college graduate would. Similarly, most college graduates today would probably outearn the typical high school graduate in a parallel universe where they did not go to college. Thus, the true "return" to a college education is probably far less than the raw earnings gaps suggest.

The ideal approach to measuring the return to college would involve a crystal ball. You would look at future parallel universes to measure how much a given individual would earn with a high school versus a college degree. That difference would reveal how much higher education would be worth.

Without a crystal ball, social scientists can use various econometric techniques to account for unobserved differences between high school and college graduates. One analysis by economist Seth Zimmerman exploited the admissions policy at Florida International University (FIU), which uses a high school GPA cutoff to determine admission. Students just above the cutoff are probably similar to those just below it, with the main difference being that those just above had the chance to earn a bachelor's degree. Comparing the two groups' outcomes gets us much closer to comparing parallel universes.[5]

Zimmerman figures that attending FIU boosts students' earnings by 22 percent, relative to the counterfactual of not attending college. That is a significant effect on earnings, but it is also far less than the raw 68 percent gap between high school and college graduates.

But even the 22 percent return to college is misleading because different colleges and different sorts of college degrees are worth vastly different amounts. In particular, the choice of what to major in is often a more financially consequential decision than the choice to attend college itself. Most college students are familiar with the jokes about English majors working as baristas, but indeed there is rigorous evidence to back up the reality that some majors are far more remunerative than others.

Economists Zachary Bleemer and Aashish Mehta used another GPA cutoff to measure the causal return of majoring in economics. The economics department at the University of California, Santa Cruz, requires its majors to earn a minimum 2.8 GPA in their introductory courses. Students who do not make this cutoff must find another major. Therefore, comparing the earnings of students just above and below the threshold allows Bleemer and Mehta to estimate the return to majoring in economics.[6]

They find that the economics degree boosts students' earnings by 46 percent relative to their second-choice major (usually another field in the social sciences). That 46 percent boost to earnings reflects differences between college majors, not differences between college and high school graduates or differences between colleges. It dwarfs the 22 percent overall return to college that Zimmerman found. From a financial perspective, therefore, choosing the right major can be more important than choosing whether to go to college.

A recent analysis of nearly 30,000 bachelor's degrees by one of us (Preston Cooper) finds that the returns to college are all over the map. Although 20 percent of bachelor's degrees yield a lifetime return on investment (ROI) of more than $500,000, another 28 percent have no ROI at all after accounting for college costs and the risk that the student will not finish school. Majors like engineering, computer science, and nursing typically deliver a lifetime payoff of $500,000 or more, but many others such as the arts, music, and philosophy have no financial value at all, on average.[7]

The federal government invests more than $100 billion every year in the US higher education system through student grants, loans, tax benefits, and the direct funding of institutions. Yet the results of that investment are uneven: Although some programs yield significant benefits for individuals and society, other degrees may not be worth the paper on which they are printed. Policymakers owe both students and taxpayers a decent return on their investment.

How Policy Can Better Support Education
as a Pathway to Economic Opportunity

Although students, parents, and economists alike are laser focused on economic returns from education after high school, the system of regulation that governs the higher education sector is seemingly agnostic about the issue. This indifference is evidenced by the continued existence of low- or no-ROI institutions and programs of study that retain access to taxpayer-funded subsidies. Instead of assessing institutions based on economic return and funneling subsidy dollars to those institutions that deliver economic mobility, the system of accountability for institutions of higher education is based on a process called accreditation.

For an institution to access federal Pell Grants or for its students to access federal loans, it must receive a stamp of approval from an accrediting agency. An accreditor is a third-party organization selected by the Department of Education to serve as a gatekeeper to the tax dollars available through federal student aid. Historically, the process of accreditation has not relied heavily, or even at all, on the notion of ROI. Instead, consideration is given to various aspects of the educational experience. Many accreditors require that institutions or programs satisfy certain criteria regarding the credentials of their faculty, the scope of their mission, and the nature of their curriculum, but they do not have requirements for student outcomes.[8] In contrast, other accrediting agencies, generally those that specialize in accrediting career-oriented programs, base requirements heavily on student employment and financial outcomes.[9]

This variance means that aspiring college students cannot rely on accreditation or participation in the federal student aid program as an indication of whether the school or program they have chosen will set them on a path to financial success. It also means that millions of taxpayer dollars are spent each year to support institutions and programs of study that fail to prepare their graduates to contribute financially to society.

Of course, higher education should not always aim to deliver the highest possible ROI to students. But we believe that a minimum standard of "do no economic harm" should be applied to the process of determining eligibility for access to federal student aid dollars. In other words, colleges and programs of study that consistently leave students worse off financially than when they started should not be allowed to participate in federal student aid programs, including the student loan program.

This reform would protect the financial well-being of individual students and prevent taxpayer dollars from being delivered to institutions that are failing to accomplish the mission of delivering economic opportunity. In the long run, it would even encourage colleges to set tuition at levels that could be justified by the earnings that a degree from their programs affords. For example, for a fine arts program to "do no economic harm" to its students, it would need to be sufficiently inexpensive such that the lower-than-average wages earned by graduates of these programs do not amount to a negative ROI.

Consider a fine arts program that increases its students' lifetime earnings by $60,000. If the cost of college over four years is $100,000, then graduates of this program come out $40,000 behind. An accountability system based on ROI would deny taxpayer funding to such a program. To maintain its access to grant and loan dollars, the school would have two options: Reduce its cost to less than $60,000 over four years or improve graduates' earnings prospects such that the increase in career earnings associated with the degree exceeds $100,000.[10]

Programs that leave their students worse off financially would lose access to federal grant and loan funding. Importantly, however, even if one program loses aid eligibility, other programs at the same institution could continue to receive federal funding, provided they do no economic harm to their students. Indeed, we see this as a key incentive for colleges to help their students make better educational decisions. Institutions would be able to maintain federal aid eligibility for more of their students if they encouraged them to change their majors from fine arts to nursing or engineering, for example.

This reform would radically change the status quo, but it is not without precedent. The Biden administration has put in place regulations to set new standards for a subset of programs and institutions. Under the gainful employment regulations, "career-oriented" educational programs are required to prove, according to metrics set by the Education Department, that graduates are gaining employment after graduation that will allow them to affordably repay their student loan debts. This rule represents a significant shift in the way policymakers recognize quality in higher education.

The gainful employment regulations are not perfect. For one, they are part of what seems like a vendetta against for-profit colleges, which are disproportionately affected by these new standards. (Degree programs at public and private nonprofit colleges, which enroll the vast majority of American students, were exempt.) But there is also room for improvement on the metrics used to assess outcomes.[11] These regulations are based on arbitrary thresholds of performance, whereas we would recommend holding all programs and institutions, not just those explicitly focused on career education, to the standard of leaving students no worse off financially than when they started.

Whenever student outcomes are used as an indicator of institutional quality, there is a legitimate concern about the indirect impact on access, meaning who applies and who is accepted to enroll. One way institutions might respond to an accountability regime based more on outcomes is to prevent poor outcomes by denying enrollment to the students who are least likely to find economic success after graduation.

On the one hand, that is a good thing. In the current regime, institutions are incentivized to enroll anyone and everyone who can pay— and most can, thanks to loose criteria for federal lending. The move to outcomes-based accountability would put the onus on institutions to enroll only those students who they think would succeed. Although this potentially limits some students' access to educational opportunities, it also reduces the risk that they will enroll in programs of study that are bound to leave them with unaffordable debt.

On the other hand, this dynamic could mean that the loss of access to educational opportunities would occur primarily among already disadvantaged populations, including low-income and minority groups. The answer to this challenge, however, is not to make an exception that would allow these students to enroll despite their lower likelihood of success. Instead, it is to deliver subsidies in the form of cash grants that would make enrollment an affordable proposition.

For students at greater risk of non-completion due to being part of a disadvantaged population, the cash assistance would lower the net tuition that each would be obliged to pay and thereby the "investment" against which the returns delivered to them would be assessed. This would in turn increase the likelihood that students' earnings after graduation would justify their financial investment in college, because the costs of college would be lower. Institutions enrolling disadvantaged students would therefore perform better on accountability metrics based on whether their programs leave students better off financially. The incentive for schools to produce positive ROI for their graduates would remain, but the cash assistance for disadvantaged students would provide a little more wiggle room. The subsidies, however, should be limited, so that they would not salvage degree programs that are fundamentally lacking in economic value. Wedding outcomes-based accountability to modest cash assistance for disadvantaged students would deliver aid to those who need additional support without undermining the use of admissions policies to reduce enrollments that will predictably lead to a negative ROI.

This reform would not only encourage institutions to be more effective in delivering economic opportunity but also empower aspiring students to make better educational decisions for themselves. Historically, prospective students tended to decide where to enroll in college based on superficial or reputational factors. This was partly due to a lack of available information to make decisions using alternative criteria.

The landscape for college decision-making changed dramatically in fall 2015, when the Obama administration introduced a new tool—the College Scorecard[12]—that enables aspiring applicants to see how students who previously attended every accredited institution in the country fared financially after graduation. The College Scorecard publishes average earnings among graduates from every single program of study across all accredited institutions and reports on their success in repaying their loans. Recent updates provide this information at the program level, so students can compare outcomes for economics and English majors at the same university. For the first time, aspiring students concerned with ROI can shop for their college and major based on the outcomes that students before them have experienced.

Despite this significant innovation in students' potential ability to advocate for themselves and pressure institutions to charge prices that are in line with the value they provide, it seems that students continue to make enrollment decisions based on noneconomic criteria. And even when outcomes data are targeted to students making enrollment decisions, it seems that this information does not strongly affect where they choose to enroll.[13] This behavior is seemingly at odds with the survey data indicating that ROI is an important factor for the vast majority of college students.[14]

We might be seeing a failure of students to advocate for themselves through informed decision-making because the prevailing discourse about higher education is that it is, quite simply, worth it. We have failed to deliver effectively the message that investments in education are like any other investment: risky. Just as getting a high return in the stock market requires savvy (or lucky) decision-making, so does making a high return on an investment in your education.

Enabling Innovation That Delivers Opportunity

Outcomes-based accountability can improve the prospects for students at traditional colleges and universities to earn a degree, graduate, and get a good middle-class job. But traditional higher education does not work for everyone. Some students are simply not inclined toward academics. Students with better grades in high school are vastly more likely to complete college, even after controlling for family income and other background characteristics.[15] These achievement gaps reflect a mismatch between students' individual learning styles, skills, and interests and the pedagogical approach of traditional higher education.

Moreover, a bachelor's degree is not necessary to perform many jobs, even if they require some sort of education beyond high school. Unfortunately, postsecondary education has a dearth of innovative models to supply the skills students need to do those jobs.[16] The federal government has its finger on the scales in favor of traditional colleges and universities, which receive the vast majority of taxpayer funding. This imbalance has stunted the growth of nontraditional postsecondary education.

It is tempting to simply open federal funding to alternative programs, thereby leveling the playing field. But without a way to discipline new entrants, an unrestricted flow of taxpayer cash will attract low-quality or unscrupulous educational providers. That may leave students even worse off than they were before—and sour the reputation of good alternative programs.

In theory, accreditors should vet new institutions seeking federal funding and enforce high standards of quality. But in practice, because accreditation commissions are largely composed of representatives of the universities themselves, the system has not proved to be up to its assigned task of gatekeeping. Accreditors have a tendency to "protect their own" by maintaining approval of low-quality institutions even after serious problems become apparent.

Accreditors should not be in the business of gatekeeping for taxpayer dollars. Instead, the federal government should rely on an outcomes-based accountability system to dole out government cash. But this still leaves the problem of approving new institutions for access to student aid programs. It takes several years for student outcomes to be realized, so institutions could conceivably pocket millions of dollars in federal student aid before providing a single job placement.

The solution is a deferred-compensation system. The Department of Education would not disburse grant or loan dollars to institutions until they have a proven track record. To fund their operations in the meantime, colleges and universities could raise money privately and, if necessary, repay it after they proved their outcomes and federal dollars start coming in. Investors would vet potential new schools before extending financing—and they would do a far better job than accreditors would, because they would have their own money on the line. Deferred compensation would give innovators in education a chance to flourish while protecting taxpayers from charlatans.

The private sector can also facilitate the development and implementation of new business models in higher education. For instance, new financial products can bolster educational innovation by providing students with protection against the risk inherent in pursuing higher education. For students, much of that risk is associated with the quality of the school they attend. But some of the risk is systemic: If students happen to graduate into a recession, they may wind up with fewer job prospects through no fault of their own. This uncertainty may dissuade some students from enrolling in higher education at all, particularly if the school they are considering is a startup without an established brand name.

The Degree Insurance Corporation offers a way for colleges to protect their students against these risks. Schools can buy an insurance policy on behalf of their students, which will pay out if graduates find themselves earning below a predetermined threshold. Institutions using degree insurance can therefore promise their students they will earn at least a minimum level of income after graduation. This promise can help overcome the uncertainty associated with new institutions of higher education.

Private-sector initiatives also can establish trust between new institutions of higher education and potential students. Students pay tuition bills upfront, while the benefits of postsecondary education—job opportunities and higher salaries—come much later. Few students will take a chance on a school without an established brand name, unless it can find a credible way to win students' trust. Income-share agreements (ISAs) can build that trust.

ISAs are a new means for students to finance their education, but they lack features of a traditional student loan like a balance or interest rate. Instead, students pay a small share of their income every month for a set period toward repaying the costs of their education. ISAs reduce risk to students, because those who earn less will pay less toward their obligations. Students using ISAs will rarely be stuck with payments they cannot afford. In fact, most ISA providers do not impose any repayment requirement for students whose annual incomes fall below a certain threshold, usually between $20,000 and $50,000.[17] Students with higher incomes will pay more toward their ISA obligations, thereby cross-subsidizing the low earners.

ISAs can be provided through financial markets, but they also may be offered by educational service providers themselves. If students have to pay the school only if they find a decent job, then they will be more likely to take a chance on a new model. Some traditional colleges, including Purdue University, are now offering ISAs. But the model has made its biggest splash among nontraditional educational providers, such as coding boot camps, discussed later. New, nontraditional institutions often provide the lowest-cost way for students to gain the skills required for today's most-in-demand jobs.

ISAs can be a vehicle for innovation in higher education, but government regulations have not kept up with the market. Many regulators choose to see ISAs as no more than private student loans with a new name. The Consumer Financial Protection Bureau recently announced an enforcement action against one ISA provider for refusing to call its product a "loan." California's higher education regulator approaches ISAs as if they were traditional consumer credit products, with perverse results. The regulator forced one coding boot camp to modify its ISA in such a way that it became a worse deal for lower-income students.[18]

ISAs are different enough from traditional student loans that they require a new regulatory framework. Traditional financial regulations such as usury laws regulating interest rates do not work for ISAs, simply because they have no interest rates. New rules are necessary to protect consumers, define the proper scope of regulators' power, and give potential investors the legal certainty they need to make significant investments in ISAs.

Because an ISA is a more complicated financial product than a loan, regulations should mandate thorough disclosures of its terms, so students know what they are agreeing to. But regulations should also create a "safe harbor" provision that restricts regulators' ability to bring enforcement actions against ISA providers that offer reasonable terms. This framework provides consumer protection and avoids the capricious exercise of regulatory power. A new legal framework should also clarify the treatment of ISAs in bankruptcy and assign oversight authority to a single federal regulator.

The ISA marketplace, although tenuous because it so far lacks a regulatory framework, has already enabled the creation of innovative educational delivery models that would otherwise not have been created. One example is the exploding, yet still niche, industry of coding boot camps.

Coding boot camps are an alternative or a supplement to traditional degree programs. Their hallmark is that they provide low-cost, intensive, and short-duration training that prepares graduates for careers in computer coding. The $730 million industry, which at last known count had 115 providers, is now graduating more than 58,000 students each year[19] and placing as many as 79 percent of them in high-paying coding jobs that in the past were filled by bachelor's and master's degree-holders.[20]

In part, coding boot camps work well because the skill they aim to impart is measurable: Employers hiring someone to do coding can quickly tell whether that person has the aptitude in coding required for the job. Other occupations might require skill sets that are more difficult to observe. But another reason they have succeeded is that most boot camps have developed relationships with employers so that the training they provide is tailor-made to deliver employees who will be valued workers. This might sound like a simple innovation, but it is a far cry from the status quo in traditional higher education, which often bristles at the idea that it is simply a training ground for employment.

Boot camps are not alone in finding success with this model. Although options remain few and far between, apprenticeship programs have succeeded in training and placing workers, at a lower cost than traditional degree programs, into well-paying occupations that would not be accessible without some sort of education or training. A rigorous study of one apprenticeship program, offered by the Federation for Advanced Manufacturing Education, found that apprentices who completed the program earned almost $100,000 after five years. Apprentices' completion rates and postgraduation earnings were much higher than those of students at nearby community colleges, who were studying the same concepts in a more traditional classroom setting.[21] More apprenticeship programs like this one should be given the opportunity to prove their value.

It is our expectation that new and innovative educational pathways will continue to emerge and flourish so long as the alternative financing marketplace is not stifled by overzealous regulation.

Conclusion

Although higher education is often viewed as a golden ticket to upward mobility, the facts suggest that the returns to college and other forms of postsecondary education are uneven. The federal government already has an active role in subsidizing college, but policymakers have failed to ensure that students—and taxpayers—are receiving a return on their generous investment. Accountability for government-dependent institutions of higher education is based on inputs such as faculty credentials and curricula, rather than the economic outcomes that are of most importance to students.

We propose a reimagining of accountability around ROI. Colleges that leave their graduates worse off financially than if they had never enrolled there should not receive taxpayer money until they have lowered costs or improved outcomes enough to ensure the financial returns justify the investment. The government should also empower students to make better educational decisions for themselves by continuing to collect and disseminate data on colleges' economic outcomes. All concerned should work to dismantle the myth that postsecondary education is always a golden ticket to financial success.

Moreover, for students whose learning styles, skills, and interests do not always align with the pedagogical approach of traditional higher education, new models of learning should be encouraged. Private-sector innovations like ISAs and degree insurance can help alternative models flourish. From coding boot camps to apprenticeships, there are many options for students outside the traditional education system, and future years will undoubtedly see completely new ideas tried. Students deserve every opportunity to succeed.

Notes

1. Yuval Levin, *A Time to Build: From Family and Community to Congress and the Campus, How Recommitting to Our Institutions Can Revive the American Dream* (New York: Basic Books, 2020), 91.

2. US Department of Education, Institute of Education Sciences, National Center for Education Statistics, "Table 302.20. Percentage of Recent High School Completers Enrolled in College, by Race/Ethnicity and Level of Institution: 1960 Through 2022," August 2023, https://nces.ed.gov/programs/digest/d23/tables/dt23_302.20.asp.

3. Ellen Bara Stolzenberg et al., *The American Freshman: National Norms Fall 2019*, University of California, Los Angeles, Graduate School of Education & Information Studies, Higher Education Research Institute, 2020, https://www.heri.ucla.edu/monographs/TheAmericanFreshman2019-Expanded.pdf.

4. US Department of Labor, Bureau of Labor Statistics, "Earnings and Unemployment Rates by Educational Attainment, 2022," September 26, 2023, https://www.bls.gov/emp/chart-unemployment-earnings-education.htm.

5. Seth D. Zimmerman, "The Returns to College Admission for Academically Marginal Students," *Journal of Labor Economics* 32, no. 4 (October 2014): 711–54, https://www.jstor.org/stable/10.1086/676661.

6. Zachary Bleemer and Aashish Mehta, "Will Studying Economics Make You Rich? A Regression Discontinuity Analysis of the Returns to College Major," *American*

Economic Journal: Applied Economics 14, no. 2 (April 2022): 1–22, http://zacharybleemer. com/wp-content/uploads/2020/04/Return_to_Economics.pdf.

7. Preston Cooper, "Is College Worth It? A Comprehensive Return on Investment Analysis," Foundation for Research on Equal Opportunity, October 19, 2021, https:// freopp.org/is-college-worth-it-a-comprehensive-return-on-investment-analysis-1b2ad17f84c8.

8. The criteria used by the Higher Learning Commission are an example of accreditation criteria that exclude return on investment (ROI) or similar measures of student outcomes. Higher Learning Commission, "Criteria for Accreditation," September 1, 2020, https://www.hlcommission.org/Policies/criteria-and-core-components.html.

9. For example, the Accrediting Commission of Career Schools and Colleges bases its evaluation of programs on "the infrastructure that supports the delivery of programs as well as educational outcomes, including the rates of student achievement such as student graduation and graduate employment." Accrediting Commission of Career Schools and Colleges, "The Accreditation Process," https://www.accsc.org/ Accreditation/The-Accreditation-Process/index.aspx.

10. Calculating the "true" ROI for programs on an ongoing basis is impractical because assessing the lifetime value of a college degree requires observing earnings outcomes for decades after students graduate. An accountability policy should therefore rely on proxies for ROI that can be calculated on an ongoing basis. One promising metric is the price-to-earnings ratio, proposed by Jason D. Delisle and Jason Cohn, which compares the net price of a college degree to former students' earnings three years after leaving school. Policymakers can make an accountability system stricter by choosing a lower price-to-earnings threshold or more lenient by choosing a higher threshold. As a starting point, we recommend a threshold ratio of 1.0; if a college education costs more than students earn in a year, that program should not continue to receive access to federal funding. For more details, see Jason D. Delisle and Jason Cohn, "A Student Debt Blind Spot in the Gainful Employment Rule for College Programs," Urban Institute, March 29, 2022, https://www.urban.org/urban-wire/student-debt-blind-spot-gainful-employment-rule-college-programs.

11. Preston Cooper, "Biden's Flawed Attempt to Stem Rising Tuition Costs," Foundation for Research on Equal Opportunity, October 11, 2022, https://freopp. org/accountable-or-not-evaluating-the-biden-administrations-proposed-gainful-employment-framework-a49231683263.

12. College Scorecard, website, https://collegescorecard.ed.gov.

13. Kristin Blagg et al., *Rethinking Consumer Information in Higher Education*, Urban Institute, July 2017, https://www.urban.org/sites/default/files/publication/91666/ rethinking_consumer_information_in_higher_education_2.pdf.

14. Stolzenberg et al., *The American Freshman.*

15. Matthew M. Chingos, *What Matters Most for College Completion? Academic Preparation Is a Key Predictor of Success*, American Enterprise Institute and Third Way, May 30, 2018, https://www.aei.org/research-products/report/what-matters-most-for-college-completion-academic-preparation-is-a-key-predictor-of-success.

16. LaunchCode, a Missouri-based provider of computer science education, is a good example of such an innovative model. It combines a traditional six-month

course with a paid apprenticeship. An analysis by the Brookings Institution showed that these components in combination increased participants' incomes by $25,000 on average. As strong as those results are, such promising models may face problems scaling up. Jason Jabbari, Wenrui Huang, and Michal Grinstein-Weiss, "Apprenticeships Increase Employment, Earnings, and Optimism in the Technology Sector," Brookings Institution, January 27, 2022, https://www.brookings.edu/blog/techtank/2022/01/27/apprenticeships-increase-employment-earnings-and-optimism-in-the-technology-sector.

17. Sheila Bair and Preston Cooper, *The Future of Income-Share Agreements: Policy and Politics*, Manhattan Institute, March 12, 2019, https://www.manhattan-institute.org/future-income-share-agreements-to-finance-higher-education.

18. Preston Cooper, "California Greenlights Income-Share Agreements, but with a Caveat That Will Hurt Students," *Forbes*, August 21, 2020, https://www.forbes.com/sites/prestoncooper2/2020/08/21/california-greenlights-income-share-agreements-but-with-a-caveat-that-will-hurt-students.

19. Marc Juberg and Jenna Mercer, "State of the Bootcamp Market Report: 2023 Statistics and Share Analysis," Career Karma, June 14, 2023, https://careerkarma.com/blog/state-of-the-bootcamp-market-2023.

20. Beth Akers, *Making College Pay: An Economist Explains How to Make a Smart Bet on Higher Education* (New York: Penguin Random House, 2021).

21. Tamar Jacoby and Ron Haskins, *Kentucky Fame: Fulfilling the Promise of Apprenticeship*, Opportunity America and Brookings Institution, October 2020, https://opportunityamericaonline.org/wp-content/uploads/2020/10/KY-FAME-final-final.pdf.

4

Reviving Marriage to Promote Upward Mobility

BRAD WILCOX AND ROBERT LERMAN

Economic mobility for poor children. Mass incarceration. The racial gap in poverty. Urban violence. Deaths of despair. These are among the most important social problems facing America today.

Yet in confronting these challenges, too many scholars, policymakers, and journalists are reluctant to face squarely one of the most important factors driving them: family breakdown. For each social problem mentioned above, research suggests that family structure is a top factor.[1] Economist Raj Chetty and his colleagues, for instance, found that for poor children's economic mobility, "the strongest and most robust predictor [across communities] is the fraction of children with single parents."[2]

Too often, as one of us—Brad Wilcox—notes in his new book, *Get Married: Why Americans Must Defy the Elites, Forge Strong Families, and Save Civilization,* our cultural leaders are unwilling to openly acknowledge family as the elephant in the room.[3] As *New York Times* journalist David Leonhardt noted:

> I think that my half of the political spectrum—the left half—too often dismisses the importance of family structure. Partly out of a worthy desire to celebrate the heroism of single parents, progressives too often downplay family structure. Social science is usually messy, with correlation and causation difficult to separate. But the evidence, when viewed objectively, points strongly to the value of two-parent households.[4]

But if we are seriously interested in addressing the central challenges of our day—from the racial divide in poverty to the health of the American

Figure 1. Percentage of Children Living with Married Parents, by Income Quintile, 1967–2022

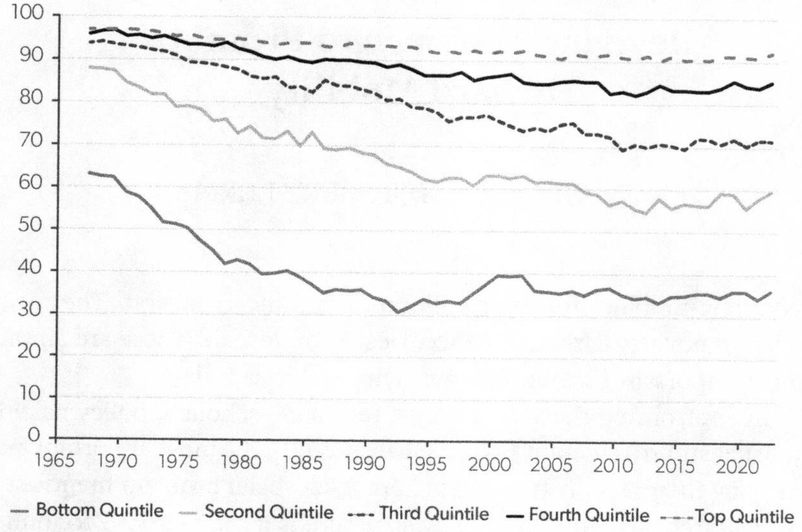

— Bottom Quintile   — Second Quintile   - - - Third Quintile   — Fourth Quintile   - - - - Top Quintile

Source: Scott Winship, "A Half-Century Decline in Marriage . . . That Ended 30 Years Ago for Disadvantaged Kids," American Enterprise Institute, April 21, 2022, https://www.aei.org/research-products/report/a-half-century-decline-in-marriage-that-ended-30-years-ago-for-disadvantaged-kids; and estimates for 2021 and 2022 provided by Scott Winship.

Dream—the data suggest we cannot ignore what is happening in homes across the country. Because married parents tend to head the most stable and happy homes, we must focus on the health of marriage.[5]

The State of Our Unions

When it comes to marriage, the state of our unions is not good. Marriage is markedly less likely than it used to be to ground and guide American children's lives. But the retreat from marriage has not affected all Americans equally. The institution has eroded most in the past five decades among poor, working-class, and middle-class Americans.

By contrast, today, marriage remains a relatively strong anchor for family life among educated and affluent Americans. Figure 1, for instance,

Figure 2. The Gap in the Marital Status of Family Heads with Children by Education, 2023

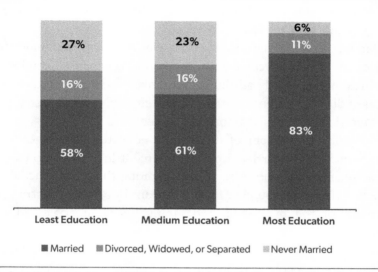

Least Education   Medium Education   Most Education

■ Married ■ Divorced, Widowed, or Separated ▨ Never Married

Source: Sarah Flood et al., Integrated Public Use Microdata Series Current Population Survey, version 11.0, 2023, https://doi.org/10.18128/D030.V11.0.

indicates that 85–90 percent of children in homes in the top two income quintiles (the top 40 percent) are living in married-parent families.[6] This means the vast majority of the affluent class can reap the substantial economic, social, and educational benefits that flow to men, women, and children in married families.[7]

But marriage among less educated and lower-income American families has eroded to create a growing class gap in the share of families headed by married parents.[8] In recent decades, as Figure 1 shows, the decline in marriage has been especially pronounced among middle- and working-class families—those headed by parents in the second and third income quintiles.

Marriage gaps by the education of family heads with children tell a similar story (Figure 2). If we divide parents by education into three roughly equal groups, the trend runs as follows. In 1970, marriage levels among family heads with the most and moderate education differed by only 6 percentage points (93 percent vs. 87 percent). By 2023, the gap had nearly quadrupled to 22 points (83 percent vs. 61 percent). The gap between heads with the most and least education grew from 9 percentage points to 25 percentage points.[9]

What has replaced marriage for poor, working-class, and middle-class Americans? A mix of cohabitation, divorce, nonmarital childbearing, and single living. Nearly all the growing marriage gaps between highly and less educated parents can be attributed to the much faster rise in never-married parenthood among the less educated.

As of 2023, 23 percent of moderately educated family heads with children had never married, up from 1 percent in 1970 and only 9 percent as recently as 1990. Also in 2023, among the least educated, the figure had risen to 27 percent from 2 percent in 1970. By contrast, only 6 percent of the most educated family heads in 2023 had never married.[10]

Nonmarital childbearing and divorce are stratified by education. Women without a college degree are much more likely to have children out of wedlock. In 2022, 62 percent of babies born to women with only a high school degree were born outside marriage, compared to just 12 percent of babies born to mothers with a four-year degree or more.[11] Divorce is also a bigger problem for less educated women; women with no more than a high school degree are half as likely as women with a bachelor's degree to see their marriage last at least 20 years.[12]

These patterns of marriage, nonmarital fertility, and divorce mean that children born into less affluent and less educated households are much more likely to live in unstable family environments than children from more advantaged homes are. In fact, having a single parent is about twice as common for children from less educated families as for children from families with college-educated parents.[13] Children and adults in many communities end up doubly disadvantaged, lacking the benefit of a stable married family and the socioeconomic resources that make it easier to flourish.[14] This, then, is one reason many important social ills—from deaths of despair to urban violence—are concentrated in poor and working-class communities.

Why Divided?

The marriage divide has arisen for a host of economic, policy-related, and cultural reasons. Some observers focus on changes in men's and women's relative labor market positions, which may have made men less attractive as husbands. When Fatih Guvenen and his colleagues compared the cohort entering the workforce in 1957 with the cohort entering in 1983, they found that men's lifetime earnings had been relatively stagnant, while women's earnings had increased 59 percent.[15] This study suggests that flat starting wages have largely driven men's economic stagnation.

Commentators and political factions suggest various explanations for male wage stagnation: bad trade deals, declines in manufacturing jobs, automation, an uncompetitive tax and regulatory environment, lax immigration enforcement, and safety-net disincentives, to cite some of the common culprits named.[16]

Meanwhile, men with a BA or higher degree have fared far better than less educated workers have. Men without college degrees are more likely than other men to face spells of unemployment, be underemployed, or stop working entirely.[17] Their distance from full-time work has increased in the past four decades. The share of 25- to 54-year-old men with moderate education (some college or an associate degree) working full-time fell from 85 percent to 77 percent between 1980 and 2019.[18]

Earnings trends among men and women have also diverged by class. According to Guvenen et al., while men's lifetime earnings were stagnant at the median and fell by 7 percent at the 25th percentile, they rose by 20 percent at the 80th percentile. In contrast, women's lifetime earnings rose 47 percent at the 25th percentile and 73 percent at the 80th percentile.[19]

Practically, these gendered shifts in work and income mean that men, especially those without college degrees, may be less economically appealing or necessary as marriage partners. That's because women are much more likely to marry men who are good providers and stay married to men who remain stably employed.[20] Thus, many men are less marriageable today—if not in absolute terms, then at least when comparing their earnings to what women can make themselves.[21]

Too many public policies are not marriage friendly. One contributing factor is the weakness of the US secondary and postsecondary education and job-training systems in preparing many students, especially those who do not graduate from college, for well-paying jobs and rewarding careers. This failure has contributed to the employment and earnings challenges that may have made men less marriageable.[22]

Another problem is that many means-tested programs, such as the earned income tax credit (EITC), Medicaid, and childcare subsidies, penalize marriage among lower-income couples.[23] These penalties hit working-class couples with children especially hard. One study found that more than 70 percent of American families with young children in the second and third income quintiles—that is, working- and middle-class families—faced marriage penalties related to cash welfare, food stamps, or Medicaid.[24]

These penalties can reduce the likelihood that couples with children will marry; one survey found that about one in 10 unmarried lower-income Americans report not marrying for fear of incurring penalties related to "government benefits."[25] Here is an example of a government policy that discourages marriage and disproportionately targets some of the very groups that have seen the greatest erosion in marriage in the past four decades.

The culture has also turned away from supporting marriage. According to Gallup, in 2020, 29 percent of Americans said it was very important that couples with children be legally married, down from 49 percent in 2006.[26] The share of adults agreeing that those who want children should get married fell from 74 percent in 1988 to 43 percent in 2022.[27] This decline in normative support for marriage means the general public perceives the institution as less obligatory for having and raising children.

This erosion of normative support for marriage has been most consequential for less educated and less affluent Americans. One survey found that while almost 70 percent of Californians with a college degree agreed that "it's very important for me, personally, to be married before having my children," only about 60 percent of Golden Staters who were not college educated took a similar view.[28] The same Gallup survey referenced above found that the share of adults without a college degree who believed it is very important for couples to marry if they plan to spend the rest of their lives together fell by 20 percentage points between 2006 and 2020.[29] In contrast, this belief fell by only 7 percentage points among college-educated respondents.

Meanwhile, the Pew Research Center found that men and women with less income and education continue to be more likely than more advantaged men and women to say a man must be a good provider to marry.[30] This cultural orientation stands in tension with the deteriorating economic status of less educated and lower-income men noted above. Thus, less educated and less affluent Americans now hold views about *both* children and breadwinning that make them less likely to see marriage as normative.

In sum, a range of economic, policy-related, and cultural currents have come together to not just erode the role of marriage in anchoring American family life but also disparately affect working-class and poor Americans.[31]

Doubly Disadvantaged

Regardless of the causes of America's marriage divide, the data above make clear that the costs of the retreat from marriage have fallen especially hard on the most vulnerable—poor and working-class children. This is particularly troubling because it renders these children doubly disadvantaged—navigating life with fewer socioeconomic resources and an absent parent.[32]

Why should the marriage divide concern policymakers? We know from decades of social science literature that children are far more likely to flourish emotionally, socially, economically, and educationally when raised by two married parents.[33] Children in single-parent families are about four times as likely to be poor as children raised by married parents are.[34] By growing up in a non-intact family, girls are about two times more likely to end up pregnant in adolescence, and boys are approximately two times more likely to end up incarcerated before they turn 30.[35] Children raised in non-intact families are also significantly less likely to graduate from college and realize the American Dream, achieving a better financial status than their parents.[36]

A Pew study found that only 26 percent of lower-income children with divorced parents experienced upward economic mobility as adults; by contrast, 50 percent of lower-income children with stably married parents reached the middle or upper class as adults.[37] Data from the National Longitudinal Survey of Youth indicate that black and white young adults raised in intact families are about 60 percent more likely to graduate from college than their peers from non-intact families are.[38]

Family structure does not just matter for individual men, women, and children; it is also crucial for communities' health. As noted above, Chetty and his colleagues found that a top predictor of poor children's economic mobility is the share of two-parent families in the community.[39] They also found the difference in economic mobility between black and white boys is smaller in communities with a greater share of present fathers and married adults. And sociologist Robert Sampson concluded that "family structure is one of the strongest, if not the strongest, predictor of . . . urban violence across cities in the United States."[40] The erosion of strong and stable families, then, has imposed a devastating cost on not just individual poor and working-class children, men, and women but also the communities they live and work in.

Five Solutions to Close the Marriage Divide

Given the importance of stable marriage, what can be done to revive the family fortunes of poor and working-class Americans? We outline five policy proposals aimed at the public and private sectors to advance this goal. Some are a familiar part of the family policy conversation on the center right. Others are new to that conversation.

Keep in mind that these recommendations seek to address the issues at the root of the marriage gap in America, not just play defense against the marriage disincentives built into public policy today. Progress on family life in America demands more: We must seek to reshape the conditions that drive young adults from marriage in the first place. We must renew marriage's educational, economic, policy, and cultural foundations to enable and encourage young adults to take a leap of faith and start building the families they desire.

Increase Funding for Apprenticeships and Other Forms of Career-Focused Learning. Building a policy landscape friendly to family formation in America will require significant improvements in preparing young adults for rewarding careers. Policymakers' most vigorous efforts should focus on the 60 percent of young people who lack a BA. In recent years, women have far surpassed men in college graduation. In 2020, among 25- to 34-year-olds, 44 percent of women but only 36 percent of men had earned BAs. The rates were far lower among minority men; only about 20–25 percent of African American and Hispanic young men had completed BAs.[41]

A lot has changed in the relations between the sexes in America since the 1960s, but the vast majority of women still consider it important to marry a man who can provide financially for a family.[42] In fact, four in five women say they consider it very important for a man to have a "steady job" when they are choosing a potential spouse.[43]

Unfortunately, a growing share of men without college degrees have left the labor force entirely.[44] With a wave of service, health, and information technology jobs replacing a shrinking manufacturing sector, many find themselves ill prepared for higher-paying positions that employers are eager to fill.[45] Far too many men cannot or do not take advantage of opportunities to enter a rewarding career early in life, become attractive marriage partners, and build families from a position of financial stability.

The "college for all" framework that dominates the culture exacerbates this problem.[46] Nearly two-thirds of high school graduates enter college degree programs.[47] While many thrive in college, large portions fail to graduate, especially those starting in two-year programs. And in 2019, even among those who graduated with an associate degree, median earnings were only about $30,000.[48]

Still, educational attention and dollars overwhelmingly focus on the college track.[49] Buttressed by federal and state funding, public four-year colleges spend 68 percent more per student on instruction than public two-year colleges do.[50]

K–12 curricula and schools are failing to offer less academically minded children the training and skills they need to build flourishing lives. Too often, schools fail to engage young people in their studies, partly because educators ignore lessons from cognitive science about how people learn.[51]

As a result, many young men spend their years in school just getting by—struggling through classes that do not capture their interests and turning to video games, social media, and other activities for a sense of place and purpose.[52] After graduating, too many drift into low-wage jobs without good prospects of upward mobility, at least in the near term, thus making them poor candidates for marriage.[53]

But things do not have to be this way. Even today, hundreds of thousands of quality, skill-based jobs are unfilled. Career and technical education programs are addressing this gap, teaching students real-world skills such as coding and car repair.[54] For example, high school career academies offer struggling students rigorous, career-oriented courses; on-the-job internships; and work-based learning opportunities.[55] Young men who participate in these programs earn more than their peers who do not.[56] Moreover, these programs prepare young men for successful relationships: Research shows that young men who attend a career academy are more likely to marry.[57]

Scaling apprenticeships is an especially attractive alternative to the college-only approach in formal education programs. Apprenticeships are highly effective in helping individuals learn relevant academic, employability, and occupational skills. The approach is cost-effective, because apprentices contribute to production while learning.[58] Apprenticeships encourage student engagement, increase incentives for good performance in academic courses, improve the match between workers' skills and labor market demands, encourage employers to upgrade their mix of jobs, and widen access to rewarding careers for workers who prefer learning by doing. Early apprenticeships can even help engage youth and build their identities.[59]

Yet government funding for apprenticeships has been minimal. Only recently has the federal government spent more on these programs than the inconsequential $30 million allocated to the Department of Labor's Office of Apprenticeship.[60] The goal should be to create a system that offers apprenticeship opportunities and occupational certifications for one-third of each student cohort.

This would mean increasing the number of civilian apprenticeships from about 510,000 to 3.3 million (assuming apprenticeships last an average of 2.5 years). Since employers will not only pay apprentices a wage but bear much of the work-based learning's cost, such an ambitious effort would require an annual government outlay of about $10–$12 billion, or about $3,000 per apprentice per year.[61] Though substantial, this amount is $1,500 less than what the federal government spends per student for Pell Grants alone.

Such an approach would require intermediaries to help employers adopt and implement apprenticeships and help high schools and community colleges offer relevant courses, enhanced counseling, and recognized skill credentials.[62] A modest number of high schools and community colleges are already taking the lead to sponsor apprenticeships and other training in close collaboration with employers.[63] Scaling these efforts requires substantially more funding—but far less than what the US spends on the purely academic approach to postsecondary education.

The opportunity at hand is a world where the potential of nonacademically minded young men and women is more fully realized—where they can build the skill sets they need to access flourishing careers that offer stable pay and a firm financial footing to marry and start a family. With a good job and no college debt, more young adults will be in a financial position to marry and form families and to start them earlier without spending years in school first.

Expand the Child Tax Credit Without Discouraging Marriage. A second step to encourage the formation of strong and stable families would be to expand and reform the child tax credit. An expanded credit, rightly designed, could help working- and middle-class families afford the challenges of raising children in the 21st century and reinforce the value of marriage and work.

In 2021, President Joe Biden sought to strengthen the financial foundations of family life by expanding the child tax credit in the American Rescue Plan. His policy sent $250 per school-age child and $300 per young child to almost all parents monthly.[64]

The president's plan was designed to help ordinary families keep up with the rising costs of raising children—such as food, housing, and childcare expenses. It was a symbolic and practical sign that the nation appreciated the opportunity costs many families incur by having one parent step away from full-time work once children come along.

As Patrick Brown and Wilcox noted in a *First Things* article, this policy move is valuable at a time when fertility is hitting record lows and families are getting less cultural support than they once did for parents' vital work: "Meaningful economic support for family life ... makes a statement about what government should be for: alleviating the pressures facing those raising the next generation."[65] The expanded child tax credit, then, was a step toward getting the republic to acknowledge and financially support the sacrifices of parents raising the nation's next generation.

Going forward, the child tax credit should be more generous toward parents of young children, given many parents' financial sacrifices to be at home or pay for childcare. Specifically, the Family Security Act proposed by former Sen. Richard Burr (R-NC) and Sens. Steve Daines (R-MT) and Mitt Romney (R-UT) is a good model for federal policy. Their credit would provide $350 per month for young children and $250 per month for school-age children.[66]

The Family Security Act avoids the Biden-style credit's primary mistake: Biden's American Rescue Plan provided cash support to families with no workers. In so doing, the Biden administration did not appreciate the lessons learned from welfare reform. By ending cash support for nonworking families, as recent research by Scott Winship and Robert Rector suggests, the 1996 welfare reform apparently helped halt the almost-relentless rise of single parenthood that America had witnessed since the 1960s.[67] Indeed, in the wake of welfare reform, the two-parent family stopped losing ground in the United States, and the country saw a slight rise in the share of children in lower-income families raised by married parents.[68]

Moreover, a recent study from Alaska provides additional evidence that moving toward an almost universal child tax credit, as the Biden administration sought to do, is not wise. A study of the Alaska Permanent Fund, which offers all the state's citizens a dividend from oil sales in Alaska, suggests that a universal benefit given without regard for work or income boosts unmarried childbearing in the Last Frontier.[69]

So in providing more help to married-parent families with one or two workers, the United States should not make the mistake of providing more cash to single-parent families with no workers, as was common with welfare before 1996.[70] Instead, any expanded child tax credit should target families striving to abide by the nation's classic commitment to the value of work. The Family Security Act does this by phasing in fully for families with incomes of at least $10,000 in the previous year (adjusted for inflation). And to minimize costs without penalizing marriage, the proposed act does not extend to the most affluent families, phasing out above $200,000 for single filers and $400,000 for joint filers.[71]

By supporting working families without penalizing marriage, the Family Security Act models the policy approach that should guide efforts to expand and reform the child tax credit. Other models, such as American Compass's family income supplemental credit and the American Enterprise Institute's working family credit, also provide approaches to reforming the child tax credit to reinforce work and marriage.[72] Because the credit provides valuable financial support to America's families, reforming the credit to reinforce the value of work and marriage should be a top priority for Congress.

Reduce Marriage Penalties from Means-Tested Tax and Transfer Programs in the US. A third step would be to reform the US social safety net so it no longer penalizes couples for marrying. Despite decades of social science research confirming the crucial role of marriage in building healthy communities and fostering positive childhood development, means-tested tax and transfer programs in the US often penalize marriage among lower-income families.[73] Marriage penalties arise when two lower-income single adults—one or both of whom might qualify for public benefits when they apply separately—become ineligible for federal benefits when they marry because their combined income pushes them above the benefit threshold.[74]

Many unmarried couples today face losing crucial federal supports and tax benefits if they choose to marry, which incentivizes cohabitation and discourages marriage.

While the research on how marriage penalties affect behavior is mixed, the literature generally suggests marriage penalties are associated with less marriage and more cohabitation.[75] One study found that every $1,000 of marriage penalties was generally associated with a 1.7 percentage point decrease in the probability a couple would marry. This figure rose to 2.7 percentage points for those without a college degree.[76] When studying

EITC-eligible single mothers, another study found that mothers facing a marriage penalty were 2.5 percentage points more likely to cohabit and 2.7 percentage points less likely to marry than were mothers who did not face a marriage penalty.[77]

Further, several federal programs have expanded their reach in recent decades, meaning a growing share of low-income families now receive some means-tested benefit. Today, more than four in 10 American families with children receive some kind of means-tested benefit or tax credit,[78] which means working-class couples with children are more likely to face marriage penalties than they once were.

The evidence suggests that the burden of marriage penalties falls on couples whose income is between 100 percent and 250 percent of the poverty line—that is, working-class Americans, who have already seen the greatest erosion in marriage of any group in the nation in the past three decades.[79]

The financial burden of marriage penalties is not small. Research suggests that marriage penalties can exceed 30 percent of some couples' income.[80] And nearly 40 percent of cohabiting parents with young children may face marriage penalties in programs such as the Supplemental Nutrition Assistance Program, Medicaid, and Temporary Assistance for Needy Families.[81]

Clearly, marriage penalties should be an unwelcome part of federal policy among conservatives. Policies should encourage and reward marriage—not penalize it. And for something as important to human flourishing as marriage, policymakers should concentrate the strongest behavioral incentives in the most vulnerable communities. The current arrangement makes marriage more costly for individuals in these communities. Policymakers must address marriage penalties in the safety net and tax code.

The first obvious policy candidate for reducing marriage penalties is the EITC. Most proposals for marriage-penalty reduction have centered on this crucial vehicle for cash support to families. Proposals by Angela Rachidi and Winship at the American Enterprise Institute, for instance, provide models for how to address this EITC problem.[82]

Doubling the income threshold for married families seeking to qualify for other major safety-net benefits (such as Medicaid, the

Supplemental Nutrition Assistance Program, and Section 8 housing) relative to single-parent families would greatly reduce the chances that a working-class couple would be penalized for marrying. But such a proposal's cost rises quickly. Adding a whole new group of middle-income married families to the list of federal beneficiaries is not inexpensive. To limit these costs, threshold extensions should be restricted to married-parent families with children under age 5. This would concentrate added costs in the immediate years after a couple's decision to marry while funneling additional support to married families in their highest-cost years of parenthood.

Give More Families the Power to Choose an Education That Will Prepare Their Children for a Strong Family Life. It is no secret that public schools are failing millions of children from poor and working-class backgrounds. In 2020, Katharine Stevens highlighted the widespread failure of public school reforms in recent decades to meaningfully reduce the achievement gap and improve low-income students' academic performance.[83] The failure of so many public schools to offer in-person education to lower-income students during the COVID-19 pandemic only added to frustrations about public schools' inability to provide all students with a good education.[84] After all, closed schools and inadequate remote learning offerings fell particularly hard on low-income and minority students.[85]

But public schools have not just failed vulnerable children academically. Many are not doing their part to prepare their students to build strong and stable families. Admittedly, education about family life is fraught with controversy—and not without good reason. Educators must be sensitive to the variety of family environments their students are raised in. But many schools respond to the challenges of contemporary family life by avoiding conversations about marriage and family formation entirely.

Too many schools fail to recognize that they have tremendous influence over a child's moral development. In the words of James Hunter and Ryan Olson, social institutions such as schools have "distinctive ideals, beliefs, obligations, prohibitions, and commitments—many implicit and some explicit," which "form a 'moral ecology.'"[86] Different kinds of schools, with different moral ecologies, set children up for success or failure in areas of life outside the classroom. Chief among these is family life.

A research report on schooling and family outcomes coauthored by Wilcox suggests different school types' moral ecologies influence students' family formation later in life. Students who attend private schools are more likely to forge strong and stable marriages and have children in marriage.[87] For example, as adults, only 11 percent of Protestant school attendees in the dataset had had a child out of wedlock, compared with more than a quarter of those who attended public school. And only 42 percent of public school attendees said they had married, compared with 53 percent of secular private school attendees and 63 percent of Protestant school attendees. Although the report controlled for a number of confounding factors, the association between these family outcomes and private schooling could be at least partially attributable to differences in the kinds of families that resorted to private schooling, especially religious schooling.

In family life, private schools—especially Protestant ones—seem to offer a clear advantage to children. But the educational system boxes the vast majority of poor and working-class students into public schools that fail to cultivate their academic and relational development. Policymakers should pursue school choice to open pathways to strong and stable families for vulnerable students who want to place themselves in a better environment.

Scholars have put forward many viable approaches to school choice, but one promising policy is education savings accounts (ESAs).[88] Arizona was the first state to authorize ESAs. When a parent removes their child from an Arizona public school, they are given a restricted-use debit card with a percentage (usually 90 percent) of the money a state would otherwise spend on their child's education at a district-run public school. Parents can use these funds toward numerous private educational ends—such as paying tuition at a local private school, paying for music lessons, or purchasing textbooks to homeschool their child. In Arizona, participation in the ESA program has increased dramatically since it was launched in 2011.[89]

An ESA's cash value—averaging more than $7,000 per Arizona child in the 2022–23 school year—can go a long way in helping families realize a better education for their children than they could otherwise afford. Federal policymakers could compound states' efforts by implementing a similar policy nationally, adding the federal government's per-pupil spending (currently about $1,200 per public school student) on top of state dollars for families in any state that chooses to pursue an ESA model.[90] Such efforts could empower families to send their children to schools that not only offer stronger academic development but also cultivate the moral ecology that will set their students up for success in family life down the road.

Launch a New Public and Private Campaign Around the Success Sequence. As noted above, one important angle of fraying family life is the rising share of young men and women having children outside marriage. Today, around 40 percent of infants were born to unwed mothers.[91] This crisis of nonmarital births is especially concentrated among poor and working-class mothers. In 2016, women with just a high school degree were nearly six times as likely to have a child outside marriage as were those with at least a bachelor's degree.[92]

Estimates suggest as many as 62 percent of children born outside marriage have biological parents who are cohabiting at their birth.[93] Cohabiting unions are far less stable than married unions, with children born in cohabiting unions about twice as likely to see their parents split up before they reach age 12.[94]

Further, we know from a wealth of research that children raised by cohabiting parents are disadvantaged on several fronts. Children born to these parents are far more likely to experience family instability and increasingly complex family arrangements.[95] Likewise, they are four times more likely to be abused.[96] And they experience worse social, emotional, and educational outcomes later in life.[97] But nonmarital childbearing is not just bad for children; young adults are also far less likely to succeed financially in life if they put the baby carriage before marriage.[98]

Most young adults desire to build committed, healthy relationships; three in four high school seniors say having a strong marriage is "extremely important" to them.[99] However, many youth lack sufficient knowledge of how to realize these desires and build strong families. Long before they intend to marry, they are thrust into situations in which they must make important decisions about sex and relationships that they are not prepared to make.[100]

Public policies should seek to empower more young adults to make informed decisions about their future. Thankfully, a powerful framework exists to help young Americans build healthy, stable family lives. Termed the "success sequence" by Brookings Institution scholars Ron Haskins and Isabel Sawhill, this framework describes a series of crucial life decisions surrounding education, work, marriage, and childbearing that are powerfully linked to a person's chance of ending up poor.[101] In research with Wendy Wang, Wilcox found that only 3 percent of millennials who completed their education with at least a high school degree, worked full-time, and waited until marriage to have children were in poverty by the time they reached adulthood.[102]

The success sequence offers an accessible framework, compelling narrative, and launching pad for teachers and mentors to engage young adults in crucial conversations about decisions related to education, work, relationships, and sex. Policymakers should launch a national public and private campaign teaching students the success sequence and building space for them to critically consider the decisions that will pave their pathways to success.

Already, rigorous evaluations of curricula teaching the success sequence show promising results. One randomized control trial evaluating a curriculum on healthy relationships that taught the success sequence showed a 46 percent reduction in teen pregnancy 12 months after the intervention.[103] Teens who participated in the course were less likely to have had sex six months after it and had fewer sex partners than those in the control group.[104]

The difficulty will be scaling successful small-scale interventions such as the one described above into a multifaceted, national, public, *and* private campaign. A national campaign must balance different stakeholders' interests. Some partners, such as churches and nonprofits, may prefer to use moral or religious language when applying the success sequence framework to family formation and relationship classes. Others, such as public schools, will likely prefer a descriptive model—teaching students the data on outcomes associated with different decisions and avoiding overly moralistic language. A successful initiative will leave room for a wide range of applications for this framework.

Campaigns against smoking and teenage pregnancy have shown that sustained efforts to change behavior can work. A campaign organized around the success sequence—receiving widespread support from educational, civic, media, pop cultural, and religious institutions—might meet the same level of success as the recent national campaign to prevent teen pregnancy, which apparently helped drive down the teen pregnancy rate by more than 65 percent since the 1990s.[105]

Conclusion

In recent decades, America has become a nation where the clear majority of well-educated and affluent children continue to enjoy the benefit of being raised by married parents, while a large share of working-class and poor children do not. Too many children in low- and middle-income families are growing up in homes without both parents. Given the importance of a stable, two-parent home for a range of economic, emotional, educational, and social outcomes across the country, this deficit leaves too many children doubly disadvantaged, with less access to socioeconomic resources *and* without a stable, married home.

To bridge this marriage divide, policymakers should pass and implement a variety of educational, economic, and cultural policies to help renew the marriage and family fabric of poor and working-class communities. Federal policies cannot aim to just "stop the bleeding" by responding defensively to the marriage disincentives built into welfare and education policies for decades. Policymakers must take steps to ensure the current and next generation of Americans are all afforded ample opportunities to access the building blocks they need to build strong, fulfilling family lives.

The policy ideas presented here are designed to make it easier for young men and women to forge strong and stable marriages. We can think of nothing more important for the state of our union than renewing the state of our unions—families.

Acknowledgments

The authors give special thanks to Peyton Roth for his research assistance.

Notes

1. Raj Chetty et al., "Where Is the Land of Opportunity? The Geography of Intergenerational Mobility in the United States," *Quarterly Journal of Economics* 129, no. 4 (November 2014): 1553–623, https://academic.oup.com/qje/article/129/4/1553/1853754; Brad Wilcox, Joseph Price, and Jacob Van Leeuwen, "The Family Geography of the American Dream: New Neighborhood Data on Single Parenthood, Prisons, and Poverty," Institute for Family Studies, October 17, 2018, https://ifstudies.org/blog/the-family-geography-of-the-american-dream-new-neighborhood-data-on-single-parenthood-prisons-and-poverty; John Iceland, "Racial and Ethnic Inequality in Poverty and Affluence, 1959–2015," *Population Research and Policy Review* 38, no. 5 (October 2019): 615–54, https://www.ncbi.nlm.nih.gov/pmc/articles/PMC6934366; Robert J. Sampson, "Unemployment and Imbalanced Sex Ratios: Race Specific Consequences for Family Structure and Crime," in *The Decline in Marriage Among African Americans: Causes, Consequences, and Policy Implications*, ed. M. Belinda Tucker and Claudia Mitchell-Kernan (New York: Russell Sage Foundation, 1995); Melvin L. Oliver, "Commentary," in *The Decline in Marriage Among African Americans: Causes, Consequences, and Policy Implications*, ed. M. Belinda Tucker and Claudia Mitchell-Kernan (New York: Russell Sage Foundation, 1995); and Philip N. Cohen, "The Rising Marriage Mortality Gap Among Whites" (working paper, University of Maryland, College Park, MD, November 2, 2019), https://doi.org/10.31235/osf.io/8374m.

2. Chetty et al., "Where Is the Land of Opportunity?"

3. Brad Wilcox, *Get Married: Why Americans Must Defy the Elites, Forge Strong Families, and Save Civilization* (New York: Broadside Books, 2024).

4. David Leonhardt, "A One-Question Quiz on the Poverty Trap," *New York Times*, October 4, 2018, https://www.nytimes.com/2018/10/04/opinion/child-poverty-family-income-neighborhood.html.

5. Richard V. Reeves and Eleanor Krause, "Cohabiting Parents Differ from Married Ones in Three Big Ways," Brookings Institution, April 5, 2017, https://www.brookings.edu/research/cohabiting-parents-differ-from-married-ones-in-three-big-ways; AEI-Brookings Working Group on Childhood in the United States, *Rebalancing: Children First*, American Enterprise Institute and Brookings Institution, February 8, 2022, https://www.aei.org/research-products/report/rebalancing-children-first; and Paul Taylor, ed., *The Decline of Marriage and Rise of New Families*, Pew Research Center, November 18, 2010, https://assets.pewresearch.org/wp-content/uploads/sites/3/2010/11/pew-social-trends-2010-families.pdf.

6. Scott Winship, "A Half-Century Decline in Marriage . . . That Ended 30 Years Ago for Disadvantaged Kids," American Enterprise Institute, April 21, 2022,

https://www.aei.org/research-products/report/a-half-century-decline-in-marriage-that-ended-30-years-ago-for-disadvantaged-kids; and estimates for 2021 and 2022 provided by Scott Winship.

7. John Iceland, "US Disparities in Affluence by Household Structure, 1959 to 2017," *Demographic Research* 44 (April 1, 2021): 653–98, https://www.demographic-research.org/articles/volume/44/28; Brad Wilcox et al., eds., *The State of Our Unions 2010: When Marriage Disappears; The New Middle America*, Institute for American Values and National Marriage Project, 2010, http://www.stateofourunions.org/2010/index.php; and Rachel Sheffield and Scott Winship, *The Demise of the Happy Two-Parent Home*, US Congress, Joint Economic Committee, July 23, 2020, https://www.jec.senate.gov/public/index.cfm/republicans/2020/7/the-demise-of-the-happy-two-parent-home.

8. AEI-Brookings Working Group on Childhood in the United States, *Rebalancing*.

9. Authors' tabulations from the March 1970 and 2023 Current Population Surveys. We accessed the data through Sarah Flood et al., Integrated Public Use Microdata Series Current Population Survey, version 11.0, 2023, https://doi.org/10.18128/D030.V11.0. We created education groups by ranking civilian adults not in group quarters and not in school by educational attainment and dividing them into thirds. Because educational attainment is "lumpy," people with the same educational attainment can end up in different thirds; each third has the same number of adults.

10. Authors' tabulations; see endnote 9.

11. Authors' calculations from US Department of Health and Human Services, Centers for Disease Control and Prevention, National Center for Health Statistics, Natality Public-Use Data 2016–22, http://wonder.cdc.gov/natality-expanded-current.html.

12. Wendy Wang, "The Link Between a College Education and a Lasting Marriage," Pew Research Center, December 4, 2015, https://www.pewresearch.org/fact-tank/2015/12/04/education-and-marriage.

13. This figure compares children of mothers and fathers with and without a bachelor's degree. Brad Wilcox, Jeffrey P. Dew, and Betsy VanDenBerghe, *State of Our Unions 2019: iFidelity; Interactive Technology and Relationship Faithfulness*, National Marriage Project, Wheatley Institution, and School of Family Life, 2019, http://nationalmarriageproject.org/wp-content/uploads/2019/07/SOU2019.pdf.

14. Sara McLanahan, "Diverging Destinies: How Children Are Faring Under the Second Demographic Transition," *Demography* 41, no. 4 (November 2004): 607–27, https://www.jstor.org/stable/1515222?seq=3.

15. Fatih Guvenen et al., "Lifetime Earnings in the United States over Six Decades," *American Economic Journal: Applied Economics* 14, no. 4 (October 2022): 446–79.

16. In a review of factors affecting the 1999–2016 decline in labor force participation, Katharine Abraham and Melissa Kearney find that trade and the penetration of robots are most important. See Katharine G. Abraham and Melissa S. Kearney, "Explaining the Decline in the US Employment-to-Population Ratio: A Review of the Evidence," *Journal of Economic Literature* 58, no. 3 (September 2020): 585–643, https://www.aeaweb.org/articles?id=10.1257/jel.20191480. For a critique of demand-side explanations for the longer-term decline in male labor force participation and wage stagnation, see Christina King, Scott Winship, and Adam N. Michel, *Reconnecting Americans to the Benefits of Work*, US Congress, Joint Economic Committee, October 27, 2021, https://www.

jec.senate.gov/public/_cache/files/5ac0a254-ff00-4a18-baf0-bdfedb9bb154/connections-to-work.pdf.

17. David Autor and Melanie Wasserman, *Wayward Sons: The Emerging Gender Gap in Labor Markets and Education*, Massachusetts Institute of Technology, Blueprint Labs, March 2013, https://blueprintlabs.mit.edu/research/wayward-sons-the-emerging-gender-gap-in-labor-markets-and-education; and Wilcox et al., eds., *The State of Our Unions 2010*.

18. Authors' tabulations from the March 2020 Current Population Survey. Flood et al., Integrated Public Use Microdata Series Current Population Survey.

19. Guvenen et al., "Lifetime Earnings in the United States over Six Decades."

20. Frances Kobrin Goldscheider and Linda J. Waite, "Sex Differences in the Entry into Marriage," *American Journal of Sociology* 92, no. 1 (July 1986): 91–109, https://www.jstor.org/stable/2779718; and Alexandra Killewald, "Money, Work, and Marital Stability: Assessing Change in the Gendered Determinants of Divorce," *American Sociological Review* 81, no. 4 (August 2016): 696–719, https://www.asanet.org/wp-content/uploads/attach/journals/aug16asrfeature.pdf.

21. William Julius Wilson, "Prisoners of the Economy," *New York Times*, October 25, 1987, https://archive.nytimes.com/www.nytimes.com/books/98/12/06/specials/wilson-disadvantaged.html; Robert Lerman and Brad Wilcox, *For Richer, for Poorer: How Family Structures Economic Success in America*, American Enterprise Institute and Institute for Family Studies, October 28, 2014, https://www.aei.org/research-products/report/for-richer-for-poorer; and Scott Winship, *Bringing Home the Bacon: Have Trends in Men's Pay Weakened the Traditional Family?*, American Enterprise Institute, December 14, 2022, https://www.aei.org/research-products/report/bringing-home-the-bacon-have-trends-in-mens-pay-weakened-the-traditional-family.

22. Ariel J. Binder and John Bound, "The Declining Labor Market Prospects of Less-Educated Men," *Journal of Economic Perspectives* 33, no. 2 (Spring 2019): 163–90, https://www.ncbi.nlm.nih.gov/pmc/articles/PMC7745920/pdf/nihms-1601100.pdf.

23. Adam Carasso and C. Eugene Steuerle, "The Hefty Penalty on Marriage Facing Many Households with Children," *Future of Children* 15, no. 2 (Fall 2005): 157–75, https://futureofchildren.princeton.edu/sites/g/files/toruqf2411/files/media/marriage_and_child_wellbeing_15_02_fulljournal.pdf.

24. Brad Wilcox, Joseph Price, and Angela Rachidi, *Marriage, Penalized: Does Social-Welfare Policy Affect Family Formation?*, American Enterprise Institute and Institute for Family Studies, July 26, 2016, https://www.aei.org/research-products/report/marriage-penalized-does-social-welfare-policy-affect-family-formation.

25. Wendy Wang, "Money Is Not the Main Reason Why Americans Who Desire Marriage Remain Single," Institute for Family Studies, November 9, 2021, https://ifstudies.org/blog/money-is-not-the-main-reason-why-americans-who-desire-marriage-remain-single.

26. Jeffrey M. Jones, "Is Marriage Becoming Irrelevant?," Gallup, December 28, 2020, https://news.gallup.com/poll/316223/fewer-say-important-parents-married.aspx.

27. Michael Davern et al., General Social Survey Data Explorer, 1972–2022, https://gssdataexplorer.norc.org.

28. Brad Wilcox and Wendy Wang, *State of Contradiction: Progressive Family Culture, Traditional Family Structure in California*, Institute for Family Studies, January 14, 2020, https://www.aei.org/research-products/report/state-of-contradiction-progressive-family-culture-traditional-family-structure-in-california.

29. Jones, "Is Marriage Becoming Irrelevant?"

30. Taylor, ed., *The Decline of Marriage and Rise of New Families*.

31. David T. Ellwood and Christopher Jencks, "The Spread of Single-Parent Families in the United States Since 1960" (working paper, Harvard University, John F. Kennedy School of Government, Cambridge, MA, June 11, 2004), https://papers.ssrn.com/sol3/papers.cfm?abstract_id=517662.

32. McLanahan, "Diverging Destinies."

33. Paul R. Amato, "The Impact of Family Formation Change on the Cognitive, Social, and Emotional Well-Being of the Next Generation," *Future of Children* 15, no. 2 (Fall 2005): 75–96, https://futureofchildren.princeton.edu/sites/g/files/toruqf2411/files/media/marriage_and_child_wellbeing_15_02_fulljournal.pdf; and Sara McLanahan and Isabel Sawhill, "Marriage and Child Wellbeing Revisited: Introducing the Issue," *Future of Children* 25, no. 2 (Fall 2015): 3–9, https://futureofchildren.princeton.edu/sites/g/files/toruqf2411/files/media/marriage_and_child_wellbeing_revisited_25_2_full_journal.pdf.

34. Melissa S. Kearney, *The Two-Parent Privilege: How Americans Stopped Getting Married and Started Falling Behind* (Chicago: University of Chicago Press, 2023); and Ron Haskins, "The Family Is Here to Stay—or Not," *Future of Children* 25, no. 2 (Fall 2015): 129–53, https://futureofchildren.princeton.edu/sites/g/files/toruqf2411/files/media/marriage_and_child_wellbeing_revisited_25_2_full_journal.pdf.

35. Bruce J. Ellis et al., "Does Father Absence Place Daughters at Special Risk for Early Sexual Activity and Teenage Pregnancy?," *Child Development* 74, no. 3 (May 16, 2003): 801–21, https://srcd.onlinelibrary.wiley.com/doi/abs/10.1111/1467-8624.00569?sid=nlm; Amato, "The Impact of Family Formation Change on the Cognitive, Social, and Emotional Well-Being of the Next Generation"; and Cynthia C. Harper and Sara McLanahan, "Father Absence and Youth Incarceration," *Journal of Research on Adolescence* 14, no. 3 (September 2004): 369–97.

36. Melissa S. Kearney and Phillip B. Levine, "The Economics of Non-Marital Childbearing and the 'Marriage Premium for Children'" (working paper, National Bureau of Economic Research, Cambridge, MA, March 2017), https://www.nber.org/papers/w23230; R. Kelly Raley, Michelle L. Frisco, and Elizabeth Wildsmith, "Maternal Cohabitation and Educational Success," *Sociology of Education* 78, no. 2 (April 2005): 144–64, https://www.jstor.org/stable/4148901?seq=3; Lerman and Wilcox, *For Richer, for Poorer*; and Thomas DeLeire and Leonard M. Lopoo, *Family Structure and the Economic Mobility of Children*, Pew Charitable Trusts, April 2010, https://www.pewtrusts.org/-/media/legacy/uploadedfiles/pcs_assets/2010/familystructurepdf.pdf.

37. DeLeire and Lopoo, *Family Structure and the Economic Mobility of Children*.

38. Brad Wilcox, Wendy Wang, and Ian Rowe, "Less Poverty, Less Prison, More College: What Two Parents Mean for Black and White Children," Institute for

Family Studies, June 17, 2021, https://ifstudies.org/blog/less-poverty-less-prison-more-college-what-two-parents-mean-for-black-and-white-children.

39. Raj Chetty et al., "Race and Economic Opportunity in the United States: An Intergenerational Perspective" (working paper, National Bureau of Economic Research, Cambridge, MA, December 2019), https://www.nber.org/papers/w24441.

40. Sampson, "Unemployment and Imbalanced Sex Ratios," 229–54.

41. Authors' tabulations from the March 2020 Current Population Survey. Flood et al., Integrated Public Use Microdata Series Current Population Survey. See endnote 9.

42. Wendy Wang and Kim Parker, "Record Share of Americans Have Never Married: As Values, Economics and Gender Patterns Change," Pew Research Center, September 24, 2014, https://www.pewresearch.org/social-trends/2014/09/24/record-share-of-americans-have-never-married.

43. Wang and Parker, "Record Share of Americans Have Never Married."

44. Nicholas Eberstadt, "Education and Men Without Work," *National Affairs*, Winter 2020, https://www.nationalaffairs.com/publications/detail/education-and-men-without-work.

45. Richard Reeves, *Of Boys and Men: Why the Modern Male Is Struggling, Why It Matters, and What to Do About It* (Washington, DC: Brookings Institution Press, 2022).

46. Oren Cass, "The Misguided Priorities of Our Educational System," *New York Times*, December 10, 2018, https://www.nytimes.com/2018/12/10/opinion/college-vocational-education-students.html.

47. US Department of Labor, Bureau of Labor Statistics, "College Enrollment and Work Activity of Recent High School and College Graduates—2022," press release, April 26, 2023, https://www.bls.gov/news.release/pdf/hsgec.pdf.

48. Authors' tabulations from the March 2020 Current Population Survey. Flood et al., Integrated Public Use Microdata Series Current Population Survey.

49. Richard Fry, Ruth Igielnik, and Eileen Patten, "How Millennials Today Compare with Their Grandparents 50 Years Ago," Pew Research Center, March 16, 2018, https://www.pewresearch.org/short-reads/2018/03/16/how-millennials-compare-with-their-grandparents.

50. US Department of Education, Institute of Education Sciences, National Center for Education Statistics, Digest of Education Statistics, "Table 334.10. Total Expenditures of Public Degree-Granting Postsecondary Institutions, by Purpose and Level of Institution: Fiscal Years 2009–10 Through 2020–21," https://nces.ed.gov/programs/digest/d22/tables/dt22_334.10.asp.

51. Lauren B. Resnick, "The 1987 Presidential Address: Learning in School and Out," *Educational Researcher* 16, no. 9 (December 1987): 13–20, 54, https://www.researchgate.net/publication/237128256_Learning_In_School_and_Out.

52. Warren Farrell and John Gray, *The Boy Crisis: Why Our Boys Are Struggling and What We Can Do About It* (Dallas, TX: BenBella Books, 2018).

53. Todd Gabe, Jaison R. Abel, and Richard Florida, *Can Low-Wage Workers Find Better Jobs?*, Federal Reserve Bank of New York, April 2018, https://www.newyorkfed.org/medialibrary/media/research/staff_reports/sr846.pdf; and Michael A. Schulz, "The

Wage Mobility of Low-Wage Workers in a Changing Economy, 1968 to 2014," *Russell Sage Foundation Journal of the Social Sciences* 5, no. 4 (September 2019): 159–89, https://www.rsfjournal.org/content/5/4/159.

54. Catherine Gewertz, "What Is Career and Technical Education, Anyway?," *Education Week*, July 31, 2018, https://www.edweek.org/teaching-learning/what-is-career-and-technical-education-anyway/2018/07.

55. James J. Kemple and Cynthia J. Willner, *Career Academies: Long-Term Impacts on Labor Market Outcomes, Educational Attainment, and Transitions to Adulthood*, MRDC, June 2008, https://www.mdrc.org/sites/default/files/full_50.pdf.

56. Kemple and Willner, *Career Academies*.

57. Kemple and Willner, *Career Academies*.

58. Christopher Dula, "Registered Apprenticeships Continue to Deliver Substantial Returns on Investment," Washington Workforce Training and Education Coordinating Board, https://www.lni.wa.gov/licensing-permits/apprenticeship/agenda-docs/R10WorkForceTrainingandEducationCoordinatingBoard.pdf.

59. Robert Halpern, *The Means to Grow Up: Reinventing Apprenticeship as a Developmental Support in Adolescence* (New York: Routledge, 2009).

60. Robert Lerman, *Scaling Apprenticeship to Increase Human Capital*, Aspen Institute, February 4, 2019, https://www.aspeninstitute.org/longform/expanding-economic-opportunity-for-more-americans/scaling-apprenticeship-to-increase-human-capital.

61. Lerman, *Scaling Apprenticeship to Increase Human Capital*.

62. Lerman, *Scaling Apprenticeship to Increase Human Capital*.

63. John Marotta, Zach Boren, and Myca San Miguel, "Iowa High School Apprenticeships: Creating Pathways to Promising Careers," Urban Institute, June 19, 2020, https://www.urban.org/research/publication/iowa-high-school-apprenticeships-creating-pathways-promising-careers.

64. White House, "The Child Tax Credit," https://www.whitehouse.gov/child-tax-credit.

65. Patrick T. Brown and Brad Wilcox, "The Child Tax Credit Should Promote Work and Marriage," *First Things*, December 19, 2022, https://www.firstthings.com/web-exclusives/2022/12/the-child-tax-credit-should-promote-work-and-marriage.

66. Office of Sen. Mitt Romney, "The Family Security Act 2.0: A New National Commitment to Working American Families," https://www.romney.senate.gov/wp-content/uploads/2022/06/family-security-act-2.0_one-pager_appendix.pdf.

67. Winship, "A Half-Century Decline in Marriage . . . That Ended 30 Years Ago for Disadvantaged Kids"; and Robert Rector, "Marriage, Abortion, and Welfare," Heritage Foundation, May 22, 2023, https://www.heritage.org/sites/default/files/2023-05/SR271_0.pdf.

68. Winship, "A Half-Century Decline in Marriage . . . That Ended 30 Years Ago for Disadvantaged Kids."

69. Sarah K. Cowan and Kiara Wyndham Douds, "Examining the Effects of a Universal Cash Transfer on Fertility," *Social Forces* 101, no. 2 (December 2022): 1003–30, https://academic.oup.com/sf/article/101/2/1003/6537059.

70. Brown and Wilcox, "The Child Tax Credit Should Promote Work and Marriage."

71. Office of Sen. Mitt Romney, "The Family Security Act 2.0."

72. Oren Cass and Wells King, *The Family Income Supplemental Credit: Expanding the Social Compact for Working Families*, American Compass, February 18, 2021, https://americancompass.org/the-family-income-supplemental-credit; and Angela Rachidi, "A Simpler Safety Net for Families: Consolidating Child Tax Credits into a Working Family Credit," American Enterprise Institute, May 23, 2022, https://www.aei.org/research-products/report/a-simpler-safety-net-for-families-consolidating-child-tax-credits-into-a-working-family-credit.

73. Douglas J. Besharov and Neil Gilbert, "Marriage Penalties in the Modern Social-Welfare State," R Street Institute, September 2015, https://welfareacademy.umd.edu/pubs/family/Marriage_Penalties_in_the_Modern_Social-Welfare_State.pdf; Carasso and Steuerle, "The Hefty Penalty on Marriage Facing Many Households with Children"; Elaine Maag and Gregory Acs, "The Financial Consequences of Marriage for Cohabiting Couples with Children," Urban Institute, September 8, 2015, https://www.urban.org/research/publication/financial-consequences-marriage-cohabiting-couples-children; and Wilcox, Price, and Rachidi, *Marriage, Penalized*. See also Elias Ilin, Laurence Kotlikoff, and M. Melinda Pitts, "Paying the Poor to 'Live in Sin'—a New Look at the Marriage Tax," Laurence Kotlikoff, https://kotlikoff.net/wp-content/uploads/2022/01/Paying-the-Poor-to-Live-in-Sin-1-17-22.pdf.

74. C. Eugene Steuerle, "The Widespread Prevalence of Marriage Penalties," testimony before the US Senate Committee on Appropriations, Subcommittee on the District of Columbia, May 3, 2006, https://www.urban.org/sites/default/files/publication/51096/900952-the-widespread-prevalence-of-marriage-penalties.pdf.

75. James Alm and Leslie A. Whittington, "Shacking Up or Shelling Out: Income Taxes, Marriage, and Cohabitation," *Review of Economics of the Household* 1, no. 3 (September 2003): 169–86; and Hayley Fisher, "The Effect of Marriage Tax Penalties and Subsidies on Marital Status," *Fiscal Studies* 34, no. 4 (December 12, 2013): 437–65.

76. Fisher, "The Effect of Marriage Tax Penalties and Subsidies on Marital Status."

77. Katherine Michelmore, "The Earned Income Tax Credit and Union Formation: The Impact of Expected Spouse Earnings," *Review of Economics of the Household* 16, no. 2 (June 2018): 377–406.

78. Wilcox, Price, and Rachidi, *Marriage, Penalized*.

79. Andrew J. Cherlin, *Marriage, Divorce, Remarriage* (Cambridge, MA: Harvard University Press, 1992); Brad Wilcox, "When Marriage Disappears: The Retreat from Marriage in Middle America," in Brad Wilcox et al., eds., *The State of Our Unions 2010: When Marriage Disappears; The New Middle America*, Institute for American Values and National Marriage Project, 2010, 13–60, http://www.stateofourunions.org/2010/index.php; and authors' calculations from Steven Ruggles et al., Integrated Public Use Microdata Series USA, version 11.0, 2021, https://doi.org/10.18128/D010.V11.0.

80. Besharov and Gilbert, "Marriage Penalties in the Modern Social-Welfare State."

81. Wilcox, Price, and Rachidi, *Marriage, Penalized*.

82. Rachidi, "A Simpler Safety Net for Families"; and Scott Winship, "Reforming the EITC to Reduce Single Parenthood and Ease Work-Family Balance," Institute for Family Studies, July 10, 2023, https://ifstudies.org/blog/reforming-the-eitc-to-reduce-single-parenthood-and-ease-work-family-balance.

83. Katharine B. Stevens and Meredith Tracy, *Still Left Behind: How America's Schools Keep Failing Our Children*," American Enterprise Institute, September 12, 2020, https://www.aei.org/research-products/report/still-left-behind.

84. Morgan Polikoff, "Parent Dissatisfaction Shows Need to Improve School Communication During Coronavirus Pandemic," Brookings Institution, July 23, 2020, https://www.brookings.edu/articles/parent-dissatisfaction-shows-need-to-improve-school-communication-during-coronavirus-pandemic.

85. Nat Malkus, "8,000 Districts Point to 5 Trends in Instructional Offerings," AEIdeas, March 2, 2021, https://www.aei.org/education/8000-districts-point-to-5-trends-in-instructional-offerings; and Nat Malkus, *Too Little, Too Late: A Hard Look at Spring 2020 Remote Learning*, American Enterprise Institute, October 6, 2020, https://www.aei.org/research-products/report/too-little-too-late-a-hard-look-at-spring-2020-remote-learning.

86. James Davison Hunter and Ryan S. Olson, eds., *The Content of Their Character: Inquiries into the Varieties of Moral Formation* (Charlottesville, VA: Finstock & Tew, 2017), 11.

87. Albert Cheng et al., *The Protestant Family Ethic: What Do Protestant, Catholic, Private, and Public Schooling Have to Do with Marriage, Divorce, and Non-Marital Childbearing?*, American Enterprise Institute and Institute for Family Studies, September 16, 2020, https://www.aei.org/research-products/report/the-protestant-family-ethic.

88. Jason Bedrick and Lindsey M. Burke, "The Next Step in School Choice," *National Affairs*, Winter 2015, https://www.nationalaffairs.com/publications/detail/the-next-step-in-school-choice; and Lindsey M. Burke, *Grand Reforms in the Grand Canyon State: Education Savings Accounts Bring Civil Society to Life in Arizona*, R Street Institute, November 20, 2019, https://www.rstreet.org/research/grand-reforms-in-the-grand-canyon-state-education-savings-accounts-bring-civil-society-to-life-in-arizona.

89. EdChoice, "Arizona: Empowerment Scholarship Accounts," January 17, 2023, https://www.edchoice.org/school-choice/programs/arizona-empowerment-scholarship-accounts.

90. Melanie Hanson, "U.S. Public Education Spending Statistics," Education Data Initiative, September 8, 2023, https://educationdata.org/public-education-spending-statistics.

91. Joyce A. Martin et al., "Births: Final Data for 2019," National Institutes of Health, National Library of Medicine, National Center for Biotechnology Information, April 2021, https://pubmed.ncbi.nlm.nih.gov/33814033.

92. Elizabeth Wildsmith, Jennifer Manlove, and Elizabeth Cook, "Dramatic Increase in the Proportion of Births Outside of Marriage in the United States from 1990 to 2016," Child Trends, August 8, 2018, https://www.childtrends.org/publications/dramatic-increase-in-percentage-of-births-outside-marriage-among-whites-hispanics-and-women-with-higher-education-levels.

93. Esther Lamidi, *A Quarter Century Change in Nonmarital Births*, Bowling Green State University, National Center for Family and Marriage Research, 2016, https://scholarworks.bgsu.edu/ncfmr_family_profiles/46.

94. Brad Wilcox and Laurie DeRose, "In Europe, Cohabitation Is Stable . . . Right?," Brookings Institution, March 27, 2017, https://www.brookings.edu/articles/in-europe-cohabitation-is-stable-right.

95. Princeton University, "Fragile Families and Child Wellbeing Study: Fact Sheet," https://fragilefamilies.princeton.edu/sites/fragilefamilies/files/ff_fact_sheet.pdf; and Sara McLanahan and Christopher Jencks, "Was Moynihan Right? What Happens to Children of Unmarried Mothers," *Education Next* 15, no. 2 (Spring 2015): 14–20, https://www.educationnext.org/was-moynihan-right.

96. Andrea J. Sedlak et al., "Fourth National Incidence Study of Child Abuse and Neglect (NIS-4)," National Data Archive on Child Abuse and Neglect, 2012, https://www.ndacan.acf.hhs.gov/datasets/dataset-details.cfm?ID=147.

97. Susan L. Brown, "Marriage and Child Well-Being: Research and Policy Perspectives," *Journal of Marriage and the Family* 72, no. 5 (October 1, 2010): 1059–77, https://www.ncbi.nlm.nih.gov/pmc/articles/PMC3091824; and Brad Wilcox et al., "Why Marriage Matters: Thirty Conclusions from the Social Sciences," Institute for American Values, 2011, https://nationalmarriageproject.org/blog/resources/why-marriage-matters.

98. Wendy Wang and Brad Wilcox, "The Millennial Success Sequence: Marriage, Kids, and the 'Success Sequence' Among Young Adults" (working paper, American Enterprise Institute, Washington, DC; Institute for Family Studies, Charlottesville, VA, June 14, 2017), https://www.aei.org/research-products/working-paper/millennials-and-the-success-sequence-how-do-education-work-and-marriage-affect-poverty-and-financial-success-among-millennials; and Ellwood and Jencks, "The Spread of Single-Parent Families in the United States Since 1960."

99. Alan J. Hawkins, "Shifting the Relationship Education Field to Prioritize Youth Relationship Education," *Journal of Couple & Relationship Therapy* 17, no. 3 (2018): 165–80, https://www.tandfonline.com/doi/full/10.1080/15332691.2017.1341355.

100. Hawkins, "Shifting the Relationship Education Field to Prioritize Youth Relationship Education"; Galena K. Rhoades, Scott M. Stanley, and Howard J. Markman, "The Pre-Engagement Cohabitation Effect: A Replication and Extension of Previous Findings," *Journal of Family Psychology* 23, no. 1 (February 2009): 107–11, https://psycnet.apa.org/record/2009-01435-003; and Karen Carver, Kara Joyner, and J. Richard Udry, "National Estimates of Adolescent Romantic Relationships," in *Adolescent Romantic Relations and Sexual Behavior: Theory, Research, and Practical Implications*, ed. Paul Florsheim (Mahwah, NJ: Lawrence Erlbaum Associates, 2003), 23–56.

101. Ron Haskins and Isabel Sawhill, *Creating an Opportunity Society* (Washington, DC: Brookings Institution Press, 2009); and Wilcox and Wang, "The Millennial Success Sequence."

102. Wilcox and Wang, "The Millennial Success Sequence."

103. Anita P. Barbee et al., "Impact of Two Adolescent Pregnancy Prevention Interventions on Risky Sexual Behavior: A Three-Arm Cluster Randomized Control Trial," *American Journal of Public Health* 106, no. S1 (September 2016): S85–90; and Anita P. Barbee, "Impact of Two Adolescent Pregnancy Prevention Interventions on Risky Sexual Behavior," MedicalResearch.com, October 14, 2016, https://medicalresearch.com/pediatrics/impact-two-adolescent-pregnancy-prevention-interventions-risky-sexual-behavior.

104. Barbee, "Impact of Two Adolescent Pregnancy Prevention Interventions on Risky Sexual Behavior."

105. Melissa S. Kearney and Phillip B. Levine, "Media Influences on Social Outcomes: The Impact of MTV's 16 and Pregnant on Teen Childbearing" (working paper, National Bureau of Economic Research, Cambridge, MA, August 2015), https://www.nber.org/papers/w19795; Joyce A. Martin et al., "Births: Final Data for 2015," US Department of Health and Human Services, Centers for Disease Control and Prevention, January 5, 2017, https://www.cdc.gov/nchs/data/nvsr/nvsr66/nvsr66_01.pdf; Joyce A. Martin et al., "Births: Final Data for 2016," US Department of Health and Human Services, Centers for Disease Control and Prevention, January 31, 2018, https://stacks.cdc.gov/view/cdc/51199; and US Department of Health and Human Services, Centers for Disease Control and Prevention, National Center for Health Statistics, Natality Public-Use Data 2007–17, https://wonder.cdc.gov/natality-current.html.

5

A Federal Safety Net to Build a Better Future for Low-Income Children

ANGELA RACHIDI AND MATT WEIDINGER

In response to the challenges of the pandemic that began in 2020 and public health measures to stem its effects, federal policymakers generated an unparalleled expansion in government assistance for American households in the years that followed. Federal policymakers provided a large amount of assistance on a temporary basis, with much focused on households that suffered employment and income loss. Most of those expansions expired when the pandemic subsided; however, some policymakers have used the experience to advocate permanent increases in taxpayer-funded assistance to low-income households.

While increasing federal spending on low-income families, as seen during the pandemic, may alleviate certain short-term material hardships, it is unlikely to resolve the long-term issues hindering American children from realizing their full potential. The most vocal movements from both the right and left calling for permanent expansions to government assistance too often ignore the safety net's successes and failures in recent decades. These proposals also do not recognize that limited upward mobility for families remains one of the fundamental challenges our nation faces today.

If policy efforts to reduce hardship end up limiting economic growth while discouraging work and marriage—long the cornerstones of family financial security—they could unintentionally undermine efforts to permanently lift children out of poverty and help them lead flourishing lives into adulthood. What lessons can we draw from current federal efforts—which, even before the pandemic, involved over $500 billion per year in spending on children[1]—for how to best promote positive outcomes for children? How should those lessons guide policymakers—including

97

conservative policymakers—in their approach to reforming the safety net so all children can thrive? How can we ensure federal antipoverty efforts are fiscally responsible—and thus sustainable?

In what follows, we review the US safety net for children, explore the answers to these and other key questions, and offer our recommendations for reorienting the safety net to improve child outcomes. Our recommendations provide an immediate pathway to enhancing the well-being of low-income families with children. Additionally, they lay the groundwork for safety-net reforms that would continue to enhance outcomes for children in the future.

The Size and Scope of the Federal Government's Safety Net for Children

The pandemic response dramatically expanded what was already a vast and growing pre-pandemic safety net for children. In the decades since President Lyndon Johnson declared the War on Poverty, the federal government has created dozens of assistance programs to address a variety of needs, including housing, food, and shelter. Any discussion of how to reform the safety net to boost child outcomes should start with a review of the current safety net, especially the part conferring means-tested benefits on families with children.

A Vast and Growing Pre-Pandemic Safety Net. The public narrative often disregards how much the safety net has grown since the mid-20th century. Today, the federal safety net's scope is vast in terms of programs, annual spending, and the number of individuals who receive assistance. The nonpartisan Congressional Research Service estimates that federal and state governments currently operate over 80 programs providing food, housing, health care, job training, education, energy, and cash assistance to low-income Americans.[2] Among the beneficiaries are millions of families with children. Figure 1 displays this complex system by major area of spending as of fiscal year 2018.

With so many programs across multiple federal agencies, it is unsurprising that federal spending on benefits and services for low-income individuals, including children, has increased substantially in recent decades. Even before the pandemic started in early 2020, federal benefits were more generous and reached a greater share of families and children than ever before. For example, federal spending on children in select programs primarily serving low-income populations increased nearly fourfold in real terms between 1990 and 2019, with the largest increases coming from refundable tax credits and health-related spending (Figure 2).[3]

Federal expenditures on all children, not only those living in low-income households, show similar increases since the 1960s, with the federal government spending over three times as much on programs for children in recent years as it did in 1980. A review in the National Academies of Sciences, Engineering, and Medicine report *A Roadmap to Reducing Child Poverty* reported that total federal expenditures on children reached $481.5 billion in 2017, up from $60.5 billion in 1960 and $151.5 billion in 1980, in constant dollars.[4]

Figure 3 provides a more detailed breakdown of federal spending on all children in the US. In total, the federal government spent $761 billion on assistance programs for children in 2022, for an average of $10,400 per child.[5] Figure 3 includes support for families far above the official poverty line, such as tax relief through the child tax credit (CTC) and the tax exclusion for employer-sponsored health insurance. Excluding those amounts suggests that means-tested support for children in low-income families totaled over $600 billion per year.[6]

Returning to federal spending on low-income children, the trends highlighted in Figure 2 reflect the US safety net's growing focus in recent decades on tax expenditures linked to earnings, especially among low-income parents. These tax expenditure programs have included new benefits such as the earned income tax credit (EITC), which was created in 1975 and significantly expanded in 1978, 1986, 1990, and 1993; the CTC, which was created in 1997 and significantly expanded in 2001, 2017, and (temporarily) 2021; and Affordable Care Act health insurance tax credits, which were created in 2010.[7]

Expanding benefits have reshaped the safety net. Take, for example, the rapidly growing Medicaid program, which now covers millions of working parents, such as those who left welfare for work in the wake of 1996 reforms. Because of this expansion, the very meaning of the safety net has

Figure 1. Benefits and Services for Low-Income Individuals, Fiscal Year 2018

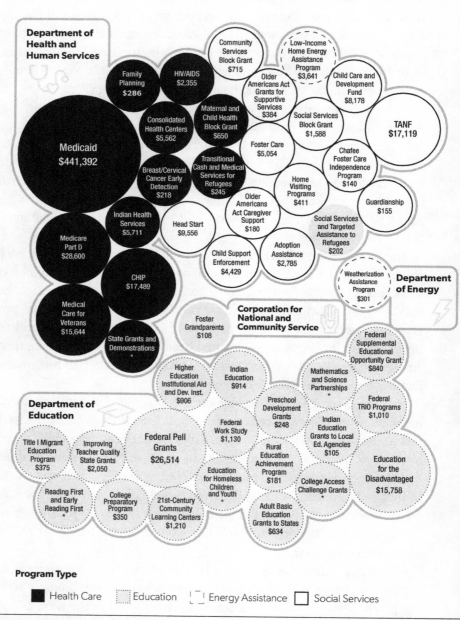

Program Type

■ Health Care　▦ Education　⌐⌐ Energy Assistance　□ Social Services

Note: The numbers indicate annual program budgets, in millions of US dollars. * Programs have annual obligations of less than $100 million, according to the Congressional Research Service. "CHIP" stands for Children's Health Insurance Program. "WIC" stands for "Women, Infants, and Children."

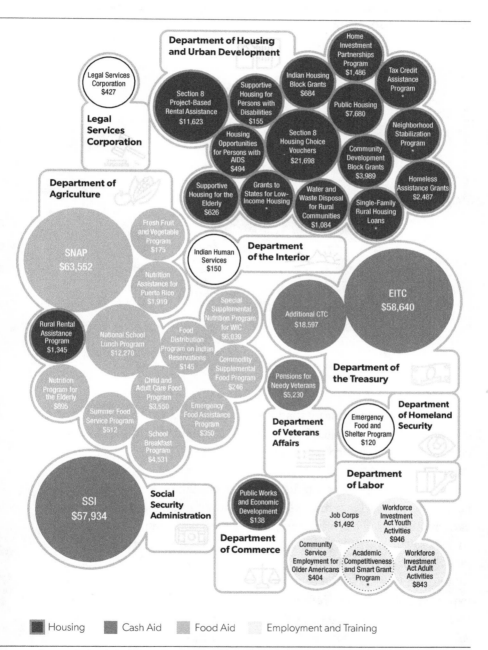

Department of Housing and Urban Development

Home Investment Partnerships Program $1,486

Legal Services Corporation $427

Indian Housing Block Grants $684

Tax Credit Assistance Program *

Supportive Housing for Persons with Disabilities $155

Section 8 Project-Based Rental Assistance $11,623

Public Housing $7,680

Legal Services Corporation

Housing Opportunities for Persons with AIDS $494

Section 8 Housing Choice Vouchers $21,698

Neighborhood Stabilization Program *

Community Development Block Grants $3,989

Department of Agriculture

Supportive Housing for the Elderly $626

Grants to States for Low-Income Housing *

Water and Waste Disposal for Rural Communities $1,084

Homeless Assistance Grants $2,487

Single-Family Rural Housing Loans *

Fresh Fruit and Vegetable Program $175

Indian Human Services $150

Department of the Interior

SNAP $63,552

Nutrition Assistance for Puerto Rico $1,919

Special Supplemental Nutrition Program for WIC $6,039

Additional CTC $18,597

EITC $58,640

Rural Rental Assistance Program $1,345

National School Lunch Program $12,270

Food Distribution Program on Indian Reservations $145

Commodity Supplemental Food Program $246

Pensions for Needy Veterans $5,230

Department of the Treasury

Nutrition Program for the Elderly $895

Child and Adult Care Food Program $3,550

Emergency Food Assistance Program $350

Department of Veterans Affairs

Department of Homeland Security

Emergency Food and Shelter Program $120

Summer Food Service Program $512

School Breakfast Program $4,531

Department of Labor

SSI $57,934

Social Security Administration

Public Works and Economic Development $138

Job Corps $1,492

Workforce Investment Act Youth Activities $946

Department of Commerce

Community Service Employment for Older Americans $404

Academic Competitiveness and Smart Grant Program *

Workforce Investment Act Adult Activities $843

Housing Cash Aid Food Aid Employment and Training

Source: Authors' depiction using data from Karen E. Lynch et al., *Federal Spending on Benefits and Services for People with Low Income: FY2008–FY2018 Update*, Congressional Research Service, February 5, 2020, https://crsreports.congress.gov/product/pdf/R/R46214.

Figure 2. Real Federal Spending on Low-Income Children in Select Categories, 1960–2022

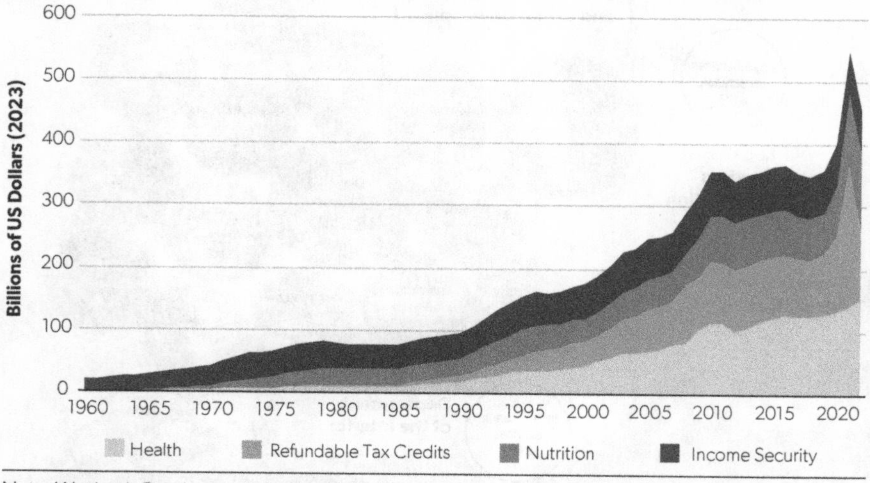

Note: We thank Cary Lou and Heather Hahn for providing the historical Kids' Share data in nominal dollars. We converted them to 2023 dollars using the Bureau of Economic Analysis's Personal Consumption Expenditures implicit price deflator.
Source: Cary Lou et al., *Kids' Share 2023: Report on Federal Expenditures on Children Through 2022 and Future Projections*, Urban Institute, November 2023, 16, Table 1, https://www.urban.org/sites/default/files/2023-11/Kids%E2%80%99%20Share%202023_Report%20on%20Federal%20Expenditures%20on%20Children%20through%202022%20and%20Future%20Projections.pdf.

evolved to encompass more than just benefits designed to assist the poorest Americans, often called simply "welfare." Increasingly, safety-net benefits also reach low-income working parents, and thus, we often call them "work supports."

Some new work supports have flowed primarily to low-income families, while others have funneled cash to low-, middle-, and high-income earners alike. Not counting the pandemic-related temporary expansions to the EITC and CTC, the Joint Committee on Taxation (JCT) projected that the federal government would spend $356 billion from 2020 to 2024 on the EITC.[8] Of that total, $313 billion (almost 88 percent) was expected in the form of refundable tax credits to families with no federal income tax liability, while only $43 billion (12 percent) was expected as tax relief to families. In contrast, JCT projected that the CTC would provide $247 billion in refundable tax credits out of $582 billion in total costs

Figure 3. Federal Expenditures on Children, by Category and Major Programs, 2022, Billions of Dollars

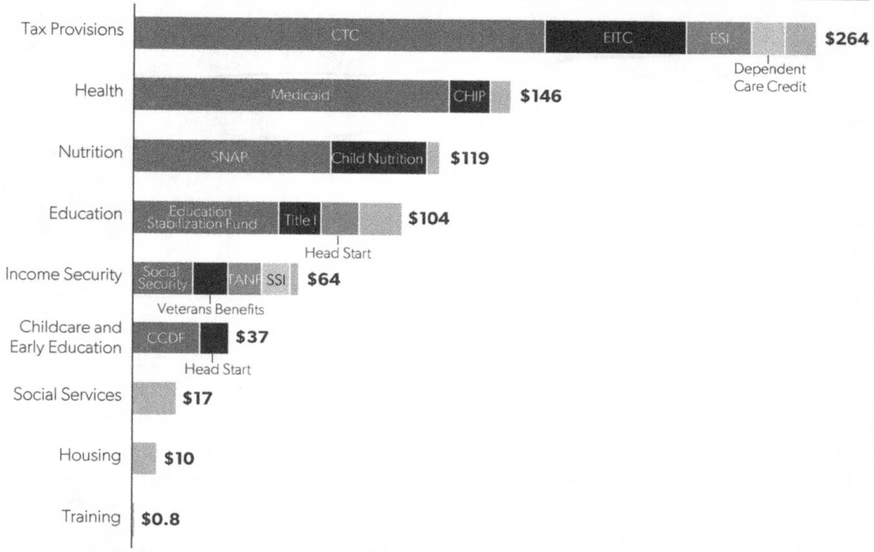

Note: Programs spending less than $10 billion are not shown separately but are included as part of "Other" (in gray) and in the totals by category. "CHIP" stands for Children's Health Insurance Program. "CCDF" stands for Child Care and Development Fund. "ESI" stands for employer-sponsored health insurance.
Source: This figure was re-created with permission based on Cary Lou et al., *Kids' Share 2023: Report on Federal Expenditures on Children Through 2022 and Future Projections*, Urban Institute, November 2023, Figure 4 and Table 2, https://www.urban.org/sites/default/files/2023-11/Kids%E2%80%99%20Share%202023_Report%20on%20Federal%20Expenditures%20on%20Children%20through%02022%20and%20Future%20Projections.pdf.

during fiscal years 2020–24, meaning the bulk of the CTC's support was projected to comprise tax relief for middle- and upper-income families.[9]

This shift toward spending on low-income *working* families has expanded the reach of federal safety-net programs and changed the composition of low-income families receiving benefits, but it has not dramatically changed the overall share of poor families with children (as defined by the official poverty measure) who receive assistance. Since at least the 1990s, a vast majority of poor families with children have received some form of cash or near-cash government assistance, even as programs shifted away from traditional "cash welfare" in favor of refundable tax credits connected to work, such as the EITC (Figure 4).

Figure 4. Percentage of Poor Families with Children That Received Selected Benefits, 1994–2012

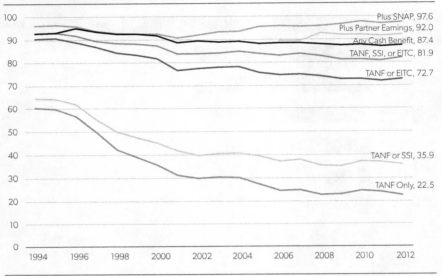

Note: "Any cash benefit" includes TANF, SSI, the EITC, CTC, unemployment compensation, and Social Security benefits.
Source: Angela Rachidi and Shijie Jin, "The Reach of the Cash-Based Safety Net for Poor Families with Children in America," American Enterprise Institute, February 28, 2017, https://www.aei.org/research-products/report/the-reach-of-the-cash-based-safety-net-for-poor-families-with-children-in-america.

A New Era of Government Expansion During the Pandemic. The onset of the pandemic and the unprecedented federal response beginning in March 2020 resulted in an unparalleled expansion in government spending on families with children—and the number receiving it. New benefits included three rounds of stimulus checks (including for children), larger Supplemental Nutrition Assistance Program (SNAP) benefits for households,[10] and the creation of Pandemic Electronic Benefits Transfer benefits for schoolchildren, which replaced government-provided school lunches when children were not physically in school. The federal government also expanded childcare funding substantially, created a public paid family leave program, and administered an unprecedented expansion to unemployment benefits, including a temporary new program offering weekly payments to adults who left work because their children's schools closed due to the pandemic, among other individuals previously ineligible for unemployment compensation. The March 2021 American Rescue Plan also modified the CTC to implement a fully refundable child allowance temporarily, greatly increasing refundable tax credits for one year at a cost of $109 billion.[11]

Poverty *fell* during the pandemic due to the massive tide of new and expanded federal benefits.[12] That flow of money was so great that, even as unemployment spiked to levels unseen since the Great Depression, personal savings actually grew—reinforcing how, for many, unprecedented benefits more than replaced lost earnings.[13] However, this result came at a staggering cost, with annual federal deficits exceeding $3 trillion and inflation rates reaching historic levels in 2022.[14]

It is particularly noteworthy that increased federal spending and program participation overlook crucial contextual factors that hinder children's ultimate success, such as family dynamics and parental employment. The safety net affects these factors—sometimes negatively, which makes long-term success more challenging. In any assessment of the safety net's effectiveness for children, the potential negative consequences for children stemming from poorly designed safety-net programs demand that we carefully consider how federal policies can shape parental behavior. Successful policies should reduce material hardship by not just providing immediate financial assistance to poor families but also ensuring that assistance does not undermine employment and the formation of strong and stable families.

Recent developments raise concerns on this front, especially the temporary replacement of the work-connected CTC with a child allowance completely disconnected from parental work. While this change applied only in 2021, Democrats in Congress and President Joe Biden have called for making it permanent. Such a move would break from prior bipartisan efforts to, as President Bill Clinton often said, "make work pay" in lieu of offering welfare checks generally unconnected with—and substituting for—work by parents.[15] It would ignore the lessons we have learned from several decades of successful antipoverty policy in the US.

A study by researchers at the University of Chicago estimated that replacing the current CTC, which phases in with earnings as they increase, with the 2021 child allowance, which was a larger flat benefit for all but the highest-income families, would reduce employment by up to 1.5 million jobs.[16] The permanent extension of the 2021 policy also would cost nearly $1.6 trillion over the next 10 years alone, according to the Tax Foundation.[17]

Effectiveness of the Safety Net for Children

Given the dramatic federal safety-net expansions for low-income children in recent decades, it is important to assess how effective the safety net has been in improving outcomes for children and to what extent policy-induced behavioral responses by parents might have offset any gains.

On the bright side, before the pandemic, by most accounts children in the US were doing materially better than at any point in this country's history. Child poverty rates were at historic lows in 2019 when counting government benefits.[18] And while poverty rates remained elevated for black and Hispanic children compared to white children, the racial and ethnic gaps in poverty rates had narrowed.[19] Mortality rates were also historically low, with the most substantial improvements concentrated among children in high-poverty communities.[20] Additionally, high school graduation and college attendance rates improved similarly over time.[21]

The federal safety net for low-income children likely contributed to these gains, but the specific ways and associated costs—both in monetary terms and socially—still require further examination. A review of the literature shows that some safety-net programs increased maternal employment and family income, benefiting low-income children. But research also shows that certain components of individual programs likely counteracted these gains by discouraging employment and marriage. The literature is complex, though. For instance, some studies delve into the effects of certain policies on overarching trends through survey data analysis. Conversely, other research focuses on the impacts of specific policies on various outcomes, employing randomized controlled trials such as those conducted in welfare-to-work experiments. Understanding how all these pieces fit together is important as we consider further reforms to the safety net to improve child outcomes.

The literature on the safety net's impacts on child outcomes includes studies that assess the impacts of individual policies and programs, as well as the safety net as a whole. Such assessments involve studying direct impacts by analyzing outcomes for children exposed to safety-net policies and comparing them with outcomes for similar children who have not been exposed to the same policies. Another component involves studying the safety net's indirect effects on children, including the influence of individual programs or the safety net as a whole on parental behavior. It is also important to understand the safety net's short-term effects on parents and children and how safety-net programs affect children in the long term.

The literature reveals many ways the safety net (as a whole and through individual programs or policies) benefits children, including improved academic performance, health, behavior, and overall well-being. At the same time, however, the literature shows that certain aspects of the safety net reduce incentives for parental employment and marriage, which can harm children. It is difficult to determine empirically how these negative behavioral effects interact with the otherwise positive aspects of the safety net and even more difficult to assess the relative importance of each factor. This presents a policy challenge: How can policymakers maintain the positive aspects of the safety net for children while minimizing the negative policy-induced responses that might harm children in the end?

Child Poverty and the Safety Net. It is often underappreciated how much child poverty rates have declined in the US over the past 30 years due to policy reforms, increased federal spending on the safety net, and overall economic growth. According to *A Roadmap to Reducing Child Poverty*, using a poverty rate that accounts for cash and noncash government benefits shows the child poverty rate has declined by almost half since the late 1960s, with the majority of this decline occurring since the early 1990s. Deep-poverty (defined as below 50 percent of the federal poverty level) and near-poverty (below 150 percent) rates also fell substantially during this time (Figure 5), with black and Hispanic children experiencing the bulk of these declines.[22]

Research credits government policies and programs as the primary cause of these dramatic declines, particularly welfare reform in the 1990s

Figure 5. Percentage of Children in Near Poverty, Poverty, and Deep Poverty in the US Using the Supplemental Poverty Measure, 1967–2019

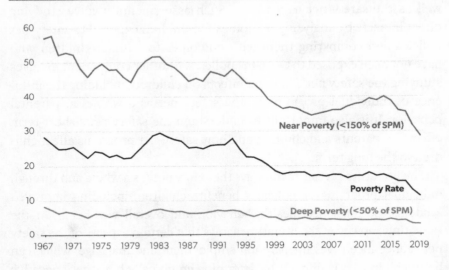

Note: "SPM" stands for Supplemental Poverty Measure.
Source: Authors' analysis of data from Columbia University, Center on Poverty and Social Policy, Historical Supplemental Poverty Measure Data, https://www.povertycenter.columbia.edu/historical-spm-data.

and subsequent expansions to the EITC and SNAP.[23] A consumption poverty rate created by economists Bruce Meyer and James Sullivan also shows dramatic declines in child poverty since the late 1990s.[24]

Still, none of these poverty rate calculations consider the effects of government programs on behavior. The result is that poverty rate calculations might over- or understate the long-term effects of safety-net programs on poverty by ignoring behavioral effects, such as changes to employment or family structure. Yonatan Ben-Shalom, Robert Moffitt, and John Scholz highlighted the importance of considering behavioral effects to fully understand the effects of the safety net on poverty, although they acknowledged the difficulty in doing so given that most US programs lack experimental evidence on their labor supply and marriage disincentives.[25]

Parental Employment and the Safety Net. For working-age people, employment (especially full-time, year-round work) typically results in higher income than government assistance alone, lifting the vast majority of people out of poverty.[26] Even if government assistance fully replaced what people could earn in the labor market, people benefit from the social and health aspects of employment in ways that can affect children, making employment preferable over government assistance.[27] For these reasons, if increasing government assistance lowers child poverty rates but hurts parental employment, families might be marginally better off with government income in the short term but prevented from reaching their full potential through their own earnings in the long term. When government assistance programs reduce labor force participation, they can also have negative macroeconomic effects, including slower economic growth.[28]

Research shows that welfare reform in 1996—which, among other changes, replaced the former Aid to Families with Dependent Children (AFDC) program with the Temporary Assistance for Needy Families (TANF) block grant—increased the employment rates of single, primarily never-married mothers.[29] TANF ended AFDC's provision of unconditional cash payments to poor families with children by imposing work-activity requirements and time limits on federal benefits. However, the relationship between welfare reform and employment is far from straightforward, even though sustained employment gains among never-married mothers are clear (Figure 6). Inconsistencies across studies remain over how much employment increased and for which groups, the specific policies that led to employment increases (e.g., time limits and work requirements), and the relative contribution of welfare reform in comparison to other policies, such as the EITC.[30]

A 2009 synthesis of the research published in *Welfare Reform* by Jeff Grogger and Lynn Karoly summarized the results from the various welfare-to-work experiments categorizing policies by their emphasis, such as those focused on financial incentives, mandatory work activities, or a combination of both. The programs most effective at improving parental employment were those that focused on mandatory work requirements, but work requirements had a smaller effect on overall income than financial incentive programs did. Nine of the 13 studies

Figure 6. Labor Force Participation Rate for Select Groups of Women Age 18–54, 1990–2022

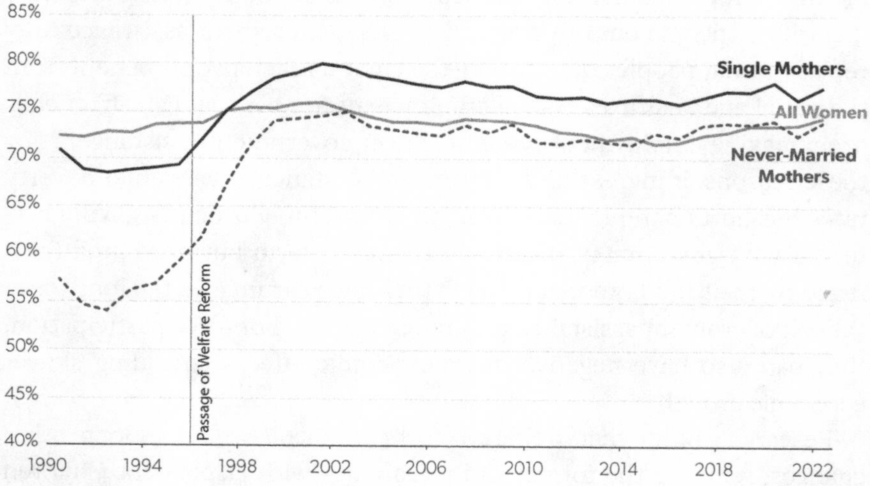

Source: Authors' analysis of the Annual Social and Economic Supplement to the Current Population Survey. Sarah Flood et al., Integrated Public Use Microdata Series, Current Population Survey, version 11.0, 2023, https://cps.ipums.org/cps.

involving programs that focused on work requirements found a statistically significant employment increase, and all but three work requirement programs had positive earnings effects.[31] While much of the evidence on work requirements comes from the 1990s welfare-to-work experiments, recent research demonstrates that work requirements remain relevant. In a study for the Congressional Budget Office, Justin Falk investigated an expansion of Alabama's work requirement to mothers of children under age 1 in 2018, finding that the policy change increased employment rates among those mothers.[32]

Additionally, the welfare-to-work experiments showed that financial incentives were less effective than work requirements at increasing employment rates, but they were more effective at increasing overall income. This highlights the need to consider both financial incentives for employment and work requirements in supporting parental employment, such as those in the EITC.

Research also shows that the EITC increased employment among single mothers after expansions in the 1990s, though gains were to employment participation rather than hours worked.[33] For married mothers, research suggests the EITC decreased employment rates, likely because a second working adult in the household pushed family income above eligibility thresholds, encouraging a one-worker arrangement.[34]

The literature on the Food Stamp Program (now called SNAP) suggests the opposite effect, likely because this program functions more like a traditional cash-based government transfer with no expectation for work or employment-like activities.[35] Hilary Hoynes and Diane Schanzenbach found that the introduction of the Food Stamp Program in the 1970s coincided with decreases in employment and hours worked among single mothers—the population most likely to receive food stamps.[36] Chloe East studied changes to the immigrant rules in the Food Stamp Program and found similar results: The reinstatement of program eligibility to immigrants in the early 2000s was associated with reduced employment among single mothers covered by the policy change.[37]

Unsurprisingly, research on other safety-net programs confirms that when government benefit programs do not require participants to work—as is generally the case with housing assistance, for instance—employment rates decline.[38] On the other hand, when benefits are contingent on working, employment rates increase, such as with childcare assistance.[39] Such findings highlight the importance of reforming the federal safety net as a whole so all programs cooperate to encourage parental employment rather than competing against one another to replace the need for employment.

One glaring problem with the safety net as it relates to employment involves the high effective marginal tax rates placed on some families when they increase their earnings. Marginal tax rates refer to the net income effect resulting from increased earnings combined with associated taxes and reduced government benefits.[40] These side effects are inherent to government supports that phase out gradually as income levels rise, but high marginal tax rates resulting from the simultaneous phaseout of multiple benefits discourage employment for low-income parents, leading some to call this dynamic a "poverty trap."[41]

A sizable number of households with children face marginal tax rates between 29 percent and 50 percent; households without children face

Figure 7. Number of Households Below 200 Percent Poverty with Various Marginal Tax Rates, After a $2,000 Earnings Increase

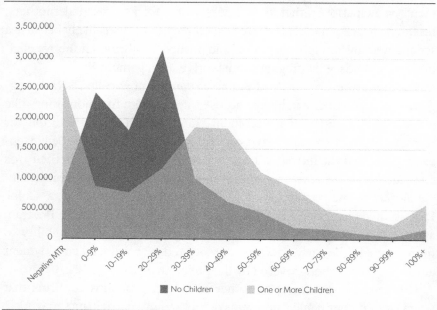

Note: "MTR" stands for marginal tax rate.
Source: Assistant Secretary for Planning and Evaluation tabulation of microdata from the Transfer Income Model, version 3, Annual Social and Economic Supplement to the Current Population Survey, 2015, as reported in Nina Chien and Suzanne Macartney, "What Happens When People Increase Their Earnings? Effective Marginal Tax Rates for Low-Income Households," US Department of Health and Human Services, Office of the Assistant Secretary for Planning and Evaluation, March 2019, https://aspe.hhs.gov/sites/default/files/private/aspe-files/260661/brief2-overviewmtranalyses.pdf.

much lower rates (Figure 7).[42] Nina Chien and Suzanne Macartney found that a $2,000 earnings increase would result in marginal tax rates between 40 percent and 50 percent for households with children at income levels between 100 percent and 200 percent of the federal poverty level, well above the marginal tax rates experienced by similar households without children.[43]

Scholars debate whether marginal tax rates affect employment behaviors among low-income families, especially in the context of the safety net's otherwise positive aspects and the large overall cost of enacting reforms required to reduce marginal tax rates.[44] These challenges have largely prevented policymakers from pursuing solutions.

Family Structure and the Safety Net. Another way the safety net can hurt children is by discouraging the formation of two-parent families or encouraging their dissolution. This makes understanding the relationship between safety-net programs and fertility and marriage important. As discussed in the preceding chapter of this volume, research concludes that children do better on average living with two married parents than with a single parent,[45] but estimating the effects of the safety net broadly on family structure brings out difficulties similar to those involved in trying to study employment effects; multiple programs exist, and each affects fertility and marriage differently. Moreover, a plethora of factors beyond the safety net influence fertility and family-formation trends, including cultural and social factors.

Nonetheless, the literature suggests that welfare reform (including the shift from AFDC to TANF and changes to the Child Support Enforcement program) likely lowered fertility among single mothers because of declining benefit values and other program reforms. On the other hand, because SNAP and the EITC contain marriage penalties (i.e., they can be more generous to unmarried than to married families), these programs might have counteracted the fertility and marriage effects associated with welfare reform in ways difficult to detect empirically.

One way to assess the relationship between the safety net and fertility is to explore birth trends among single mothers. Between the 1960s and the mid-1990s, the share of births to unmarried mothers displayed a steady rise (Figure 8). That was interrupted by a decade-long deceleration before the rate accelerated again and then plateaued—ultimately declining slightly in the years following the Great Recession. Such trends suggest that welfare reform in the mid-1990s may have played a role in stemming the prior decades-long rise in the share of births to unmarried mothers but also that other factors—including cultural norms and immigration—played significant roles, making it difficult to determine empirically the safety net's precise impact on these trends.

Much of the research on the relationship between safety-net policies and family structure studies individual policies within a program. The most studied policy is variation in AFDC or TANF benefit levels, including "family caps" that prevented benefits from rising due to subsequent births.[46] A review of mostly nonexperimental literature before welfare

Figure 8. Percentage of Births to Unmarried Women, 1940–2022

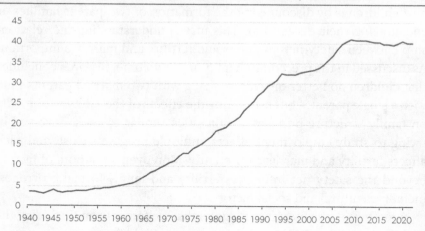

Source: Stephanie J. Ventura and Christine A. Bachrach, "Nonmarital Childbearing in the United States, 1940–99," *National Vital Statistics Reports* 18, no. 48 (October 2000): 1–40, https://pubmed.ncbi.nlm. nih.gov/11060989; and US Department of Health and Human Services, Centers for Disease Control and Prevention, CDC Wonder Natality Dataset, 2016–2022 Expanded for 2022. See also *National Vital Statistics Reports* for 2000–21.

reform by Robert Moffitt found the literature inconclusive but suggestive of an association between welfare generosity and family structure in the expected direction; the more generous the benefit, the higher the incidence of unmarried childbearing.[47] A later review by James Ziliak largely concluded the same.[48]

Not reviewed by Ziliak, however, was experimental research from a few states, which provides stronger evidence that welfare policies affect fertility and marriage decisions. Radha Jagannathan and Michael J. Camasso used data from an AFDC demonstration project in New Jersey, which implemented a family cap. They found that the family cap policy reduced births for black mothers but not white or Hispanic mothers while also increasing abortions for black mothers. The overall effect was a fertility decline among black single mothers receiving AFDC in New Jersey.[49]

Camasso used the same New Jersey experimental data and found birth reductions and abortion increases as well, but only for short-term welfare users. David Fein used data from an AFDC demonstration project in Delaware to study marital and childbearing decisions 18 months after random assignment. Although the follow-up period was short, he found policy-related effects on marital cohabitation and marital and childbearing expectations and effects on fertility for one subgroup, perhaps because of the short follow-up period.[50]

Jagannathan studied the effects of three policies on fertility patterns from 1992 to 2005 across the 50 states using panel data on welfare policies and vital statistics, including policies related to family caps, work requirements, and time limits. She found that family caps had the strongest effect on reducing the percentage of births to unmarried parents, the nonmarital birth rate, and pregnancies, while work requirements were associated with increased abortions and reduced overall pregnancies.[51]

In other studies published after Ziliak's TANF review, a relationship between welfare reform and fertility emerged. Ho-Po Crystal Wong used birth data from 1989 to 2012 and found that welfare reform led to substantial reductions in nonmarital births among teenagers.[52] Furthermore, Cody Vaughn used Panel Study of Income Dynamics (PSID) data on children from 1997 through early adulthood in 2015, finding that children's welfare reform exposure led to increased odds of their later being married and decreased odds of having a child outside of marriage, with stronger effects for women.[53]

Beyond research on welfare reform, studies of the Alaska Permanent Fund Dividend also suggest that unrestricted cash payments can affect fertility decisions.[54] However, sociologists Sarah Cowan and Kiara Wyndham Douds found that the Alaska Dividend increased fertility only among unmarried mothers, while it decreased fertility among married mothers.[55]

One particularly bright spot for children over the past three decades has been the significant decline in births to teenagers in the US, which research shows has led to positive outcomes for young adults.[56] The birth rate per 1,000 teens age 15–19 has steadily declined since the 1990s, especially in the past 15 years, reaching a record low in recent years (Figure 9). The reasons for the steep decline are many, including reduced sexual activity among teens and more contraception use.[57]

The research on the safety net's role in declining births to teenagers is mixed, however.[58] Like the broader research on welfare and fertility, the literature suggests that reduced welfare benefits and specific policies around

Figure 9. Births and Birth Rates for US Females Age 15–19, 1990–2022

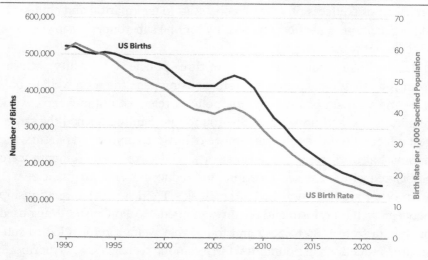

Source: US Department of Health and Human Services, Centers for Disease Control and Prevention, National Center for Health Statistics, U.S. and State Trends on Teen Births, 1990–2019, https://www.cdc. gov/nchs/data-visualization/teen-births; and US Department of Health and Human Services, Centers for Disease Control and Prevention, CDC Wonder Natality Dataset, 2016–2022 Expanded for 2022. See also *National Vital Statistics Reports* for 2020–22.

teen mothers as part of TANF likely contributed to lower fertility among teenagers in the US, but some studies found welfare reform had no effect on teen fertility, while other studies found statistically significant effects.[59]

Research has also shown that increased child support enforcement stemming from welfare reform reduced nonmarital births, with Irwin Garfinkel and coauthors finding a substantial decline in nonmarital births with stricter state-level child support enforcement policies and declines related to reducing the generosity of welfare benefits.[60] Similarly, Robert D. Plotnick and coauthors found that states with more effective child support policies—such as higher expenditures on child support enforcement and greater collections as a percentage of what is owed—had lower nonmarital fertility rates, with the strongest effects among younger women.[61]

Although the research is mixed, much of the experimental and nonexperimental literature suggests that welfare policies (or unrestricted cash payments more broadly, such as the Alaska Dividend) affect fertility and marriage decisions among populations exposed to them. The magnitude of the effects depends on the specific policy and other demographic and community factors. These findings should raise concern among policy-makers interested in expanding cash benefits without considering the effects on fertility outside marriage and among teenagers, which can considerably affect poverty and mobility over the long term.

A smaller literature exists related to other safety-net programs and family structure outcomes, including the effects of SNAP and the EITC on fertility and marriage. A study on the rollout of the Food Stamp Program in the 1970s found small, statistically insignificant effects on the total number of live births, but the direction suggested an increase in births, which supports the idea that increased government resources increase fertility.[62] Janet Currie and Enrico Moretti found a similar result studying the rollout of the Food Stamp Program in California.[63] A study on the fertility effects of EITC expansions in the 1990s found no statistically significant results, but the direction of the relationship suggested a reduction in births, which would contradict the theory that cash assistance from the government increases births.[64] However, research on the EITC shows that it increased employment among single mothers, which might explain the reduction in births found in the study.

The structure of means-tested programs such as the EITC, SNAP, and TANF penalizes marriage because when cohabiting couples marry, the income from both parents counts toward program eligibility, whereas most programs count the income only of custodial parents in cohabiting couples. This dynamic is well-known in the literature, but there is little agreement on whether marriage penalties affect marriage behavior.[65] A 2016 study found that Medicaid, SNAP, and TANF had only small effects on marriage decisions.[66]

The Persistence of Poverty and the Intergenerational Transfer of Welfare Receipt. Most measures focus on poverty rates in a single year rather than following income dynamics among the same families and individuals over time. Ignoring the persistence of poverty can heavily skew our understanding of the safety net's impacts on children because research shows that long-term poverty has particularly harmful effects, such as worsened physical health, cognitive difficulties, and increased risky behavior among children.[67]

Similarly, researchers have long cautioned that welfare dependency can be harmful to children, with particular concerns over the intergenerational transmission of welfare receipt.[68] Research finds that the condition of poverty explains much of the intergenerational transmission of welfare receipt (i.e., poverty is passed on through generations, which condition leads to greater welfare receipt), but research also finds that some of the transmission is due to parental participation in welfare programs itself (i.e., welfare programs encourage future welfare receipt).[69]

Research links safety-net benefits to declines in persistent poverty for children, although like the research on point-in-time poverty rates, this evidence does not consider negative behavioral effects that might also influence persistent poverty rates. Using data from the PSID, Sara Kimberlin found that the chronic poverty rate for children (i.e., being in poverty during four or more years in a six-year period) declined from 11.4 percent to 2.5 percent when all safety-net benefits were counted in the poverty calculation. The EITC, SNAP, and housing subsidies had the largest effects on reducing chronic poverty rates for children.[70] However, it was unclear how much persistent poverty would have declined (or might have declined even further) if not for behavioral effects, such as changes to parental employment or fertility.

Research on welfare reform's influence over the intergenerational transmission of dependency on government benefits is mixed. The only study to date that explores the transmission of welfare dependency post-TANF finds that welfare reform dramatically reduced the intergenerational transmission of cash-welfare receipt but did not reduce the transmission of a broader array of government benefits, including SNAP and Supplemental Security Income (SSI).[71]

Child Outcomes and the Safety Net. Like the evidence on the safety net's effects on parental behavior, the research exploring the effects on child outcomes shows many positive results, along with some findings suggesting no effects on children at all. Much of the research on child outcomes focuses on how SNAP, the EITC, and TANF influence children's academic outcomes, physical health, and behavioral health.

Research on SNAP consistently finds that the introduction of the Food Stamp Program improved child and adult health.[72] Douglas Almond, Hoynes, and Schanzenbach studied the phased implementation of the Food Stamp Program in the 1970s and found that children with access to the program were less likely to experience low birth weight and had better health outcomes as adults, including lower incidence of obesity and other chronic diseases.[73] East studied the implications of SNAP restrictions on immigrants and found that immigrant groups who gained access to SNAP through reinstated eligibility in the early 2000s had children with higher birth weights and better parent-reported health than immigrant groups without access to SNAP did.[74]

East also found that children of immigrants with access to SNAP had fewer chronic school absences than similar children of immigrants without access to SNAP. The estimated effects were relatively large: Every $1,000 increase in benefits received resulted in a 15 percent reduction in parental reports of fair, poor, or good health (compared to very good or excellent), for example. However, the measured outcomes were based on self-reported measures of health and school absences.[75]

The literature also links the EITC to positive child outcomes. Austin Nichols and Jesse Rothstein reviewed the literature and summarized the areas in which the EITC was associated with positive child outcomes.[76] Studies have linked the EITC to increased birth weight and better maternal health.[77] Raj Chetty, John Friedman, and Jonah Rockoff found that a higher EITC benefit was related to higher test scores among New York City public school students.[78] Similarly, Jacob Bastian and Katherine Michelmore found a link between larger EITC payments during childhood and improved high school completion rates, college attendance, and employment in young adulthood.[79]

Researchers attribute the EITC's impacts on child outcomes to increased income—resulting from greater parental employment and the tax credit itself,[80] although increased employment independent of higher income could also explain better child outcomes. For example, research credited welfare-to-work programs in the 1990s with improved child outcomes regardless of income effects because maternal employment led to increased use of quality childcare.[81]

The evidence linking welfare reforms to child outcomes, specifically reforms to AFDC, is less straightforward, although many studies have found positive impacts on children associated with welfare reform, including improved academic performance, increased high school completion, and reduced risky behavior. Other studies found no impacts, and a few found negative impacts.[82] In summarizing the results specific to the welfare-to-work experiments, Grogger and Karoly concluded there was "no clear pattern of beneficial or harmful effects for children up to age 14 across domains."[83]

Researchers have continued studying the effects of welfare reform on various outcomes, and recent studies point to generally positive effects. For example, a recent paper found that, in the next generation exposed to it, welfare reform reduced food insecurity.[84] Moreover, another study examined changes in material well-being among single-mother households from 1984 to 2019 and found that the well-being of single-mother households improved after welfare reform across a range of consumption measures.[85]

Additionally, studies have identified varying effects for different groups. For example, child outcomes were generally better when single mothers found employment and increased their family income due to welfare reform, while child outcomes went unchanged (or were sometimes negatively affected) when mothers left welfare without employment.[86] It is also important to note that these studies examined changes to AFDC and assessed whether reforms resulted in better outcomes compared to AFDC policies. That does not necessarily mean that TANF, for example, was optimally designed or would result in better outcomes compared to something other than AFDC.

The most rigorous research involving evaluations of specific welfare-to-work programs throughout the 1990s (often referred to as AFDC demonstration projects or waivers) found overall positive effects on school achievement for children, with stronger effects for young children.[87] Authors of these studies noted that individual programs produced different results and that programs that increased parental employment and income through earnings supplements yielded positive results for children, while programs that increased employment only (and not income) had no effect on children.

Many of the welfare-to-work evaluations followed children for only a few years, limiting the ability to study any long-term effects. However, one study in Milwaukee followed children for eight years after exposure to welfare reform. Children in the treatment group experienced improved school achievement five years after random assignment. This faded by year eight but had lasting positive effects on other school measures, such as school progress, school engagement, and improved behaviors, especially among boys.[88]

The evidence on changes to child support enforcement after welfare reform is also largely positive. Child support collections increased following welfare reform, benefiting thousands of children. Research links increased child support to better child outcomes, such as fewer behavioral problems and better school performance.[89]

Not all the evidence related to welfare reform was positive, however. In Ziliak's 2015 literature review, he notes several studies linking welfare reform to poor health outcomes for children, including reduced breast-feeding rates, less prenatal care, lower birth weights, and increased child maltreatment.[90] However, it is possible that these outcomes stemmed from reduced participation in Medicaid as a tertiary effect of welfare reform—participation declines that were short-lived.[91] Ziliak also noted several observational (or nonexperimental) studies that found no effects of welfare reform on child academic performance, behaviors, or health.[92]

Finally, the literature most relevant for understanding the impacts of the safety net on children and upward mobility comes from studies that have explored the long-term effects of these policies on individuals exposed as children, compared with otherwise similar children not exposed to these programs. This research generally finds long-term positive effects among such children. For example, Almond, Hoynes, and Schanzenbach found that exposure to the Food Stamp Program as a child (i.e., compared to no federal food-related government assistance) led to better health and better economic outcomes as an adult, such as higher earnings and family income, more employment, and lower poverty.[93]

Research also consistently finds positive long-term effects of the EITC on children. Bastian and Michelmore exploited changes to the EITC over time and found that a larger EITC during childhood increased high school completion, college attendance, and employment in young adulthood.[94]

Similarly, a study by Day Manoli and Nicholas Turner and another by Michelle Maxfield found that EITC receipt as a child increased college attendance and employment later in life.[95] Few studies have explored the long-term impacts of TANF exposure. However, Vaughn used PSID data and found that the educational gains for children affected by welfare reform led to higher college-completion rates as young adults.[96]

Conservative Principles for Safety-Net Reform

The literature shows generally positive, although mixed, success regarding the safety net's impact on children. It suggests that safety-net programs improve child outcomes, reduce point-in-time poverty, support better health, and improve academic performance, in both the short and long terms, when compared to nothing at all or poorly designed programs such as AFDC. However, researchers have also identified negative behavioral effects, such as decreased parental employment and increased nonmarital childbearing, which might counteract the safety net's otherwise positive aspects. Notably, research on safety-net programs does not generally assess the cost-benefit implications of such programs, largely because the indirect costs and the long-term benefits are difficult to quantify.[97]

A conservative safety-net reform agenda should seek to maximize the poverty-reducing aspects of safety-net programs and limit the negative behavioral effects while also organizing and administering safety-net programs efficiently and improving program integrity. Most importantly, all reforms should work toward one overarching goal: supporting the healthy development of children by helping families achieve sufficient income through work and, when necessary, efficient government programs. Reaching this goal requires, first, an expectation that every family maximize its own self-reliance. In our view, we best achieve this goal when policies incorporate specific principles: the promotion of work and personal responsibility, a long-term perspective on poverty alleviation, and a focus on efficiency, effectiveness, and sustainability.

Promoting Work and Personal Responsibility. The first principle of conservative social policy reform to improve child outcomes is orienting policies toward work and personal responsibility for work-capable adults. This philosophy manifests itself most obviously in work or activity requirements, such as those included in the 1996 welfare reform law. Welfare reform replaced the open-ended AFDC program with TANF, which conditioned eligibility for most beneficiaries on participation in work, training, or other positive activities.

Similar activity requirements were then established as a condition of eligibility for food stamp benefits for some able-bodied adults without dependents. In 2018, during President Donald Trump's administration, officials proposed expanding work requirements to other programs, including housing and health insurance assistance.[98] However, beyond welfare reform, few federal policies have incorporated work requirements,[99] and one of the most consequential benefit program reforms in recent years, 2021's temporarily expanded CTC, actually further disconnected benefits from work.

Work requirements are far from the only way policymakers have promoted parental employment as a primary response to child poverty. Key benefit programs such as the EITC and CTC (outside of the 2021 expansion) promote work by conditioning benefit payments on earnings and offering greater assistance for the lowest-income working parents as they work and earn more. Promoting work in these ways reinforces the long-held American conviction that advancement is both obtainable by all and best procured through work and individual initiative. It also acknowledges that the best path toward family upward mobility involves parental employment.

Focusing on Permanent Pathways out of Poverty. The second conservative principle of reform to improve outcomes for children is the understanding that poverty reduction involves more than alleviating immediate financial needs; it requires helping families escape poverty permanently. Indeed, some efforts that focus only on immediate assistance to families can actually increase dependence and stifle upward mobility. The former AFDC program provides a clear illustration of this phenomenon. Though ostensibly aimed at aiding needy families, its low expectations for adult recipients frequently led to prolonged dependency on benefits and limited engagement in work-related activities.[100]

Other features of this longer-term focus include promoting asset building and bolstering the ideals of education, employment, and strong families, along the lines of the "success sequence" discussed in the preceding chapter of this volume.

Maintaining Fiscal Responsibility and Program Sustainability. The third principle of conservative reform to improve child outcomes is a focus on policies that are fiscally responsible and produce sustainable results for benefit recipients and taxpayers. This involves ensuring the federal government pays for its share of benefit programs without adding to the federal deficit or substantially increasing the tax burden on working families. Policymakers should focus on ending or curtailing underperforming programs to offset new spending and reforming inefficient programs to reduce wasted costs. This principle also recognizes that the federal government is not the only source of support for needy families and that state and local governments, nonprofits, and private charities often deliver more effective and appropriate support. Other essential conservative goals include ensuring benefits are administrable, effective, and resistant to fraud or abuse and preventing duplication with other benefit programs.

A Conservative Safety-Net Reform Agenda to Boost Child Outcomes

While all the above principles underlie our approach, the central feature of our proposed reforms is improving outcomes for children. We believe this is important not only because today's children determine our country's future but also because we have a moral obligation to ensure our society produces healthy and happy children. We propose two broad reforms consistent with this vision.

At the core of our reform agenda is the acknowledgment that having the federal government simply send families money undermines the three principles we outlined. It especially undermines parental employment and marriage, which can jeopardize upward mobility and the long-term success of children. It is also fiscally irresponsible and unsustainable in the current fiscal environment.[101]

At the same time, however, we acknowledge the evidence that additional government resources can have positive effects on children. For this reason, we propose consolidating child-related federal tax credits to better support parental employment and marriage, while allowing state and local governments the flexibility to help families progress toward upward mobility, accompanied by robust federal accountability measures that ensure states meet that goal.

Working Family Credit. We propose consolidating the EITC and CTC into one working family credit (WFC) that rises as earnings increase for low-income families while ending the head-of-household filing status. (Single parents would use the single filing status.) The WFC would maintain many of the same features of the current EITC and CTC but be structured in a way that aligns them. The tax filing unit, not the child, would serve as the basis for the credit, although like current policies, the WFC would be more generous for larger families.

As we outline in Table 1, the WFC could maintain approximately the same level of current benefits for very low-income families, which is already quite substantial, but could start phasing maximum benefits out at slightly higher income levels, especially for married families, and phase them out more slowly than the current EITC. The goal of this approach would be to partly address the current EITC's marriage penalties and maintain employment incentives higher up the income scale. However, policymakers could adjust the specific WFC parameters depending on the most pressing policy priorities and available funds.

We believe a consolidated benefit offers several advantages over the current structure. One of the most important is that a WFC would simplify the existing system of multiple child-related tax credits by aligning program rules and parameters. It would also increase transparency and the overall understanding of the size and scope of child-related tax credits. Combining the EITC and CTC into one tax credit would allow policymakers to address policy priorities with a single tool.

For example, we suggest a WFC that matches the maximum benefit levels from current policy for very low-income families but increases the start of the phaseout from approximately $20,000 for single filers and $25,000 for married filers to $30,000 and $50,000, respectively (using

Table 1. Proposed WFC Parameters

	Single, One Child	Single, Two Children	Single, Three or More Children	Married, One Child	Married, Two Children	Married, Three or More Children
Phase-In Rate (Percentage)	45	55	65	45	55	65
Maximum WFC Amount	$6,000	$9,000	$12,000	$6,000	$9,000	$12,000
Income at Which Phaseout Starts	$30,000	$30,000	$30,000	$50,000	$50,000	$50,000
Phaseout Rate (Percentage)	7.0	7.0	7.0	7.0	7.0	7.0
Credit Floor	$1,000	$2,000	$3,000	$1,000	$2,000	$3,000
Income at Which Credit Floor Is Reached	$105,000	$130,000	$160,000	$125,000	$150,000	$180,000
Current EITC Phase-In (Percentage)	34	40	45	34	40	45
Current EITC Phaseout (Percentage)	16	21	21	16	21	21

Source: Authors' proposed parameters for a working family credit based on 2021 policy without the American Rescue Plan Act changes.

2021 income levels). For simplicity, in Table 1 we reproduce a proposal developed in 2021 using EITC and CTC policy before the temporary CTC expansion.[102] At the time, this translated into a maximum WFC of $6,000 for families with one child, $9,000 for families with two children, and $12,000 for families with three or more children, following a schedule included in Table 1 and illustrated in Figure 10.[103] Current parameters would reflect annual inflation adjustments since 2021.

Compared to current EITC and CTC policy, the maximum WFC would cover a slightly wider span of low- and middle-income households before phasing out more gradually than current benefits as household earnings

Figure 10. Proposed WFC Amounts

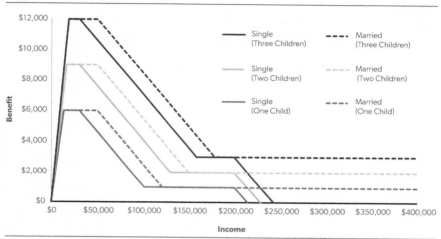

Source: Authors' calculations using the working family credit parameters outlined in Table 1 based on 2021 policy without the American Rescue Plan Act changes.

rise, minimizing the effective marginal tax rate on additional earnings until the credit reaches a floor equal to $1,000 per child, eventually phasing down to $0. However, the elimination of the head-of-household tax-filing status reduces the overall tax benefit to higher-income single-parent households in favor of lower-income single parents (Figure 11, Panel A). Our proposal also partly addresses the current marriage penalty in the EITC by extending the maximum benefit higher up the income scale for married families. However, it does not address the "vertical" marriage penalty.[104]

We recognize that this would raise taxes on higher-income families by reducing the current $2,000-per-child CTC, which replaced the dependent exemption in the 2017 Tax Cuts and Jobs Act. Our intent behind reducing the current CTC for higher-income families is to control the overall cost of the proposal and shift this particular tax benefit toward middle-income families. An alternative policy could maintain a floor of $2,000 at current CTC income levels, which would add to the overall cost.

We also recommend that the IRS take a number of important steps to improve the integrity of these reformed programs. According to the Treasury Department's 2020 audit, more than a quarter of total EITC payments

Figure 11. WFC vs. Current Benefits for Tax Filers with Two Qualifying Children

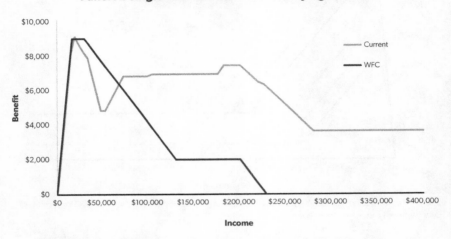

Panel A. Single Tax Filer with Two Qualifying Children

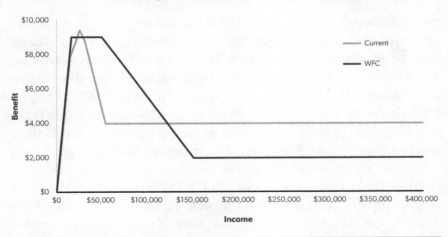

Panel B. Married, Filing Jointly Tax Filer with Two Qualifying Children

Source: Authors' calculations using the working family credit parameters outlined in Table 1 and 2021 earned income tax credit, child tax credit, and head-of-household parameters without the American Rescue Plan Act changes.

in fiscal year 2019 were improper, and nearly one-sixth of additional CTC payments (i.e., the refundable portion of the CTC) were improper, totaling more than $20 billion in improper payments.[105] Improper payments stem primarily from misreported income on tax filings and qualifying children, but benign errors also contribute to the problem due to the complicated nature of benefit-eligibility rules.[106] A 2016 report by Steve Holt offered several recommendations for improving the integrity of the EITC program that Congress could pursue, including simplifying the rules around qualifying children, better regulating tax preparers, developing alternative data sources to verify eligibility, and verifying eligibility before dispersing funds.[107]

Opportunity Demonstration Projects. While the federal government is well suited to transfer income to low-income working families through existing tax credits (or our preference of a consolidated benefit), state and local governments are in the best position to help families achieve upward mobility over time. State leaders have a direct interest in ensuring that resident families find and sustain employment, because it helps build a strong economy and supports strong communities. State and local leaders are also in the best position to design approaches that meet the needs of their constituents, coordinating job training, education, and other benefit programs. Toward this end, we propose a series of demonstration projects that are similar to efforts leading up to welfare reform in 1996 but that involve a wider array of safety-net programs than TANF alone.

Opportunity demonstration projects would give states the latitude to design and implement pilot projects aimed at increasing opportunity for low-income families for the betterment of children. The main goal would be to allow states to combine program funding streams—including TANF, SNAP, housing assistance, the Child Care and Development Block Grant, the Social Services Block Grant, and the Workforce Innovation and Opportunity Act—to address high effective marginal tax rates, employment and marriage disincentives, and ineffective job-training program approaches.

One example of a demonstration project could be a state program that consolidates TANF, SNAP, utility assistance, childcare, and housing assistance. Participants could receive financial assistance to meet their individual needs with state programs developing a consolidated-aid budget that addresses high marginal tax rates and work disincentives. State agencies could design the program so the assistance budget is most generous when the family includes a worker—amplified by the WFC described above. When work is not possible, the program would expect the parent to participate in education, training, or other similar activities as a condition of assistance to set him or her on a path toward employment.

Another demonstration project might involve a state testing ways to publicize, promote, and help more young people follow the success sequence of completing high school, engaging in full-time work, and avoiding parenthood outside marriage.

Granted, the flexibility inherent in this approach would allow states to test programs with questionable evidence of success, such as guaranteed income programs. However, all demonstration projects would require a rigorous evaluation to explore impacts related to employment, earnings, and income changes over time; family structure effects; and child outcomes over the pilot period to include a long-term follow-up period. After a pilot period, the evaluation would help determine whether the program continues and informs possible national policy changes. As with the 1996 welfare reforms, such federal policy changes would be based on practical lessons from the states about what has worked to improve outcomes for children and families.

Additional Reforms. In addition to the reforms outlined above, long-term success for children involves more than simply focusing on parental employment and family structure. We also need policies that promote greater asset building among low-income families and that ensure families have the ability to move where employment opportunities are most abundant, including housing and school choice reform.

One tool Congress could incorporate into federal tax policy is flexible savings accounts that allow families to save pretax dollars for a variety of family-related expenses, such as paid parental or family care leave, childcare or educational expenses, a down payment on a home, or work-related expenses such as transportation. The federal government could match initial savings for low-income families that fund these accounts, along the lines of the current saver's credit for retirement.[108] State agencies would ignore families' savings (but not government matching funds) when determining eligibility for other means-tested benefits.

We also see a need to reform housing-assistance programs so families are better able to relocate from neighborhoods characterized by concentrated, endemic poverty.[109] Ideally, one or more opportunity demonstration projects would address the need to ensure that housing assistance allows families to select more income-diverse neighborhoods so that they can better achieve upward mobility. However, in the meantime, Congress could reallocate funding from project-based housing assistance—that is, assistance tied to a particular dwelling—toward tenant-based assistance, which gives flexibility to individuals to choose their own housing.[110]

Cost Implications and Funding Offsets. One of our underlying principles for reforming the safety net to improve child outcomes is that reforms must be fiscally responsible and sustainable. Throwing more federal tax dollars at the problem of poverty each year might achieve some short-term reductions in the poverty rate, but unintended consequences, such as lower parental employment and fewer two-parent families, could worsen problems for low-income children in the end. This approach reflects fiscal irresponsibility in addressing the needs of low-income children and is ultimately unsustainable, particularly if Congress neglects to pay for increased spending, a scenario that occurs too frequently.

We believe increasing federal assistance to low- and middle-income working families through a consolidated tax credit is appropriate, but only by offsetting the increased costs through other spending reductions and program consolidations. Our WFC proposal would have cost approximately $25 billion more in 2022 than the combination of tax credits under current policy, with inflation adjustments projected to increase the cost of the proposal to $28 billion by 2025 and more thereafter, given the expiration of the temporary expansion in the CTC included in the Tax Cuts and Jobs Act of 2017.[111]

The cost estimate considers offsetting reductions due to the elimination of the head-of-household filing status and reducing the current CTC for high-income families.[112] To pay for this spending increase, we propose a cost-sharing arrangement between the federal and state governments in major benefit programs, including SSI, SNAP, and housing assistance, which would require states to contribute more but also give them more incentive to contain costs and improve outcomes.[113]

We also believe that better aligning job training and education programming across TANF, SNAP, and housing assistance could result in improved program performance and cost savings that Congress could reallocate to a child-related tax benefit like the WFC. Finally, we need TANF reforms to revive work-activity requirements, which have weakened over time, and ensure states contribute their proper share of program funds, which is especially appropriate given the federal government's increasing assistance for low-income families.[114]

Conclusion

In the midst of the pandemic, the federal government spent $761 billion annually on children, with the vast bulk flowing to children in lower-income families. That includes some of the $140 billion that the federal government temporarily added under the March 2021 American Rescue Plan by expanding the CTC, the EITC, and childcare spending.[115] This approach continues a trend seen over the past few decades of addressing poverty by increasing federal spending for existing programs, broadening eligibility criteria, and expanding the amount of assistance provided. But that misses the broader point: While transferring more taxpayer resources to low-income families might meet their short-term material needs, it does little to help low-income families and their children achieve long-term success. In fact, it may impede that goal.

To ensure that low-income children thrive, it is appropriate for the government to provide assistance, particularly by providing vital health and educational resources. But more importantly, that goal requires families and communities to offer an environment conducive to childhood success. We believe this is most attainable when parents work and, when possible, form two-parent families.

For this reason, we recommend a two-pronged approach. First, improve federal assistance to low- and middle-income parents through a consolidated tax credit. Second, provide greater flexibility for state and local governments to design and implement programs that seek to achieve long-term child success. Implementing these measures, among others, would lead to both immediate and sustainable improvements in the well-being of low-income children. Even more important, they would pave the way for more upward mobility and long-term success.

Notes

1. Heather Hahn et al., *Kids' Share 2020: Report on Federal Expenditures on Children Through 2019 and Future Projections*, Urban Institute, July 28, 2020, https://www. urban.org/research/publication/kids-share-2020-report-federal-expenditures-children-through-2019-and-future-projections.

2. Patrick A. Landers et al., *Federal Spending on Benefits and Services for People with Low Income: FY2008–FY2020*, Congressional Research Service, December 8, 2021, https://crsreports.congress.gov/product/pdf/R/R46986/3.

3. We thank Cary Lou and Heather Hahn for providing the historical Kids' Share data in nominal dollars. See also Angela Rachidi, "American Exceptionalism? Five Ways Government Spending on Low-Income Children and Child Poverty Is Misunderstood," American Enterprise Institute, November 12, 2019, https://www.aei.org/research-products/report/american-exceptionalism-five-ways-government-spending-on-low-income-children-and-child-poverty-is-misunderstood.

4. Greg Duncan and Suzanne Le Menestrel, eds., *A Roadmap to Reducing Child Poverty* (Washington, DC: National Academies Press, 2019), https://nap.nationalacademies. org/catalog/25246/a-roadmap-to-reducing-child-poverty.

5. US Census Bureau, America's Families and Living Arrangements: 2022, 2022, https://www.census.gov/data/tables/2022/demo/families/cps-2022.html.

6. Cary Lou et al., *Kids' Share 2023: Report on Federal Expenditures on Children Through 2022 and Future Projections*, Urban Institute, November 2023, 16, Table 1, https://www.urban.org/sites/default/files/2023-11/Kids%E2%80%99%20Share%20 2023_Report%20on%20Federal%20Expenditures%20on%20Children%20through %202022%20and%20Future%20Projections.pdf. According to the data analyzed, federal expenditures on children in 2022 totaled $761 billion, including tax relief. Of this total, expenditures on children from households with higher incomes totaled $152 billion, including $94 billion for tax relief through the child tax credit and $25 billion through employer-sponsored health insurance.

7. Margot L. Crandall-Hollick, *The Earned Income Tax Credit (EITC): A Brief Legislative History*, Congressional Research Service, March 20, 2018, https://crsreports. congress.gov/product/pdf/R/R44825/8.

8. Joint Committee on Taxation, "Estimates of Federal Tax Expenditures for Fiscal Years 2020–2024," November 5, 2020, https://www.jct.gov/publications/2020/jcx-23-20.

9. Joint Committee on Taxation, "Estimated Revenue Effects of H.R. 1319, the 'American Rescue Plan Act of 2021,' as Amended by the Senate, Scheduled for Consideration by the House of Representatives," March 9, 2021, https://www.jct.gov/

publications/2021/jcx-14-21. The March 2021 American Rescue Plan increased the child tax credit so that for tax year 2021, its maximum benefit was as much as $3,600 per child, which was entirely refundable for millions of families for the first time. During just fiscal years 2021 and 2022, this change increased spending under the child tax credit program by $109 billion, of which $84 billion, or over 80 percent, involved refundable benefits focused on lower-income parents, including some who would receive the benefit for the first time despite having no earnings at all. See Joint Committee on Taxation, "JXC-12-31," March 4, 2021, https://www.jct.gov/publications/2021/jcx-13-21.

10. US Department of Agriculture, "USDA to Provide Critical Nutrition Assistance to 30M+ Kids over the Summer," press release, April 26, 2021, https://www.usda.gov/media/press-releases/2021/04/26/usda-provide-critical-nutrition-assistance-30m-kids-over-summer.

11. US Congressional Budget Office, "Estimated Budgetary Effects of H.R. 1319, American Rescue Plan Act of 2021," March 6, 2021, https://www.cbo.gov/publication/57056; and Matt Weidinger, "Child Allowances Make the IRS America's Number One Welfare Agency," RealClearPolicy, June 9, 2021, https://www.aei.org/op-eds/child-allowances-make-the-irs-americas-number-one-welfare-agency. The American Rescue Plan Act also modestly expanded the earned income tax credit.

12. Bruce D. Meyer and James X. Sullivan, "Near Real Time COVID-19 Income and Poverty Dashboard," Poverty Measurement, http://povertymeasurement.org/covid-19-poverty-dashboard; Michael Karpman and Stephen Zuckerman, "Average Decline in Material Hardship During the Pandemic Conceals Unequal Circumstances," Urban Institute, April 14, 2021, https://www.urban.org/research/publication/average-decline-material-hardship-during-pandemic-conceals-unequal-circumstances; and John Creamer et al., *Poverty in the United States: 2021*, US Census Bureau, September 13, 2022, https://www.census.gov/library/publications/2022/demo/p60-277.html.

13. Mitchell Barnes et al., *Bolstered Balance Sheets: Assessing Household Finances Since 2019*, Brookings Institution, March 22, 2022, https://www.brookings.edu/research/bolstered-balance-sheets-assessing-household-finances-since-2019.

14. US Congressional Budget Office, "An Update to the Budget and Economic Outlook: 2021 to 2031," July 1, 2021, https://www.cbo.gov/publication/57218; and US Department of Labor, Bureau of Labor Statistics, Consumer Price Index, https://www.bls.gov/cpi.

15. See Bill Clinton, "Statement on Signing the Personal Responsibility and Work Opportunity Reconciliation Act of 1996," August 22, 1996, https://www.presidency.ucsb.edu/documents/statement-signing-the-personal-responsibility-and-work-opportunity-reconciliation-act-1996.

16. Kevin Corinth et al., "The Anti-Poverty, Targeting, and Labor Supply Effects of the Proposed Child Tax Credit Expansion" (working paper, National Bureau of Economic Research, Cambridge, MA, October 2021), https://www.nber.org/papers/w29366.

17. Erica York and Huaqun Li, "Making the Expanded Child Tax Credit Permanent Would Cost Nearly $1.6 Trillion," Tax Foundation, March 19, 2021, https://taxfoundation.org/expanded-child-tax-credit-permanent.

18. Richard V. Burkhauser et al., "Evaluating the Success of the War on Poverty Since 1963 Using an Absolute Full-Income Poverty Measure," *Journal of Political Economy* 132, no. 1 (January 2024): 1–47, https://www.journals.uchicago.edu/doi/epdf/10.1086/725705.

19. Duncan and Le Menestral, eds., *A Roadmap to Reducing Child Poverty*, Appendix D, 2–8.

20. Janet Currie and Hannes Schwandt, "Mortality Inequality: The Good News from a County-Level Approach" (working paper, National Bureau of Economic Research, Cambridge, MA, April 2016), https://www.nber.org/papers/w22199.

21. See US Department of Education, Institute of Education Sciences, National Center for Education Statistics, "Public High School Graduation Rates," May 2021, https://nces.ed.gov/programs/coe/indicator/coi/high-school-graduation-rates; and US Census Bureau, "CPS Historical Time Series Tables on School Enrollment," Table A-5a, December 20, 2022, https://www.census.gov/data/tables/time-series/demo/school-enrollment/cps-historical-time-series.html.

22. Duncan and Le Menestral, eds., *A Roadmap to Reducing Child Poverty*.

23. Duncan and Le Menestral, eds., *A Roadmap to Reducing Child Poverty*, Appendix D, 2–9.

24. Bruce D. Meyer and James X. Sullivan, "Five Decades of Consumption and Income Poverty" (working paper, National Bureau of Economic Research, Cambridge, MA, March 2009), https://www.nber.org/papers/w14827.

25. Yonatan Ben-Shalom, Robert Moffitt, and John Karl Scholz, "An Assessment of the Effectiveness of Antipoverty Programs in the United States," in *The Oxford Handbook of the Economics of Poverty*, ed. Philip N. Jefferson (Oxford, UK: Oxford University Press, 2012), 709–49, https://academic.oup.com/edited-volume/36327/chapter-abstract/318699934.

26. Liana E. Fox and Kalee Burns, "The Supplemental Poverty Measure: 2020," US Census Bureau, September 2021, https://www.census.gov/content/dam/Census/library/publications/2021/demo/p60-275.pdf. According to the US Census Bureau, 1.9 percent of full-time, year-round workers were considered poor according to the supplemental poverty measure in 2020 and 3.9 percent in 2019.

27. Maaike van der Noordt et al., "Health Effects of Employment: A Systematic Review of Prospective Studies," *Occupational and Environmental Medicine* 71, no. 10 (August 2014): 730–36, https://oem.bmj.com/content/71/10/730.

28. Mary Daly and Tali Regev, "Labor Force Participation and the Prospects for U.S. Growth," Federal Reserve Bank of San Francisco, November 2, 2007, https://www.frbsf.org/economic-research/publications/economic-letter/2007/november/labor-force-participation-us-growth.

29. Robert F. Schoeni and Rebecca M. Blank, "What Has Welfare Reform Accomplished? Impacts on Welfare Participation, Employment, Income, Poverty, and Family Structure" (working paper, National Bureau of Economic Research, Cambridge, MA, March 2000), https://www.nber.org/papers/w7627; Robert A. Moffitt, Brian J. Phelan, and Anne E. Winkler, "Welfare Rules, Incentives, and Family Structure" (working paper, National Bureau of Economic Research, Cambridge, MA, March 2018), https://www.nber.org/papers/w21257; and James P. Ziliak, "Temporary Assistance for Needy

Families," in *Economics of Means-Tested Transfer Programs in the United States, Volume 1,* ed. Robert A. Moffitt (Chicago: University of Chicago Press, 2015).

30. Jeffrey Grogger, Lynn A. Karoly, and Jacob Alex Klerman, *Consequences of Welfare Reform: A Research Synthesis* (Santa Monica, CA: RAND Corporation, 2002), https://www.rand.org/pubs/drafts/DRU2676.html; Jeffrey Grogger and Lynn A. Karoly, *Welfare Reform: Effects of a Decade of Change* (Cambridge, MA: Harvard University Press, 2005); and Henrik Kleven, "The EITC and the Extensive Margin: A Reappraisal" (working paper, National Bureau of Economic Research, Cambridge, MA, September 2022), https://www.nber.org/papers/w26405.

31. Grogger and Karoly, *Welfare Reform.*

32. Justin Falk, *The Effects of Work Requirements on the Employment and Income of TANF Participants* (working paper, Congressional Budget Office, Washington, DC, March 2023), https://www.cbo.gov/system/files/2023-03/58867-TANF.pdf.

33. Hilary Hoynes, "The Earned Income Tax Credit," *ANNALS of the American Academy of Political and Social Science* 686, no. 1 (November 2019): 180–203, https://journals.sagepub.com/toc/ann/686/1.

34. Nada Eissa and Hilary W. Hoynes, "Behavioral Responses to Taxes: Lessons from the EITC and Labor Supply," in *Tax Policy and the Economy, Volume 20,* ed. James Poterba (Cambridge, MA: MIT Press, 2006), https://www.nber.org/books-and-chapters/tax-policy-and-economy-volume-20/behavioral-responses-taxes-lessons-eitc-and-labor-supply.

35. The Supplemental Nutrition Assistance Program has a work-related time limit that applies to able-bodied adults without dependent children. Able-bodied adults without dependent children can receive Supplemental Nutrition Assistance Program benefits for only three months out of a three-year period unless they are working or engaging in a work activity, as allowed by the state. However, the law allows states to waive the time limit when jobs are scarce, including when the unemployment rate is high.

36. Hilary Williamson Hoynes and Diane Whitmore Schanzenbach, "Work Incentives and the Food Stamp Program," *Journal of Public Economics* 96, nos. 1–2 (February 2012): 151–62, https://www.sciencedirect.com/science/article/abs/pii/S0047272711001472.

37. Chloe N. East, "The Effect of Food Stamps on Children's Health: Evidence from Immigrants' Changing Eligibility," *Journal of Human Resources* 55, no. 2 (Spring 2020): 387–427, http://jhr.uwpress.org/content/early/2018/09/04/jhr.55.3.0916-8197R2.abstract.

38. Brian A. Jacob and Jens Ludwig, "The Effects of Housing Assistance on Labor Supply: Evidence from a Voucher Lottery," *American Economic Review* 102, no. 1 (February 2012): 272–304, https://www.aeaweb.org/articles?id=10.1257/aer.102.1.272.

39. Taryn W. Morrissey, "Child Care and Parent Labor Force Participation: A Review of the Research Literature," *Review of Economics of the Household* 15, no. 1 (March 2017): 1–24, https://link.springer.com/article/10.1007/s11150-016-9331-3.

40. Nina Chien and Suzanne Macartney, "What Happens When People Increase Their Earnings? Effective Marginal Tax Rates for Low-Income Households," US Department of Health and Human Services, Office of the Assistant Secretary for Planning and Evaluation, March 2019, https://aspe.hhs.gov/sites/default/files/private/aspe-files/260661/brief2-overviewmtranalyses.pdf.

41. The Congressional Budget Office concluded that we should expect individuals to reduce their work hours as effective marginal tax rates rise—including men and single women and to a lesser extent married women. See Robert McClelland and Shannon Mok, "A Review of Recent Research on Labor Supply Elasticities" (working paper, Congressional Budget Office, Washington, DC, October 2012), https://www.cbo.gov/sites/default/files/112th-congress-2011-2012/workingpaper/10-25-2012-recentresearchonlaborsupplyelasticities.pdf; and Congressional Budget Office, "How the Supply of Labor Responds to Changes in Fiscal Policy," October 2012, https://www.cbo.gov/sites/default/files/112th-congress-2011-2012/reports/43674-laborsupplyfiscalpolicy.pdf. Regarding poverty traps, see Charles Hughes, "New Study Finds More Evidence of Poverty Traps in the Welfare System," Cato Institute, December 30, 2014, https://www.cato.org/blog/new-study-finds-more-evidence-poverty-traps-welfare-system.

42. Chien and Macartney, "What Happens When People Increase Their Earnings?"

43. Chien and Macartney, "What Happens When People Increase Their Earnings?"

44. Sharon Parrott and Robert Greenstein, "Policymakers Often Overstate Marginal Tax Rates for Lower-Income Workers and Gloss Over Tough Trade-Offs in Reducing Them," Center on Budget and Policy Priorities, December 3, 2014, https://www.cbpp.org/research/policymakers-often-overstate-marginal-tax-rates-for-lower-income-workers-and-gloss-over.

45. David C. Ribar, "Why Marriage Matters for Child Wellbeing," *Future of Children* 25, no. 2 (September 2015): 11–27, https://files.eric.ed.gov/fulltext/EJ1079374.pdf.

46. Robert A. Moffitt, "The Role of Nonfinancial Factors in Exit and Entry in the TANF Program," *Journal of Human Resources* 38 (2003): 1221–54, https://www.jstor.org/stable/3558986.

47. Moffitt, "The Role of Nonfinancial Factors in Exit and Entry in the TANF Program."

48. Ziliak, "Temporary Assistance for Needy Families."

49. Radha Jagannathan and Michael J. Camasso, "Family Cap and Nonmarital Fertility: The Racial Conditioning of Policy Effects," *Journal of Marriage and Family* 65, no. 1 (February 2003): 52–71, https://www.jstor.org/stable/3600050.

50. David J. Fein, "Will Welfare Reform Influence Marriage and Fertility? Early Evidence from the ABC Demonstration," *Evaluation and Program Planning* 24, no. 4 (November 2001): 427–44, https://www.sciencedirect.com/science/article/abs/pii/S0149718901000374.

51. Radha Jagannathan, "A Latent Growth Curve Model of Nonmarital Births, Abortions, and Pregnancies: Did Welfare Reform Play a Role in Changing the Trajectories?," *Marriage & Family Review* 48, no. 4 (May 2012): 363–85, https://www.tandfonline.com/doi/abs/10.1080/01494929.2012.674481.

52. Ho-Po Crystal Wong, "The Quantity and Quality Adjustment of Births When Having More Is Not Subsidized: The Effect of the TANF Family Cap on Fertility and Birth Weight" (working paper, West Virginia University Department of Economics, Morgantown, WV, 2015), https://ideas.repec.org/p/wvu/wpaper/15-04.html.

53. Cody Vaughn, "Long-Run Impact of Welfare Reform on Educational Attainment and Family Structure," University of Wisconsin–La Crosse, September 6, 2022, https://

papers.ssrn.com/sol3/papers.cfm?abstract_id=4131589; and Catalina Amuedo-Dorantes, Susan L. Averett, and Cynthia A. Bansak, "Welfare Reform and Immigrant Fertility" (working paper, Institute of Labor Economics, Bonn, Germany, April 2014), https://www.econstor.eu/bitstream/10419/98987/1/dp8153.pdf. Catalina Amuedo-Dorantes, Susan L. Averett, and Cynthia A. Bansak studied the impact of welfare reform's restriction on benefits for immigrant groups and their fertility decisions using Current Population Survey data. They found that immigrant women (primarily of Hispanic ethnicity) had lower fertility when states did not replace discontinued federal benefits.

54. Nishant Yonzan et al., "Economic Incentives Surrounding Fertility: Evidence from Alaska's Permanent Fund Dividend," *Economics and Human Biology* 52 (2024): 101334, https://pubmed.ncbi.nlm.nih.gov/38070225.

55. Sarah K. Cowan and Kiara Wyndham Douds, "Examining the Effects of a Universal Cash Transfer on Fertility," *Social Forces* 101, no. 2 (2022): 1003–30, https://academic.oup.com/sf/article/101/2/1003/6537059.

56. US Department of Health and Human Services, Centers for Disease Control and Prevention, "About Teen Pregnancy," November 15, 2021, https://www.cdc.gov/teenpregnancy/about/index.htm.

57. Laura Lindberg, John Santelli, and Sheila Desai, "Understanding the Decline in Adolescent Fertility in the United States, 2007–2012," *Journal of Adolescent Health* 59, no. 5 (November 2016): 577–83, https://www.jahonline.org/article/S1054-139X(16)30172-0/fulltext.

58. Martha A. Beltz et al., "State Policy and Teen Childbearing: A Review of Research Studies," *Journal of Adolescent Health* 56, no. 2 (February 2015): 130–38, https://www.jahonline.org/article/S1054-139X(14)00709-5/fulltext.

59. For example, Paul Offner used data from the US Census Bureau's Current Population Survey and found that welfare reform increased school attendance among teens and reduced teenage childbearing. Using natality data, Leonard M. Lopoo and Thomas DeLeire compared 16- to 17-year-olds affected by new rules in the Temporary Assistance for Needy Families that required teen mothers to remain in high school and live with a parent or guardian to receive welfare benefits to 18-year-olds not affected by the rule on measures of fertility. They found that the Temporary Assistance for Needy Families rule reduced teenage fertility by 22 percent. In reviewing the decline in teenage birth rates over time, Melissa S. Kearney and Phillip Levine concluded that only two policies had effects: declining welfare benefits and Medicaid's family planning services. See Ziliak, "Temporary Assistance for Needy Families"; Paul Offner, "Welfare Reform and Teenage Girls," *Social Science Quarterly* 86, no. 2 (June 2005): 306–22, https://www.jstor.org/stable/42956065; Leonard M. Lopoo and Thomas DeLeire, "Did Welfare Reform Influence the Fertility of Young Teens?," *Journal of Policy Analysis and Management* 25, no. 2 (Spring 2006): 275–98, https://www.jstor.org/stable/30162721; and Melissa S. Kearney and Phillip Levine, "Teen Births Are Falling: What's Going On?," Brookings Institution, March 11, 2014, https://www.brookings.edu/research/teen-births-are-falling-whats-going-on.

60. Irwin Garfinkel et al., "The Roles of Child Support Enforcement and Welfare in Non-Marital Childbearing," *Journal of Population Economics* 16, no. 1 (February 2003): 55–70, https://www.jstor.org/stable/20007852.

61. Robert D. Plotnick et al., "The Impact of Child Support Enforcement Policy on Nonmarital Childbearing," *Journal of Policy Analysis and Management* 26, no. 1 (Winter 2007): 79–98, https://www.jstor.org/stable/30164085.

62. Hilary Hoynes, Diane Whitmore Schanzenbach, and Douglas Almond, "Long-Run Impacts of Childhood Access to the Safety Net," *American Economic Review* 106, no. 4 (April 2016): 903–34, https://www.aeaweb.org/articles?id=10.1257/aer.20130375.

63. Janet Currie and Enrico Moretti, "Did the Introduction of Food Stamps Affect Birth Outcomes in California?," in *Making Americans Healthier: Social and Economic Policy as Health Policy*, ed. Robert F. Schoeni et al. (New York: Russell Sage Foundation, 2008), https://www.jstor.org/stable/10.7758/9781610444873.

64. Reagan Baughman and Stacy Dickert-Conlin, "The Earned Income Tax Credit and Fertility," *Journal of Population Economics* 22, no. 3 (July 2009): 537–63, https://www.jstor.org/stable/40344745.

65. Doug J. Besharov and Neil Gilbert, "Marriage Penalties in the Modern Social-Welfare State," R Street Institute, September 2015, https://www.rstreet.org/wp-content/uploads/2018/04/RSTREET40-1.pdf.

66. Brad Wilcox, Angela Rachidi, and Joseph Price, *Marriage, Penalized: Does Social-Welfare Policy Affect Family Formation?*, American Enterprise Institute, July 26, 2016, https://www.aei.org/research-products/report/marriage-penalized-does-social-welfare-policy-affect-family-formation.

67. Greg J. Duncan, Jeanne Brooks-Gunn, and Pamela Kato Klebanov, "Economic Deprivation and Early Childhood Development," *Child Development* 65, no. 2 (April 1994): https://www.jstor.org/stable/1131385; Jeanne Brooks-Gunn and Greg J. Duncan, "The Effects of Poverty on Children," *Children and Poverty* 7, no. 2 (Summer–Autumn 1997), https://www.jstor.org/stable/1602387; Sanders Korenman and Jane E. Miller, "Effects of Long-Term Poverty on Physical Health of Children in the National Longitudinal Survey of Youth," in *Consequences of Growing Up Poor*, ed. Greg J. Duncan and Jeanne Brooks-Gunn (New York: Russell Sage Foundation, 1997); Ingrid Schoon et al., "The Influence of Context, Timing, and Duration of Risk Experiences for the Passage from Childhood to Midadulthood," *Child Development* 73, no. 5 (September–October 2002): 1486–504, https://www.jstor.org/stable/3696394; Lee Pachter et al., "Do Parenting and the Home Environment, Maternal Depression, Neighborhood, and Chronic Poverty Affect Child Behavioral Problems Differently in Different Racial-Ethnic Groups?," *Pediatrics* 117, no. 4 (April 2006): 1329–38, https://www.ncbi.nlm.nih.gov/pmc/articles/PMC1475725; and Caroline Ratcliffe and Signe-Mary McKernan, *Child Poverty and Its Lasting Consequence: Low-Income Working Families*, Urban Institute, September 2012, https://www.urban.org/sites/default/files/publication/32756/412659-Child-Poverty-and-Its-Lasting-Consequence.pdf.

68. Charles Murray, *Losing Ground: American Social Policy, 1950–1980* (New York: Basic Books, 1984).

69. Peter Gottschalk, "Is the Correlation in Welfare Participation Across Generations Spurious?," *Journal of Public Economics* 63, no. 1 (December 1996): 1–25, https://www.sciencedirect.com/science/article/abs/pii/S004727279601585X; and Phillip B. Levine and David John Zimmerman, "The Intergenerational Correlation in AFDC

Participation: Welfare Trap or Poverty Trap?," University of Wisconsin–Madison, Institute for Research on Poverty, 1996, https://ideas.repec.org/p/wop/wispod/1100-96.html.

70. Sara Kimberlin, "The Influence of Government Benefits and Taxes on Rates of Chronic and Transient Poverty in the United States," *Social Service Review* 90, no. 2 (June 2016): 185–234, https://www.journals.uchicago.edu/doi/abs/10.1086/687306.

71. Robert Paul Hartley, Carlos Lamarche, and James P. Ziliak, "Welfare Reform and the Intergenerational Transmission of Dependence," *Journal of Political Economy* 130, no. 3 (March 2022), https://www.journals.uchicago.edu/doi/epdf/10.1086/717893.

72. Hilary W. Hoynes and Diane Whitmore Schanzenbach, "Safety Net Investments in Children" (working paper, National Bureau of Economic Research, Cambridge, MA, May 2018), https://www.nber.org/papers/w24594.

73. Douglas Almond, Hilary W. Hoynes, and Diane Whitmore Schanzenbach, "Inside the War on Poverty: The Impact of Food Stamps on Birth Outcomes," *Review of Economics and Statistics* 93, no. 2 (May 2011): 387–403, https://www.jstor.org/stable/23015943.

74. Hoynes, Schanzenbach, and Almond, "Long-Run Impacts of Childhood Access to the Safety Net"; Almond, Hoynes, and Schanzenbach, "Inside the War on Poverty"; and Chloe N. East, "The Effect of Food Stamps on Children's Health: Evidence from Immigrants' Changing Eligibility," *Journal of Human Resources* 55, no. 2 (September 2018): 387–427, http://jhr.uwpress.org/content/early/2018/09/04/jhr.55.3.0916-8197R2.

75. East, "The Effect of Food Stamps on Children's Health."

76. Austin Nichols and Jesse Rothstein, "The Earned Income Tax Credit," in *Economics of Means-Tested Transfer Programs in the United States*, ed. Robert A. Moffitt (Chicago: University of Chicago Press, 2015), 1:137–218.

77. Hoynes and Schanzenbach, "Safety Net Investments in Children."

78. Raj Chetty, John N. Friedman, and Jonah Rockoff, "New Evidence on the Long-Term Impacts of Tax Credits," National Tax Association, 2011, https://www.ntanet.org/wp-content/uploads/proceedings/2011/018-chetty-new-evidence-longterm-2011-nta-proceedings.pdf.

79. Jacob Bastian and Katherine Michelmore, "The Long-Term Impact of the Earned Income Tax Credit on Children's Education and Employment Outcomes," *Journal of Labor Economics* 36, no. 4 (October 2018): 1127–63, https://www.journals.uchicago.edu/doi/abs/10.1086/697477. Other research has found similar results, including Day Manoli and Nicholas Turner, "Cash-on-Hand and College Enrollment: Evidence from Population Tax Data and the Earned Income Tax Credit," *American Economic Journal: Economic Policy* 10, no. 2 (May 2018): 242–71, https://www.aeaweb.org/articles?id=10.1257/pol.20160298; and Michelle Maxfield, "The Effects of the Earned Income Tax Credit on Child Achievement and Long-Term Educational Attainment," Michigan State University, Institute for Public Policy and Social Research, November 2013, http://ippsr.msu.edu/research/effects-earned-income-tax-credit-child-achievement-and-long-term-educational-attainment.

80. Hoynes, "The Earned Income Tax Credit."

81. Pamela A. Morris, Lisa A. Gennetian, and Greg J. Duncan, "Effects of Welfare and Employment Policies on Young Children: New Findings on Policy Experiments

Conducted in the Early 1990s," Society for Research in Child Development, 2005, https://eric.ed.gov/?id=ED521746.

82. See Amalia R. Miller and Lei Zhang, "Intergenerational Effects of Welfare Reform on Educational Attainment," *Journal of Law and Economics* 55, no. 2 (May 2012): 437–76, https://www.jstor.org/stable/10.1086/663348; Vaughn, "Long-Run Impact of Welfare Reform on Educational Attainment and Family Structure"; Morris, Gennetian, and Duncan, "Effects of Welfare and Employment Policies on Young Children"; Ziliak, "Temporary Assistance for Needy Families"; and Aletha C. Huston et al., "Impacts on Children of a Policy to Promote Employment and Reduce Poverty for Low-Income Parents: New Hope After 5 Years," *Developmental Psychology* 41, no. 6 (December 2005): 902–18, https://pubmed.ncbi.nlm.nih.gov/16351336.

83. Grogger and Karoly, *Welfare Reform*.

84. Hope Corman et al., "Effects of Welfare Reform on Household Food Insecurity Across Generations" (working paper, National Bureau of Economic Research, Cambridge, MA, July 2021), https://www.nber.org/papers/w29054.

85. Jeehoon Han, Bruce D. Meyer, and James X. Sullivan, "The Consumption, Income, and Well-Being of Single Mother Headed Families 25 Years After Welfare Reform" (working paper, National Bureau of Economic Research, Cambridge, MA, July 2021), https://www.nber.org/papers/w29188.

86. Sandra K. Danziger, "The Decline of Cash Welfare and Implications for Social Policy and Poverty," *Annual Review of Sociology* 36 (August 2010): 523–45, https://www.annualreviews.org/doi/10.1146/annurev.soc.012809.102644.

87. Morris, Gennetian, and Duncan, "Effects of Welfare and Employment Policies on Young Children."

88. Morris, Gennetian, and Duncan, "Effects of Welfare and Employment Policies on Young Children."

89. Robert Doar, "Empowering Child Support Enforcement to Reduce Poverty," in *A Safety Net That Works: Improving Federal Programs for Low-Income Americans*, ed. Robert Doar (Washington, DC: AEI Press, 2017), 63–86, https://www.aei.org/research-products/book/a-safety-net-that-works-improving-federal-programs-for-low-income-americans; Virginia W. Knox, "The Effects of Child Support Payments on Developmental Outcomes for Elementary School-Age Children," *Journal of Human Resources* 31, no. 4 (Autumn 1996): 816–40, https://www.jstor.org/stable/146148; and Paul R. Amato and Joan G. Gilbreth, "Nonresident Fathers and Children's Well-Being: A Meta-Analysis," *Journal of Marriage and Family* 61, no. 3 (August 1999): 557–73, https://www.jstor.org/stable/353560.

90. Steven J. Haider, Alison Jacknowitz, and Robert F. Schoeni found rates of breastfeeding to be 5.5 percent lower. Robert Kaestner and Won Chan Lee found lower prenatal care and low birth weight (but that could have reflected problems with Medicaid). Christina Paxson and Jane Waldfogel found increased child maltreatment due to welfare reform. See Steven J. Haider, Alison Jacknowitz, and Robert F. Schoeni, "Welfare Work Requirements and Child Well-Being: Evidence from the Effects on Breast-Feeding," *Demography* 40, no. 3 (August 2003): 479–97, https://www.jstor.org/stable/1515156; Robert Kaestner and Won Chan Lee, "The Effect of Welfare Reform on Prenatal Care and Birth Weight," *Health Economics* 14, no. 5 (September 2004): 497–511, https://

onlinelibrary.wiley.com/doi/10.1002/hec.921; and Christina Paxson and Jane Wald-fogel, "Work, Welfare, and Child Maltreatment," *Journal of Labor Economics* 20, no. 3 (July 2002): 435–74, https://www.jstor.org/stable/10.1086/339609.

91. Wendy Chavkin, Diana Romero, and Paul H. Wise, "State Welfare Reform Policies and Declines in Health Insurance," *American Journal of Public Health* 90, no. 6 (June 2000): 900–8, https://www.ncbi.nlm.nih.gov/pmc/articles/PMC1446262.

92. Ziliak, "Temporary Assistance for Needy Families."

93. Hoynes, Schanzenbach, and Almond, "Long-Run Impacts of Childhood Access to the Safety Net."

94. Bastian and Michelmore, "The Long-Term Impact of the Earned Income Tax Credit on Children's Education and Employment Outcomes."

95. Manoli and Turner, "Cash-on-Hand and College Enrollment"; and Maxfield, "The Effects of the Earned Income Tax Credit on Child Achievement and Long-Term Educational Attainment."

96. Vaughn, "Long-Run Impact of Welfare Reform on Educational Attainment and Family Structure."

97. See Nathaniel Hendren and Ben Sprung-Keyser, "A Unified Welfare Analysis of Government Policies," Opportunity Insights, February 2020, https://opportunityinsights.org/wp-content/uploads/2019/07/Welfare_paper.pdf.

98. White House, "Reducing Poverty in America by Promoting Opportunity and Economic Mobility," *Federal Register* 83, no. 72 (April 13, 2018): 15941–44, https://www.federalregister.gov/documents/2018/04/13/2018-07874/reducing-poverty-in-america-by-promoting-opportunity-and-economic-mobility.

99. Lawrence M. Mead, *Expanding Work Programs for Poor Men* (Washington, DC: AEI Press, 2011), https://www.aei.org/research-products/book/expanding-work-programs-for-poor-men.

100. Mary Jo Bane and David T. Ellwood, "Slipping into and out of Poverty: The Dynamics of Spells" (working paper, National Bureau of Economic Research, Cambridge, MA, September 1983), https://www.nber.org/papers/w1199.

101. See the Committee for a Responsible Federal Budget, "Analysis of the CBO's March 2024 Long-Term Budget Outlook," March 20, 2024, https://www.crfb.org/papers/analysis-cbos-march-2024-long-term-budget-outlook.

102. Angela Rachidi, "A Simpler Safety Net for Families: Consolidating Child Tax Credits into a Working Family Credit," American Enterprise Institute, May 23, 2022, https://www.aei.org/research-products/report/a-simpler-safety-net-for-families-consolidating-child-tax-credits-into-a-working-family-credit.

103. Rachidi, "A Simpler Safety Net for Families."

104. The "vertical" marriage penalty refers to two single parents marrying when each parent has a qualifying child for the purposes of the earned income tax credit. In this scenario, under the current earned income tax credit and under our proposal, the family would lose a similar amount in tax benefits due to the marriage.

105. US Treasury Inspector General for Tax Administration, *Improper Payment Reporting Has Improved; However, There Have Been No Significant Reductions to the Billions of Dollars of Improper Payments*, April 30, 2020, https://www.oversight.gov/sites/default/files/oig-reports/202040025fr_0.pdf.

106. Steve Holt, *The Role of the IRS as a Social Benefit Administrator*, American Enterprise Institute, July 25, 2016, https://www.aei.org/research-products/report/the-role-of-the-irs-as-a-social-benefit-administrator.

107. Holt, *The Role of the IRS as a Social Benefit Administrator*.

108. For parameters of the saver's credit, see Internal Revenue Service, "Retirement Savings Contributions Credit (Saver's Credit)," December 21, 2022, https://www.irs.gov/retirement-plans/plan-participant-employee/retirement-savings-contributions-savers-credit.

109. Raj Chetty and Nathaniel Hendren, "The Impacts of Neighborhoods on Intergenerational Mobility I: Childhood Exposure Effects" (working paper, National Bureau of Economic Research, Cambridge, MA, May 2017), https://www.nber.org/papers/w23001.

110. Edgar O. Olsen, "Reducing Poverty by Reforming Housing Policy," in *A Safety Net That Works: Improving Federal Programs for Low-Income Americans*, ed. Robert Doar (Washington, DC: AEI Press, 2017), https://www.aei.org/research-products/book/a-safety-net-that-works-improving-federal-programs-for-low-income-americans.

111. Rachidi, "A Simpler Safety Net for Families."

112. Rachidi, "A Simpler Safety Net for Families."

113. See Angela Rachidi, Matt Weidinger, and Scott Winship, "A Safety Net for the Future: Overcoming the Root Causes of Poverty," in *American Renewal: A Conservative Plan to Strengthen the Social Contract and Save the Country's Finances*, ed. Paul Ryan and Angela Rachidi (Washington, DC: AEI Press, 2022), https://americanrenpr.wpengine.com/wp-content/uploads/2022/11/AR-final.pdf.

114. Ron Haskins and Matt Weidinger, "The Temporary Assistance for Needy Families Program: Time for Improvements," *ANNALS of the American Academy of Political and Social Science* 686, no. 1 (November 6, 2019), https://journals.sagepub.com/doi/10.1177/0002716219881628.

115. Committee for a Responsible Federal Budget, "COVID Money Tracker," https://www.covidmoneytracker.org.

6

Place Belongs at the Center of an Opportunity Agenda

JOHN W. LETTIERI

M any factors influence children's development and life outcomes. However, a wide body of research reveals the multitude of ways that *place* contributes to a child's odds of success later in life. Taken together, the empirical evidence points to an inescapable conclusion: Outcomes in education, employment, health, parenthood, marriage, and more are intimately linked to the neighborhoods where children are raised. To uplift the lives of future generations, we must reduce their likelihood of growing up in economically distressed neighborhoods.

Therein lies a great American problem. For all its dazzling economic success, the United States remains woefully ineffective at improving the conditions of its most disadvantaged neighborhoods—and all too effective at producing new ones. High-poverty neighborhoods have proliferated even as individual poverty has declined and the country overall has grown ever more prosperous. Distressed communities seem increasingly disconnected from the fruits of national economic growth, with far-reaching consequences for the residents—especially children—who call them home.

Exacerbating this challenge is the proliferation of restrictive zoning and land-use regulations that have made housing less abundant and affordable in the places where it is most needed, in turn fueling the spatial concentration of poverty—the very phenomenon that harms intergenerational mobility and perpetuates a variety of social maladies. As spatial divides in well-being have grown more pronounced, America's once-vibrant geographic mobility has declined, leaving disadvantaged populations more dissatisfied, unproductive, and stuck in place than in decades past.

These challenges call for an ambitious, place-targeted policy agenda designed to tackle the spatial barriers to opportunity and social mobility from the neighborhood level on up, with the goal of greatly reducing the number of years American children spend in areas of concentrated poverty and economic distress. Such efforts should follow a two-pronged approach focused on improving the economic conditions of impoverished communities and helping families with young children move to better areas.

Why Place Matters for Children

Researchers have long understood that neighborhoods matter to childhood well-being. Children growing up in high-poverty neighborhoods[1] are disproportionately exposed to a wide range of social and economic dysfunction, from adults out of work and crumbling amenities to pervasive health maladies, crime, and violence.[2] Life expectancy is fully six years shorter in high-poverty neighborhoods than in low-poverty ones.[3]

In addition, high school graduation—a key predictor of success later in life—is positively correlated to neighborhood quality.[4] Living in low-quality neighborhoods is found to increase antisocial "externalizing behaviors" such as fighting, property damage, and stealing.[5] Exposure to environmental health hazards varies dramatically by neighborhood type. Lead exposure, which reduces vocabulary skills, is more common in children who spend extended periods of their childhood in high-poverty, disadvantaged neighborhoods.[6] High-poverty neighborhoods are also much more likely than affluent ones to be food deserts.[7]

But what about upward mobility—the chances that a child born at the bottom of the socioeconomic ladder can rise and achieve higher levels of well-being? Many of the most valuable insights on how neighborhoods influence children's social mobility come from the Moving to Opportunity (MTO) policy experiment, launched by the US Department of Housing and Urban Development in the mid-1990s, which randomly assigned vouchers to low-income families in very poor neighborhoods to enable them to relocate to better ones.[8] Research by economists Raj Chetty, Nathaniel Hendren, and their colleagues has uncovered significant benefits for the children of families that relocated to low-poverty neighborhoods. Those who made such moves were more likely to earn higher incomes, avoid single parenthood, and achieve higher levels of education.[9]

Building on these findings, Chetty and Hendren used anonymized tax records to examine the effects of moves across counties for over five million children. The result was a landmark study revealing that places affect children's chances of upward mobility and shedding new light on the characteristics of high-opportunity areas.[10]

When the move occurred is just as crucial as where. Each year that a child was exposed to a better neighborhood delivered a similar level of benefit.[11] Thus, the earlier a child moved, the more beneficial years spent in a good neighborhood and the stronger the lifetime effects they tended to experience. As Chetty put it, "Every extra year of childhood spent in a better neighborhood seems to matter."[12] The opposite held true as well: Moving to worse areas produced equivalently strong negative exposure effects for children.

Moving from high-poverty neighborhoods to lower-poverty ones when a child is young increases the likelihood of college attendance and leads to significantly higher earnings in adulthood. Those who moved to a low-poverty area before age 13 were greatly better off, with 31 percent higher earnings as adults.[13] Importantly, the children who make the move to higher-quality neighborhoods are themselves more likely to live in such neighborhoods as adults and are less likely to become single parents. This means that the positive repercussions of a child's move to opportunity-rich neighborhoods extend beyond the generation that actually moved.

The MTO studies underscore that individual poverty is only one factor in the equation of social mobility. Two equally poor children in similar households will have fundamentally different odds of achieving the American Dream, depending on their surrounding communities. What, then, are the neighborhood factors that correlate most strongly with positive outcomes for their young residents?

High-opportunity neighborhoods tend to be more affluent overall but also more economically integrated among low-income, middle-class, and affluent residents. This is corroborated by other research finding that metropolitan areas with higher levels of segregation between clusters of concentrated poverty and wealthy enclaves tend to have less economic mobility.[14] High-opportunity areas also tend to have higher concentrations of two-parent families, better schools, and low crime.[15]

Importantly, neighborhoods influence children in ways that are distinct from the effects seen in adults. Several evaluations of the MTO initiative found that adults who moved to better neighborhoods benefited in terms of physical and mental health and an improved sense of well-being.[16] However, these studies failed to identify improved long-term *economic* results, such as increased employment or higher earnings. The key window for shaping such outcomes seems to be found exclusively in early childhood.

But why? This brings us to yet another remarkable set of findings from Chetty and his colleagues, published in a 2022 paper in the journal *Nature,* that digs deeper into why some neighborhoods are so much better than others at providing a pathway to the American Dream.[17] The authors evaluated the importance of "economic connectedness"—or cross-class friendships—in different types of neighborhoods by analyzing the social media connections of 72 million US adults.

Higher-income people tend to have a heavy concentration of social connections with people of similar socioeconomic status (SES). On average, one-third of the Facebook friends of people in the top 10 percent are likewise from the top decile, compared to only 16 percent coming from the bottom five deciles combined.[18] A neighborhood's level of economic connectedness between people with high and low SES turns out to be a remarkably strong predictor of the social mobility of its low-income residents. According to the authors, "If children with low-SES parents were to grow up in counties with economic connectedness comparable to that of the average child with high-SES parents, their incomes in adulthood would increase by 20% on average."[19] Social connectedness was more important than any other neighborhood factor the researchers tested.

The bottom line is that neighborhoods matter for a child's social mobility because economic connectedness plays such a profound role in social mobility, and certain types of neighborhoods offer much stronger connectedness than others.

The Growing Challenge of Spatial Inequality
and Concentrated Poverty

Since neighborhood conditions play such a large role in shaping the lives and economic prospects of children, we should be particularly attuned to the changing nature of communities over time and the relationship between the national economy and local neighborhoods.

The United States has undoubtedly become more prosperous over the past four decades. Real gross domestic product grew to over $20 trillion in 2023, more than tripling since 1980.[20] Real gross domestic product per capita more than doubled over the same period. In 2019, real median family income exceeded $91,000 to reach its highest level on record.[21] And from June 2009 to February 2020, the US experienced the longest period of economic growth in the nation's history.

However, while the national and local economies are no doubt interconnected, people tend to experience the economy more tangibly at a local level, where national aggregates and averages are little more than an abstraction. One might expect a general rise in national prosperity to translate into a rising tide for communities at the bottom and the steady eradication of concentrated economic distress at the neighborhood level, but just the opposite has occurred. The map of economic growth has become increasingly uneven across regions and communities, while spatial clusters of poverty have multiplied.

The relationship between spatial concentration of poverty and a range of important outcomes holds true at multiple units of geography, from multicounty commuting zones down to smaller areas such as school districts and census tracts, making the poverty rate a useful gauge of the broader well-being of a neighborhood. And it is here that we return to one of America's most pernicious challenges. According to researchers August Benzow and Kenan Fikri at the Economic Innovation Group, the number of concentrated-poverty neighborhoods in metropolitan areas nationwide—ones in which 30 percent or more of the residents live in poverty—stood at just over 6,500 in 2018, more than twice the number that existed nearly four decades earlier in 1980.[22] In total, more than 24 million Americans lived in such neighborhoods in 2018, doubling the number found in 1980 even as the country's total population grew by only 44 percent.

The challenge of high-poverty neighborhoods in the United States is one of persistence and proliferation. Contrary to much of the conventional wisdom about neighborhoods' susceptibility to gentrification and rapid socioeconomic change, places tend to evolve quite slowly. Dramatic changes in fortune—either positive or negative—are relatively rare and isolated, even over decades-long timescales. As a rule, neighborhoods with elevated levels of poverty tend to stay that way: Nearly two-thirds of neighborhoods with concentrated poverty in 1980 remained persistently poor across subsequent decades and were still in such a condition in 2018.[23]

Long-running persistence in levels of economic welfare can be observed at other geographic scales using a variety of measures. For example, two-thirds of ZIP codes that scored in the highest quintile of well-being on the Economic Innovation Group's Distressed Communities Index in 2000 remained so in 2018. This pattern gets repeated at the other end of the distribution, as an identical share—66 percent—of ZIP codes that ranked in the lowest tier of well-being in 2000 remained mired at the bottom in 2018 as well.[24]

Researchers at the Hamilton Project uncovered similar results at the county level using their Vitality Index to measure economic and social well-being across places over time. Consistent with other research, they found that only 29 percent of counties in the bottom vitality quintile in 1980 had risen to a higher quintile by 2016. Meanwhile, nearly six in 10 counties in the top quintile in 1980 remained there over the period studied, and nearly 90 percent remained in the top two quintiles. Places marked by economic diversity, dense populations, high levels of human capital, limited exposure to manufacturing, and higher levels of innovative activity in 1980 tended to see durable benefits over time, as evidenced by persistently high vitality scores.[25]

In recent decades, it is much more common for stable neighborhoods to slide into high concentrations of poverty than it is for deeply impoverished communities to truly revitalize. For example, Benzow and Fikri find that for every concentrated-poverty neighborhood that experienced a steep drop in poverty between 1980 and 2018, five low-poverty neighborhoods saw their rates increase sharply to eclipse 30 percent.

Dramatically improving and deteriorating neighborhoods alike tend to be highly spatially concentrated phenomena. More than one-fifth of the nation's entire cohort of "turnaround" neighborhoods between 1980 and 2018 can be found in New York City alone—most of them in a single borough (Brooklyn). Only 53 of the country's 100 largest cities contained *even a single census tract* that went from a poverty rate of 30 percent or more to one below 20 percent over that period. At the other end of the spectrum, the economic collapse of legacy industrial cities like Detroit, Michigan; Cleveland, Ohio; and Rochester, New York, produced alarming numbers of downwardly mobile communities. In Detroit, for example, 61 percent of low-poverty neighborhoods saw their poverty rates spike to 30 percent or more over the period studied.[26]

By 2018, only 14 percent of the 1980 cohort of concentrated-poverty neighborhoods—just 464 neighborhoods—had achieved what could be considered a true turnaround, as evidenced by a poverty rate below 20 percent. This is roughly the same number of tracts as compose Cuyahoga County, Ohio, or Clark County, Nevada. Another 22 percent saw their poverty rate modestly improve, falling below 30 percent but remaining above 20 percent. Meanwhile, the country added more than 2,500 new high-poverty neighborhoods over the same period. Sustained stretches of national growth, such as the 1990s economic boom, served only to temporarily stall the multiplication of concentrated-poverty areas across the map.

The End of Convergence, the Rise of Being Stuck, and the Role of Housing Policy

The geography of economic well-being is evolving in other ways as well. The 21st-century economic map reflects an increased concentration of economic growth and dynamism in a relatively small share of places compared to previous periods. The national recovery following the Great Recession marked a sharp narrowing of economic activity as high-performing areas became dominant in ways not seen in previous periods of growth.

For example, during the first five years of recovery following the Great Recession, 20 counties alone produced fully half of the net increase in US business establishments. These places were home to only 17 percent of the national population. Previous recoveries were far more regionally balanced. During the 1992–96 recovery period, it took 125 counties, home to nearly one-third of the US population and spread widely across the map, to produce the same result.[27] ZIP codes in the most prosperous quintile of well-being, according to the Distressed Communities Index, captured 62 percent of all net new jobs added to the US economy between 2000 and 2018—more than triple the amount gained by the bottom three quintiles combined.[28]

While prosperous areas are becoming more populous and diverse, America's distressed communities appear increasingly dislocated from the rest of the nation's economic performance. Even late in a period of record economic expansion, the bottom quintile of US ZIP codes experienced net losses to employment and establishments that one would typically associate with a recession.[29]

The trajectory of the US economy from the late 19th century through the late 20th century was one of regional convergence: Places were generally becoming more alike in incomes and standards of living. Workers migrated into areas of the country rich in opportunity, while firms flowed to lower-cost, less-developed areas.[30] This geographic churn of people and firms fueled steady convergence across regions and provided a crucial way for the economy to respond to economic disruption.[31]

Both the rate of income convergence across states and rate of migration to high-income places saw striking declines beginning in the late 20th century.[32] For decade after decade following World War II, at least 6 percent of Americans moved across counties each year. Migration rates remained strong at the turn of the new century, with 6.4 percent moving to a different county in 2000. From there, however, the decline in this key measure of mobility has been precipitous, falling to 3.5 percent in the wake of the Great Recession and barely budging since—even with the great social and economic upheaval of the pandemic.[33]

As migration has steeply declined overall, it has also fractured along educational lines. Americans of all educational attainment levels used to move from low-income to high-income places. Today, high school graduates are half as likely to move to a different state as someone with a graduate degree, and, worse yet, these low-skilled workers are moving *away* from high-income, opportunity-rich places.[34] In fact, while low-skilled workers moving to productive, high-wage areas used to see a large boost to their cost-of-living-adjusted wages, today they instead receive an effective wage *penalty*.[35]

Why is this happening? After all, individual poverty itself is not on the rise; the share of Americans living in poverty has declined slightly over the past 40 years, according to the official measure, and has seen a steep drop by more comprehensive measures that take into account government benefits and transfers.[36] The answer is that restrictive zoning and land-use regulations have skyrocketed, reducing the supply of housing and stifling migration to opportunity-rich places that fueled a century or more of regional convergence and offered a reliable pathway to a better life for millions of workers.[37] As a result, affluent people have become increasingly residentially segregated from the rest of society.

Indeed, the story of American communities in recent decades is one of a steady rise in economic segregation in which affluent and low-income people have become more clustered in their respective spaces.[38] Hence the share of high-poverty *census tracts* has risen by nearly 20 percent over the past three decades, even as the share of high-poverty *counties* has steadily declined.[39]

One way to illustrate this socioeconomic sorting: In 1980, more poor Americans in metropolitan areas lived in a neighborhood with a poverty rate below 10 percent than one above 30 percent. The inverse is true today.[40] Decades of sorting and being stuck have made poor Americans more likely to start and stay in distressed areas—and therefore more exposed to the spatial disadvantages that block access to the American Dream. It should then come as no surprise that the share of Americans who report being stuck in an undesirable neighborhood has risen by almost 50 percent in the past 40 years.[41]

While the harms to low-income people caused by restrictive land-use policies are obvious, the hidden effects make the entire country poorer, slower growing, and less dynamic. For example, researchers Chang-Tai Hsieh and Enrico Moretti come to an eye-popping conclusion in a 2019 paper for the *American Economic Journal*:

> We quantify the amount of spatial misallocation of labor across US cities and its aggregate costs. Misallocation arises because high productivity cities like New York and the

San Francisco Bay Area have adopted stringent restrictions to
new housing supply, effectively limiting the number of workers
who have access to such high productivity. Using a spatial equi-
librium model and data from 220 metropolitan areas we find
that these constraints lowered aggregate US growth by more
than 36% from 1964 to 2009.[42]

In other words, not only does bad housing policy fuel racial and
economic segregation, but it is also a massive self-inflicted wound on
American prosperity.

Race and Place

As high-poverty, low-opportunity neighborhoods have proliferated, the
share of American children who call them home has fluctuated with cycles
of economic expansion and contraction. But even in periods when the
national economy is at its peak, millions of children must contend with
severe, place-based disadvantages. According to the US Census Bureau's
2022 American Community Survey five-year estimates, more than a fifth
of children in the United States live in high-poverty neighborhoods—
ones where the poverty rate is 20 percent or more. Roughly 8 percent
(5.7 million) live in areas where the poverty rate is 30 percent or greater.[43]
The share of children living in these concentrated-poverty neighborhoods
is only marginally better today than it was at the turn of the 21st century,
but in between, it spiked as high as 14 percent in the early 2010s before
steadily falling as the country continued its recovery from the Great
Recession.[44]

Childhood exposure to neighborhood disadvantage, like most national
challenges, varies considerably across states. In some, such as New Hamp-
shire and Utah, a mere 1 percent or less of children must contend with
the deep disadvantages of concentrated-poverty neighborhoods, while
in New Mexico and Mississippi, a staggering one-fifth are spending their
formative years, through no fault of their own, immersed in such areas.[45]

One cannot grapple with the marked differences in economic well-
being across racial and ethnic groups in the United States without first

understanding the highly uneven nature of childhood exposure to neigh-borhood disadvantages. Though white children vastly outnumber black children overall, just over four million white and black children alike live in high-poverty neighborhoods. Of the 19 million Hispanic children in the US, over six million reside in such communities.[46] This means that more than 40 percent of black children and 30 percent of Hispanic children live in a high-poverty neighborhood, compared to just under 12 percent of both white and Asian children.

An even more lopsided distribution is found at higher levels of neigh-borhood poverty. Only 3 percent of white and Asian children call a concentrated-poverty neighborhood home, compared to 13 percent of Hispanic children and 21 percent of black children and Native American children. At the most extreme end of neighborhood disadvantage, only one out of every 100 white or Asian children reside in neighborhoods where the poverty rate reaches 40 percent or higher, compared to one in 20 Hispanic children and one in 11 black children.[47]

If anything, these point-in-time figures understate the extent and per-sistence of place-based racial disparities. Patrick Sharkey's research finds that two-thirds of black children born from 1985 to 2000 spent their childhood in a neighborhood where the poverty rate was 20 percent or higher. The same was true of only 6 percent of white children. More-over, this gap was nearly identical to the one separating white and black children born between 1955 and 1970. Once again, this research finds that the consequences of concentrated poverty are staggering for social mobility: Spending childhood in a neighborhood with a poverty rate of 20–30 percent comes with a 52 percent higher likelihood of downward mobility, compared with being raised in an area where the poverty rate is lower than 10 percent.[48]

Massive differences in spatial disadvantage exist across racial and eth-nic divides even when confining the sample to poor children. One exhaus-tive study of children's exposure to various types of neighborhoods in the 100 largest metropolitan areas finds that fully two-thirds of poor black children and half of poor Hispanic children live in very low-opportunity neighborhoods, compared with only one-fifth of poor white children.[49] Meanwhile, a vanishingly small share of poor black children—merely one in 50—live in very high-opportunity neighborhoods, compared to more than one in eight poor white and Asian children. In fact, black children in general, regardless of their level of affluence, are only half as likely as *poor* white children to call a very high-opportunity neighborhood home.

Stark racial differences in childhood environments reverberate throughout the landscape of American life, reinforcing socioeconomic advantages and disadvantages for generation after generation.

The Return of Place-Based Policymaking

Mounting evidence of the importance of neighborhood effects and the growing severity of spatial inequality and its consequences has led to a sea change in thinking among prominent economists, who had long been skeptical of the idea that government should take an active role in revitalizing lagging areas of the country. There are no better bellwethers for the shift in conventional wisdom regarding "place-based" policy than economists Larry Summers and Edward L. Glaeser.

Research by Summers, Glaeser, and their Harvard colleague Benjamin Austin seeks to provide an affirmative rationale for place-based policies focused on boosting employment in hot spots of joblessness. They find that as the economic convergence of US regions has stalled, the share of prime-age men without work has seen a nearly threefold increase over the past 50 years, "generating a social problem that is disproportionately centered in the eastern parts of the American heartland."[50] To combat the challenges caused by spatially concentrated joblessness, they propose a work subsidy in the form of a modified version of the earned income tax credit that boosts its generosity in depressed labor markets, arguing that public spending to counter unemployment will go furthest in areas with high rates of joblessness.

The shift among leading economists regarding not just the wisdom but also the urgency of pursuing place-based policy could hardly be starker. Summers, for his part, sees spatial inequality as a driving force behind the rise of populist nationalism and anti-internationalism and believes there is "probably no issue more important for the political economy of the next 15 years" than addressing the social and economic dislocation of left-behind areas.[51] Lawmakers seem to agree, with Republicans and Democrats alike rallying behind major place-based policy initiatives during the Trump and Biden administrations in succession.

Key Pillars of a Place-Based Opportunity Agenda

The challenges described throughout this chapter call for a place-based opportunity agenda focused on reducing the share of children growing up in high-poverty areas. Such an agenda should focus on both improving the residential mobility of young families to opportunity-rich areas and promoting greater private and public investment in disadvantaged communities. Policymakers have many options at their disposal for pursuing these goals.

Improve and Standardize the Targeting of Federal Resources to High-Need Areas. The scale and quality of federal resources devoted to addressing the needs of impoverished communities are by no means commensurate with the challenge. But before Congress commits greater levels of funding, it should first ensure that existing resources are being properly targeted to the intended areas. Today, federal targeting is often disjointed and woefully incomplete, excluding millions of Americans from programs intended to help their communities.

For example, several federal programs administered by the Departments of Agriculture, Commerce, and Treasury are required to follow the "10-20-30" persistent poverty formula, by which 10 percent of funding must go to counties in which at least 20 percent of the population has been below the poverty line for at least 30 years. Research by Fikri and Benzow finds that the 10-20-30 formula excludes a whopping 40 percent of the true population living in persistently high-poverty communities, a difference of roughly 15 million people, including a large area of Houston, Texas, that is home to 500,000 residents and an area of central Los Angeles with a population of over one million.[52]

Promote Greater Experimentation. Despite a growing wealth of empirical evidence pointing to the importance of neighborhood effects and the persistent challenge of high-poverty areas, the US has relatively few concrete examples of successful place-based policies aimed at improving neighborhood conditions and mobility to high-opportunity areas for young families. We desperately need more evidence on what types of interventions work best—and where and how best to implement them. A place-centric opportunity agenda should involve a heavy dose of experimentation to translate the social science into new and innovative pilot programs, the best of which could then be scaled into a new generation of best-in-class national efforts.[53]

The need and capacity for experimentation are not limited to the federal level. States like California, Florida, and Texas have recently been awash in multibillion-dollar budget surpluses—more than enough to fund an array of research-informed initiatives to boost social mobility and spur economic revitalization in struggling neighborhoods.

Deregulate Housing Policy to Increase National Prosperity and Improve Access to High-Opportunity Areas. The intensity of land-use regulations has grown markedly since the 1970s,[54] imposing limits on every imaginable aspect of what can be built on residentially zoned land. As a result, detached single-family homes are the *only legal building option* in a large majority of residential areas in many US cities.[55] As discussed earlier, the aggregate effect of this regulatory explosion has been to shape American life in profoundly negative ways, making the US economy weaker and less dynamic and blocking access to opportunity for low-income Americans. Conservatives should recognize this for what it is: an egregious intrusion of government on the rights of property owners and an interference in the healthy functioning of the housing market.

Many cities are pursuing long-overdue housing reforms, and some already have significant results to show for it. In 2018, Minneapolis, Minnesota, moved to boost residential density by ending single-family zoning. Fast-forward to 2023, and, thanks in part to increased housing supply and restrained price increases, Minneapolis–Saint Paul became the first major metropolitan area in the country to drive inflation below the Federal Reserve's 2 percent target rate.[56]

Beyond the fundamentally important role of states and municipalities, well-designed federal incentives to adopt streamlined zoning and building codes could be a powerful tool in overcoming local hesitation to deregulate land-use rules and offsetting the potential costs of greater density.

Boost Depressed Labor Markets and Improve Returns to Work. Wherever we find concentrated poverty, we also find concentrated joblessness. Less than 2 percent of full-time, year-round workers were in poverty in 2021, compared to 30 percent of people who did not work at all.[57]

There are multiple ideas for boosting employment in distressed areas and among low-wage and marginally attached workers, including the expanded earned income tax credit proposal by Glaeser and Summers and federal wage subsidy and state-based block grant proposals. Conservative populist Oren Cass has argued that a wage subsidy—essentially a reverse payroll tax by which the federal government boosts the pay of low-income workers toward a certain target wage—would be a boon to depressed *communities* in addition to individual workers: "Rather than rely on people not working to attract dollars from Washington, the community's workers become its engine of prosperity—and all jobs within the community can be ones that generate resources."[58]

Proponents of a wage subsidy also believe it would be an effective way of offsetting the wage penalty that noncollege workers now face in cities, thereby making it easier for them to move to high-income, high-productivity areas in search of opportunity. Economist Tim Bartik of the Upjohn Institute has argued that policies targeting distressed neighborhoods (census tracts) should be coupled with ones targeting distressed labor markets (commuting zones).[59] Furthermore, Bartik favors a state-based approach as a means of encouraging greater experimentation in place-based policies and solutions designed to meet unique local conditions without the political obstacles inherent to federal legislation. To this end, he proposes two programs: a "Local Job Creation" block grant and a "Neighborhood Employment Opportunities" block grant. Each approach merits careful consideration, though each comes with its own limitations and implementation challenges.

Promote Productive, Long-Term Private Investment in Disadvantaged Areas. Any serious effort to expand the scope of economic opportunity must include policies that encourage private investment in high-poverty, disinvested communities. The US has launched several programs over the years at the state and federal levels to do just that, but they have a mixed track record.[60]

One of the few major place-based federal initiatives in recent memory is the Opportunity Zones (OZ) tax incentive passed as part of the 2017 tax reform package. The OZ model was a sharp departure from previous place-based investment incentives, eschewing the use of tax credits in favor of deferring, reducing, and eliminating the capital gains tax liability associated with long-term investments in low-income, high-poverty areas chosen by states nationwide. The OZ incentive is markedly more flexible and decentralized than are typical federal initiatives, requiring no mediation or preapproval of investments from federal agencies.

The most comprehensive studies to date on the scope and effects of the OZ incentive find highly promising results in terms of new development, business establishments, and employment activity in designated areas. According to IRS data, nearly $50 billion in private investment occurred across roughly 4,000 OZ communities by the end of 2020, less than three years after the designation of those communities, making the OZ incentive by far the largest and farthest-reaching policy of its kind in US history.

Examining 40 large cities, researcher Harrison Wheeler finds that merely being designated as an OZ led to a 20 percent jump in the likelihood of residential and commercial development activity in a given tract with no observed increase in rents.[61] Another study finds a jump in employment in designated OZ communities driven by an increase in business establishments, with the largest effects in neighborhoods with higher shares of non-white residents.[62] Crucially, rather than simply poaching activity from surrounding areas, the OZ incentive delivered positive spillovers to neighboring communities—a key measure of success for any place-based policy—in the form of increased development activity and employment.

While these results suggest the policy has achieved unprecedented scale and effects for a private investment incentive, that bar is relatively low.[63] A much larger tool kit is needed to attack the underlying challenge of community disinvestment at scale. The early success of the nimble and decentralized OZ incentive model suggests that it holds crucial lessons for future policy initiatives targeted to distressed areas.

Promote Residential Mobility for Poor Families. The promising results of research on mobility experiments like the MTO initiative have yet to make their way into policy interventions at a national scale. This is a shame, because MTO-style interventions informed by the best research on what works would be relatively cheap and easy to design and would deliver sizable benefits.

First, and most obviously, relocation vouchers should be designed to encourage families to move to low-poverty areas by linking the generosity of the assistance to the conditions of the target destination. Families willing to move to very high-opportunity areas should see the greatest benefit. This is not the case today, as most recipients of housing vouchers do not use them to relocate to significantly better areas.[64]

Second, since we know that early childhood is the crucial window for influencing long-term outcomes, families with young children—or expecting a new child—should be given top priority for assistance and counseling on what options are available to them. Local experiments in providing location counseling and additional services have generated extremely promising results. In Seattle and King County, Washington, such services increased the share of families moving to high-opportunity neighborhoods by 40 percentage points, suggesting that personal preferences and discriminatory practices alone are not responsible for residential segregation and that relatively small interventions can significantly enhance the impact of housing assistance programs.[65]

Third, the amount of support should scale with the number of young children per family. Encouragingly, the benefits of the MTO program—in terms of the estimated increase in a child's future earnings and tax revenue—appear to have far outweighed the cost to taxpayers.[66]

Conclusion

When it comes to achieving the American Dream, it matters a great deal where you live and whom you know as a child. Children, however, have little say in choosing the neighborhoods—or, by extension, the social networks—that will pave the way for a lifetime of success or struggle. Much more must be done to tackle the country's yawning spatial divides in economic well-being so that far fewer American children are hobbled with the lifetime disadvantages that come from growing up in a high-poverty, low-opportunity neighborhood. A place-based opportunity agenda can play a meaningful role in leveling the playing field.

Notes

1. For the purposes of this chapter, "high-poverty neighborhoods" refers to places where the poverty rate is 20 percent or higher, and "concentrated-poverty neighborhoods" refers to places where the poverty rate reaches or exceeds 30 percent.

2. Eric Chyn and Lawrence F. Katz, "Neighborhoods Matter: Assessing the Evidence for Place Effects," *Journal of Economic Perspectives* 35, no. 4 (Fall 2021): 197–222, https://pubs.aeaweb.org/doi/pdfplus/10.1257/jep.35.4.197.

3. August Benzow and Kenan Fikri, *The Expanded Geography of High-Poverty Neighborhoods*, Economic Innovation Group, May 2020, https://eig.org/wp-content/uploads/2020/04/Expanded-Geography-High-Poverty-Neighborhoods.pdf.

4. Kyle Crowder and Scott J. South, "Spatial and Temporal Dimensions of Neighborhood Effects on High School Graduation," *Social Science Research* 40, no. 1 (January 30, 2011): 87–106, https://pubmed.ncbi.nlm.nih.gov/21180398.

5. Mengying Li et al., "Perceived Neighborhood Quality, Family Processes, and Trajectories of Child and Adolescent Externalizing Behaviors in the United States," *Social Science and Medicine* 192 (November 2017): 152–61, https://www.sciencedirect.com/science/article/abs/pii/S0277953617304604.

6. Geoffrey T. Wodtke, Sagi Ramaj, and Jared Schachner, "Toxic Neighborhoods: The Effects of Concentrated Poverty and Environmental Lead Contamination on Early Childhood Development," *Demography* 59, no. 4 (August 2022): 1275–98, https://read.dukeupress.edu/demography/article/59/4/1275/314006/Toxic-Neighborhoods-The-Effects-of-Concentrated.

7. US Department of Agriculture, Economic Research Service, Food Access Research Atlas, 2015, https://www.ers.usda.gov/data-products/food-access-research-atlas/download-the-data.

8. National Bureau of Economic Research, "Moving to Opportunity," https://www.nber.org/programs-projects/projects-and-centers/moving-opportunity.

9. Raj Chetty, Nathaniel Hendren, and Lawrence F. Katz, "The Effects of Exposure to Better Neighborhoods on Children: New Evidence from the Moving to Opportunity Experiment," *American Economic Review* 106, no. 4 (2016): 855–902, https://pubs.aeaweb.org/doi/pdfplus/10.1257/aer.20150572.

10. Raj Chetty and Nathaniel Hendren, "The Impacts of Neighborhoods on Intergenerational Mobility I: Childhood Exposure Effects," *Quarterly Journal of Economics* 133, no. 3 (August 2018): 1107–62, https://academic.oup.com/qje/article/133/3/1107/4850660.

11. Chetty and Hendren, "The Impacts of Neighborhoods on Intergenerational Mobility I."

12. David Leonhardt, Amanda Cox, and Claire Cain Miller, "An Atlas of Upward Mobility Shows Paths out of Poverty," *New York Times*, May 4, 2015, https://www.

nytimes.com/2015/05/04/upshot/an-atlas-of-upward-mobility-shows-paths-out-of-poverty.html.

13. Chetty, Hendren, and Katz, "The Effects of Exposure to Better Neighborhoods on Children." Importantly, neighborhood effects appear to be stronger for boys than for girls. See Raj Chetty et al., "Childhood Environment and Gender Gaps in Adulthood," *American Economic Review Papers and Proceedings* 106, no. 5 (January 2016): 282–88, https://www.researchgate.net/publication/302973222_Childhood_Environment_and_Gender_Gaps_in_Adulthood.

14. Patrick Sharkey and Bryan Graham, *Mobility and the Metropolis: How Communities Factor into Economic Mobility*, Pew Charitable Trusts, December 2013, https://www.pewtrusts.org/-/media/legacy/uploadedfiles/pcs_assets/2013/mobilityandthemetropolispdf.pdf.

15. Chetty and Hendren, "The Impacts of Neighborhoods on Intergenerational Mobility I."

16. Lawrence F. Katz, Jeffrey R. Kling, and Jeffrey B. Liebman, "Moving to Opportunity in Boston: Early Results of a Randomized Mobility Experiment," *Quarterly Journal of Economics* 116, no. 2 (2001): 607–54, https://www.jstor.org/stable/2696474; Jeffrey R. Kling, Jeffrey B. Liebman, and Lawrence F. Katz, "Experimental Analysis of Neighborhood Effects," *Econometrica* 75, no. 1 (January 2007): 83–119, https://scholar.harvard.edu/lkatz/publications/experimental-analysis-neighborhood-effects; Susan Clampet-Lundquist and Douglas F. Massey, "Neighborhood Effects on Economic Self-Sufficiency: A Reconsideration of the Moving to Opportunity Experiment," *American Journal of Sociology* 114, no. 1 (July 2008): 107–43; and Jens Ludwig et al., "Long-Term Neighborhood Effects on Low-Income Families: Evidence from Moving to Opportunity," *American Economic Review Papers and Proceedings* 103, no. 3 (May 2013): 226–31, https://www.aeaweb.org/articles?id=10.1257/aer.103.3.226.

17. Raj Chetty et al., "Social Capital I: Measurement and Associations with Economic Mobility," *Nature* 608, no. 7921 (August 2022): 108–21, https://www.nature.com/articles/s41586-022-04996-4.

18. Richard V. Reeves and Coura Fall, "Seven Key Takeaways from Chetty's New Research on Friendship and Economic Mobility," Brookings Institution, August 2, 2022, https://www.brookings.edu/articles/7-key-takeaways-from-chettys-new-research-on-friendship-and-economic-mobility.

19. Chetty et al., "Social Capital I," 108.

20. Federal Reserve Bank of St. Louis, "Real Gross Domestic Product," October 26, 2023, https://fred.stlouisfed.org/series/GDPC1.

21. Federal Reserve Bank of St. Louis, "Real Median Family Income in the United States," September 12, 2023, https://fred.stlouisfed.org/series/MEFAINUSA672N.

22. Benzow and Fikri, *The Expanded Geography of High-Poverty Neighborhoods*. The authors use census tracts as the unit of measurement in their analysis.

23. August Benzow and Kenan Fikri, *The Persistence of Neighborhood Poverty: Examining the Power of Inertia and the Rarity of Neighborhood Turnaround Across U.S. Cities*, Economic Innovation Group, May 2020, https://eig.org/wp-content/uploads/2020/04/Persistence-of-Neighborhood-Poverty.pdf.

24. August Benzow et al., *The Spaces Between Us: The Evolution of American Communities in the New Century*, Economic Innovation Group, October 2020, https://eig.org/wp-content/uploads/2020/10/EIG-2020-DCI-Report.pdf.

25. Ryan Nunn, Jana Parsons, and Jay Shambaugh, "The Geography of Prosperity," in *Place-Based Policies for Shared Economic Growth*, ed. Jay Shambaugh and Ryan Nunn (Washington, DC: Brookings Institution, 2018), 11–42, https://www.brookings.edu/wp-content/uploads/2018/09/THP_PBP_web_4.pdf.

26. Benzow and Fikri, *The Persistence of Neighborhood Poverty*.

27. Economic Innovation Group, *The New Map of Economic Growth and Recovery*, May 2016, https://eig.org/wp-content/uploads/2016/05/recoverygrowthreport.pdf.

28. Benzow et al., *The Spaces Between Us*.

29. Economic Innovation Group, "Distressed Communities: Key Findings," 2022, https://eig.org/distressed-communities/key-findings.

30. Olivier Jean Blanchard and Lawrence F. Katz, "Regional Evolutions," *Brookings Papers on Economic Activity* 1 (1992), https://scholar.harvard.edu/files/lkatz/files/regional_evolutions.pdf.

31. Robert J. Barro and Xavier Sala-i-Martin, "Convergence Across States and Regions," *Brookings Papers on Economic Activity* 1 (1991), https://www.brookings.edu/wp-content/uploads/1991/01/1991a_bpea_barro_salaimartin_blanchard_hall.pdf.

32. Peter Ganong and Daniel Shoag, "Why Has Regional Income Convergence in the U.S. Declined?," *Journal of Urban Economics* 102 (November 2017): 76–90, https://www.sciencedirect.com/science/article/abs/pii/S0094119017300591.

33. US Census Bureau, "Table A-1. Annual Geographic Mobility Rates, by Type of Movement: 1948–2022," August 2023, https://www.census.gov/data/tables/time-series/demo/geographic-mobility/historic.html.

34. Ganong and Shoag, "Why Has Regional Income Convergence in the U.S. Declined?"; and Adam Ozimek, Kenan Fikri, and John W. Lettieri, *From Managing Decline to Building the Future: Could a Heartland Visa Help Struggling Regions?*, Economic Innovation Group, April 2019, https://eig.org/wp-content/uploads/2019/04/Heartland-Visas-Report.pdf.

35. Philip G. Hoxie, Daniel Shoag, and Stan Veuger, "Moving to Density: Half a Century of Housing Costs and Wage Premia from Queens to King Salmon" (working paper, American Enterprise Institute, Washington, DC, April 9, 2023), https://www.aei.org/research-products/working-paper/moving-to-density-half-a-century-of-housing-costs-and-wage-premia-from-queens-to-king-salmon.

36. From 1979 to 2019, the official poverty rate fell only 1.2 percentage points, but a more consistently measured poverty rate based on a more comprehensive income measure declined nearly 20 points. Were such a measure available at the neighborhood level, it would show a smaller increase in "poor" neighborhoods over time than the figures in this chapter. But a major reason more comprehensive and consistent measures indicate lower poverty is that they count various noncash government benefits and refundable tax credits as income. In other words, if the number of "high-poverty" neighborhoods grew by less than the official poverty measure used here indicates, it would be, in no small measure, because additional government assistance kept many neighborhoods from having higher poverty rates. Government assistance alleviates

material hardship among families and neighborhoods, but it does not necessarily diminish the myriad problems associated with geographically concentrated poverty. It may even create new problems associated with dependency and perverse incentives. For the alternative poverty measure, see Richard V. Burkhauser et al., "Evaluating the Success of the War on Poverty Since 1963 Using an Absolute Full-Income Poverty Measure," *Journal of Political Economy* 132, no. 1 (January 2024), https://www.journals. uchicago.edu/doi/10.1086/725705.

37. Ganong and Shoag, "Why Has Regional Income Convergence in the U.S. Declined?"

38. John Iceland and Erik Hernandez, "Understanding Trends in Concentrated Poverty: 1980–2014," *Social Science Research* 62 (February 2017): 75–95, https://pubmed.ncbi. nlm.nih.gov/28126115.

39. Craig Benson, Alemayehu Bishaw, and Brian Glassman, "Persistent Poverty in Counties and Census Tracts," US Census Bureau, May 2023, https://www.census.gov/ content/dam/Census/library/publications/2023/acs/acs-51%20persistent%20poverty. pdf.

40. Benzow and Fikri, *The Expanded Geography of High-Poverty Neighborhoods*.

41. Nicholas Buttrick and Shegehiro Oishi, "The Cultural Dynamics of Declining Residential Mobility," *American Psychologist* 76, no. 6 (September 2021): 904–16, https:// pubmed.ncbi.nlm.nih.gov/34914429.

42. Chang-Tai Hsieh and Enrico Moretti, "Housing Constraints and Spatial Misallocation," *American Economic Journal: Macroeconomics* 11, no. 2 (2019): 1–39, https://eml. berkeley.edu//~moretti/growth.pdf.

43. Annie E. Casey Foundation, "Children Living in High-Poverty Areas in United States," January 2023, https://datacenter.aecf.org/data/tables/6795-children-living-in-high-poverty-areas#detailed/1/any/false/2454,2026,1983,1692,1691,1607,880,11/ any/13891,13892.

44. Annie E. Casey Foundation, "Children Living in High-Poverty Areas in United States."

45. Annie E. Casey Foundation, "Children Living in High-Poverty Areas in United States." For additional data on the variation of distressed communities across states, see also Economic Innovation Group, "Distressed Communities Index," https://www. eig.org/dci; and Alemayehu Bishaw et al., "Changes in Poverty Rates and Poverty Areas over Time: 2005 to 2019," US Census Bureau, December 2020, https://www. census.gov/content/dam/Census/library/publications/2020/acs/acsbr20-008.pdf.

46. All figures were taken from the author's analysis of US Census Bureau, American Community Survey, 2018–2022 5-Year Estimates, December 7, 2023, Tables B01001B, B01001C, B01001D, B01001H, and B01001I, https://data.census.gov/table?q=acs.

47. US Census Bureau, American Community Survey, 2018–2022 5-Year Estimates.

48. Patrick Sharkey, *Neighborhoods and the Black-White Mobility Gap*, Pew Charitable Trust, July 2009, https://www.pewtrusts.org/~/media/legacy/uploadedfiles/ wwwpewtrustsorg/reports/economic_mobility/pewsharkeyv12pdf.pdf.

49. Delores Acevedo-Garcia et al., "Racial and Ethnic Inequities in Children's Neighborhoods: Evidence from the New Child Opportunity Index 2.0," *Health*

Affairs 39, no. 10 (October 2020): 1693–701, https://www.healthaffairs.org/doi/10.1377/hlthaff.2020.00735.

50. Benjamin Austin, Edward Glaeser, and Lawrence H. Summers, "Saving the Heartland: Place-Based Policies in 21st Century America," *Brookings Papers on Economic Activity* (March 8, 2018): 151–255, https://www.brookings.edu/articles/saving-the-heartland-place-based-policies-in-21st-century-america.

51. Lawrence H. Summers, "Has the Time for Place-Based Policies Finally Arrived? A Panel Discussion" (panel discussion, Federal Reserve Bank of Boston, Boston, MA, October 4, 2019), https://www.bostonfed.org/housedivided2019/agenda.

52. August Benzow et al., *Advancing Economic Development in Persistent-Poverty Communities*, Economic Innovation Group, 2023, https://eig.org/wp-content/uploads/2023/06/EIG-Persistent-Poverty-Report.pdf.

53. Jonathan Rothwell, "Sociology's Revenge: Moving to Opportunity (MTO) Revisited," Brookings Institution, May 6, 2023, https://www.brookings.edu/articles/sociologys-revenge-moving-to-opportunity-mto-revisited.

54. Ganong and Shoag, "Why Has Regional Income Convergence in the U.S. Declined?"

55. Emily Badger and Quoctrung Bui, "Cities Start to Question an American Ideal: A House with a Yard on Every Lot," *New York Times*, June 18, 2019, https://www.nytimes.com/interactive/2019/06/18/upshot/cities-across-america-question-single-family-zoning.html.

56. US Department of Labor, Bureau of Labor Statistics, "Regional Resources," https://www.bls.gov/cpi/regional-resources.htm.

57. John Creamer et al., *Poverty in the United States: 2021*, US Census Bureau, September 2022, https://www.census.gov/content/dam/Census/library/publications/2022/demo/p60-277.pdf.

58. Oren Cass, "An Anti-Poverty Program Even Conservatives Can Love: Why Subsidizing Wages Is the Best Way to Help Lower-Income Americans—and Their Communities," *Politico*, November 20, 2018, https://www.politico.com/agenda/story/2018/11/20/wage-subsidies-low-income-americans-000788.

59. Timothy J. Bartik, "How State Governments Can Target Job Opportunities to Distressed Places," W. E. Upjohn Institute for Employment Research, June 15, 2022, https://research.upjohn.org/up_technicalreports/44.

60. David Neumark and Helen Simpson, "Place-Based Policies" (working paper, National Bureau of Economic Research, Cambridge, MA, April 2014), https://www.nber.org/system/files/working_papers/w20049/w20049.pdf.

61. Harrison Wheeler, "Locally Optimal Place-Based Policies: Evidence from Opportunity Zones," November 2022, https://hbwheeler.github.io/files/JMP_HW.pdf.

62. Alina Arefeva et al., "The Effect of Capital Gains Taxes on Business Creation and Employment: The Case of Opportunity Zones," Social Science Research Network, July 4, 2023, https://papers.ssrn.com/sol3/papers.cfm?abstract_id=3645507.

63. Kenan Fikri, August Benzow, and John W. Lettieri, "Examining the Latest Multi-Year Evidence on the Scale and Effects of Opportunity Zones Investment," Economic Innovation Group, 2023, https://eig.org/wp-content/uploads/2023/03/Examining-the-Latest-Multi-Year-Evidence-on-Opportunity-Zones-Investment.pdf.

64. Robert Collinson and Peter Ganong, "How Do Changes in Housing Voucher Design Affect Rent and Neighborhood Quality?," *American Economic Journal: Economic Policy* 10, no. 2 (May 2018): 62–89, https://www.aeaweb.org/articles?id=10.1257/pol.20150176.

65. Opportunity Insights, "Reducing Segregation and Increasing Upward Mobility in American Cities, One Housing Voucher at a Time," August 4, 2019, https://opportunity-insights.org/updates/cmto.

66. Chetty, Hendren, and Katz, "The Effects of Exposure to Better Neighborhoods on Children."

7

Kids and Community Violence: Costs, Consequences, and Solutions

JOSHUA CRAWFORD

On Saturday, December 1, 2018, gunshots rang out in the Smoketown neighborhood in Louisville, Kentucky. From a vehicle outside, assailants sprayed three townhomes with AK-47 rounds. Unfortunately, that night wasn't an anomaly. In 2018 alone, 355 Louisville residents were shot non-fatally.[1] Thankfully, on the night of December 1, no one was hit.

Inside one of those three townhomes were the daughter and four young grandchildren of community activist Christopher 2X, who has been a mainstay in Louisville for almost 25 years, promoting peace in some of the city's toughest neighborhoods. He helps families navigate life after violence comes to their doorstep, and he helps children avoid the poor decisions that can lead to a life unfulfilled. 2X himself hasn't always followed the straight and narrow; in 2020, he was pardoned by President Donald Trump for a decades-old drug charge.

The families 2X works with could be discussed in many of the chapters in this book: They come from disadvantaged neighborhoods, have low educational attainment, and lack educational options and opportunities. The children also often live in single-parent homes. But the thing that brings each of these families into 2X's orbit is their shared experience of neighborhood or street violence. The families fall into a few categories: parents whose children have been murdered; children, sometimes as young as elementary school students, who find themselves on the path to gang membership and a violent lifestyle; and young kids who find themselves surrounded by—but not directly implicated in—violence.

An estimated 3.5 million kids in the US live in neighborhoods identified as "unsafe" by their parents.[2] These children's lives are cut short, fundamentally altered, or otherwise worsened by exposure to this violence.

Government at all levels should therefore protect public safety and preserve public order—not only as a necessary function for its own sake but also as a necessary precondition for prosperity.

Why Focus More on Public Safety and Public Order?

Walk into any suburban coffee shop in a low-crime neighborhood and look around. You'll quickly notice the tables are populated by tens of thousands of dollars' worth of laptops and smartphones, and designer purses sit on the floor. These items often go unguarded when patrons pick up their coffees or go to the bathroom. It's the normal course of business in these establishments. No one fears these items will be stolen. There is an unconscious presupposition of public safety. This is what happens when the public order is upheld.

When this presumption of safety falls apart, however, people change their behavior. Following the expansion of remote work during the coronavirus pandemic, workers in New York City cited violence and crime as the primary reasons for not wanting to return to the office.[3] Research on crime avoidance also finds that households will pay a premium to avoid violence. One 2011 study of families in the San Francisco Bay Area in California found that the average household was willing to pay $472 per year to avoid a 10 percent increase in violent crime.[4]

The United States has had varying degrees of success in public safety over the years.[5] In the modern context, violent crime peaked in the United States in 1991 with 758.1 instances per 100,000 people, an increase of more than 470 percent from 1960. Homicide, the most destructive and permanent of the violent offenses, peaked in 1980 with a rate of 10.2 per 100,000 residents and in 1991 with a rate of 9.8 per 100,000 residents; in 1960, the murder rate had been almost half that at 5.1 per 100,000 residents.

After 1991, as a result of a number of changes in policing and sentencing and a wide array of other hotly debated factors, homicide and violent crime declined significantly in cities across the country (Figures 1 and 2). This decline continued until 2014, when the homicide rate reached 4.4 per 100,000 and the violent-crime rate was 379.4 per 100,000. While this was

Figure 1. US Homicide Rate per 100,000 People, 1960–2022

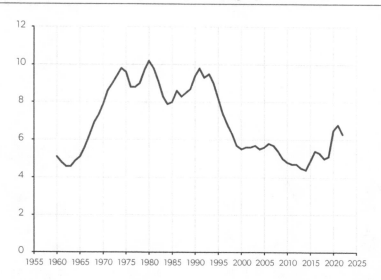

Source: Nathan James, *Recent Violent Crime Trends in the United States*, Congressional Research Service, June 20, 2018, https://sgp.fas.org/crs/misc/R45236.pdf; and Federal Bureau of Investigation, Crime Data Explorer, https://cde.ucr.cjis.gov/LATEST/webapp/#/pages/explorer/crime/crime-trend.

a huge improvement from the highs of 1991, the violent-crime rate in 2014 was still more than double the rate in 1960. It has trended in the wrong direction in recent years, with a jump in homicides in 2020.[6]

While the long-run decline in crime is important, it is ultimately not too reassuring because no one lives in "the nation." Aggregated data erase important variations from state to state, city to city, and neighborhood to neighborhood. People live in communities, not the whole nation.

Despite these declines in violent crime often being disproportionately experienced in disadvantaged neighborhoods,[7] violence continues to concentrate at the sub-city level. One study of gun violence in Boston, Massachusetts, for example, found that these crimes were concentrated in less than 5 percent of one-block street segments and intersections.[8] The "law of crime concentration" generally states that in large cities, about 50 percent of crime occurs in about 5 percent of street segments.[9] Crime

Figure 2. US Violent-Crime Rate per 100,000 People, 1960–2022

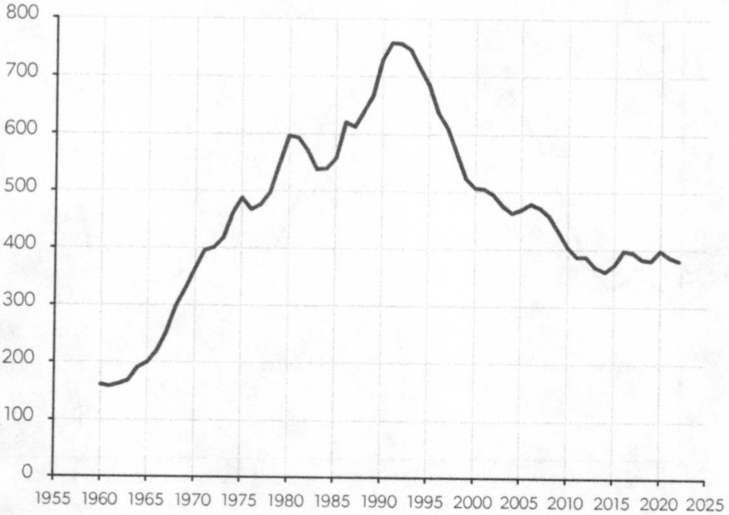

Source: Nathan James, *Recent Violent Crime Trends in the United States*, Congressional Research Service, June 20, 2018, https://sgp.fas.org/crs/misc/R45236.pdf; and Federal Bureau of Investigation, Crime Data Explorer, https://cde.ucr.cjis.gov/LATEST/webapp/#/pages/explorer/crime/crime-trend.

is even more concentrated in smaller cities, where, on average, between 2 percent and 4 percent of street segments are responsible for 50 percent of violence.[10] These micro-communities lack the minimum levels of safety and order that are precursors for human flourishing, and the effects of their violence propagate beyond these few hot zones.

　　Philosopher and political theorist James Burnham observed:

> Human beings must have at least a minimum security in life and property, must be able to move through the streets and between the cities, must accept certain common rules in their mutual intercourse, or civilization does not exist. If this necessary order is subverted, the civilization is destroyed, whether the subversion takes place from the best or worst of motives, whether or not it is in some supposedly moral sense

justified, whether it is carried out by saints or devils. At some point the guardians of a civilization must be prepared to draw the line.[11]

For far too many children, this kind of order has been inconsistent at best and nonexistent at worst. For children in these neighborhoods, violence is pervasive and affects them both directly and indirectly. Those directly affected are the youth who join criminal street gangs and become perpetrators, as well as those who are either victimized themselves or kin to victims. Those indirectly affected are those who neither become perpetrators nor victims but who contend with the persistent fear, stress, and isolation that come with growing up in a community with high rates of violence.

The Directly Affected

The degrading of public order directly affects crime victims, their immediate families, and the offenders themselves. In fact, many offenders are previous victims themselves. This is the group most obviously influenced by changes to public safety in a neighborhood and most likely to be seen on the evening news related to a crime.

The Victims. On May 21, 2017, 7-year-old Dequante Hobbs Jr. was sitting at his kitchen table, eating a piece of cake and reading on his tablet. Across the street, a dice game was taking place behind an abandoned building. A dispute broke out, and a bullet flew through the window of Dequante's home, striking him. As he screamed out in pain, his mother, Micheshia Norment, ran to the kitchen to find her son crawling on the floor into the hallway. There was blood everywhere. Micheshia tried to perform CPR, but her son threw up in her mouth. She spit it out and kept going. He died several hours later at a children's hospital in Louisville.

The following day, 2X received a call from Dequante's great-aunt. He had already been working with her because her two teenage grandsons, Dequante's cousins, were murdered earlier that year. The family would have to deal with the violent loss of yet another child.

Dequante's death rocked Louisville, not just because of his innocence but because his murder was hardly anomalous. In 2021 alone, 123 children under age 18 were shot in Louisville; 24 of them died. But Louisville isn't an anomaly either. Some of the cases garner national headlines, like 8-year-old Secoriea Turner in Atlanta, Georgia, and 4-year-old Mychal Moultry Jr. in Chicago. From 1980 to 2008, 10 percent of all homicide victims in the United States were children under age 18.[12]

Homicides of young people are pervasive enough to reduce the life expectancy of entire city populations. In Los Angeles County, California, homicide reduced life expectancy by 0.4 years for all residents and by 2.1 years for black males from 2001 to 2006.[13] The impact on life expectancy was even higher in low-income neighborhoods. In some low-income urban neighborhoods, homicide was estimated to decrease the life expectancy of black males by nearly five years.[14] Nationwide, the decline in homicides from 1991 to 2014 is credited with a 10-month increase in black male life expectancy and a 17 percent reduction in the life expectancy gap between white and black males.[15]

It has also long been understood that violent-crime victimization, especially homicide victimization, has ripple effects in families and other close networks. Each homicide leaves behind, on average, seven to 10 close family members, friends, neighbors, or other associates.[16] These individuals, often referred to as "co-victims," are left to deal with the funeral, law enforcement, and court proceedings, all while trying to process loss and grieve.

For the victims and co-victims, the emotional and physical costs of violence are obvious, but violence has significant financial costs as well. A number of studies have attempted to calculate the total cost that a homicide exacts on its victims, the surrounding community, and society at large. Two separate studies found the total cost of a homicide to the victim and society was just under $9 million in 2008 and 2010 dollars, respectively.[17] This number considers both tangible and intangible costs including direct victim costs, criminal justice costs, opportunity costs associated with the offender's decision to engage in criminal behavior, and the loss of productivity and earning potential from a lost life.

Some researchers, however, have found a much larger cost associated with murder. Matt DeLisi, a professor of criminal justice and sociology, found that the average cost of a homicide exceeded $17.25 million per instance.[18] The study used a sample of 654 convicted and incarcerated murderers and found that the most prolific and violent of these individuals cost victims and society upward of $150 million each.[19]

Violence is costly. For the victims it affects, it is life ending or life altering, but they are not the only group affected.

The Offenders. In fall 2021, teachers and administrators at Engelhard Elementary School asked 2X to meet with a group of young boys who displayed troubling behaviors.

He spoke to an 8-year-old first. The child expressed his desire to go to Chicago because he could make something of himself there—not in business or family but on the street. He assured 2X that it would be OK if he died in Chicago because that would be "better than dying in Louisville."

A 9-year-old told 2X he was a member of the Bloods. While the notorious gang is best known for its activities in Los Angeles, there are gangs in cities all over the country that claim the "Blood" name with varying degrees of affiliation with the Los Angeles gangs. The 9-year-old wore this status like a badge of honor. In his mind, his future was certain: He was a Blood, which meant whatever the Bloods did, he would do. Their issues were his issues.

2X spent time with each boy, trying to explain to them the benefits of a more productive life path. The boys weren't immediately convinced, but 2X will keep working with them as he has with so many others.

For kids in neighborhoods with high levels of violence, learning how to navigate life comes with some unique challenges not faced by kids in neighborhoods with low levels of crime. One of the most difficult is how to navigate gang membership.

Youth gang members typically range in age from 12 to 24,[20] but some as young as 5 find themselves recruited into gangs.[21] Kids join gangs for a variety of reasons: perceived economic benefit, reputation and prestige, and a desire for structure.[22] One of the most widely cited reasons youth join gangs, though, is for protection.[23]

Unfortunately, this calculation ends up being misguided. Far from providing safety, gang membership significantly increases the likelihood of victimization. Gang-affiliated youth are nearly 50 percent more likely to be victimized compared to youth who aren't affiliated with gangs.[24] Gang members are three times as likely as those unaffiliated to be victims of robbery and nearly five times more likely to be victims of aggravated assault.[25]

Gang members also criminally offend at higher rates relative to their unaffiliated counterparts.[26] According to the National Gang Intelligence Center, in 2011, gangs were responsible for 48 percent of violent crime in most states and upward of 90 percent of violence in some states.[27] Gang members are also more likely than unaffiliated at-risk youth to commit acts of serious violence, such as drive-by shootings and homicides. A comparison of gang-affiliated youth with unaffiliated at-risk youth in Cleveland, Ohio, found that 40 percent of the gang members had participated in a drive-by shooting, while only 2 percent of the unaffiliated at-risk cohort had.[28] That study also found that 64 percent of gang members surveyed in Colorado and Florida said that members of their gang had committed homicide, while only 6–7 percent of unaffiliated at-risk youth in those states said that their friends had done so.[29]

For those who become gang members or otherwise violent offenders, criminal conviction becomes likely, and lifetime career earnings decrease considerably. Convicted felons who do not serve jail time see an average decrease in lifetime wages of 22 percent.[30] For convicted felons who do serve time in prison, lifetime earnings fall by 52 percent.[31] High rates of offending in communities with high rates of violence lead to high rates of incarceration. Communities with high rates of parent-aged men cycling in and out of prison have weaker informal social controls and weaker social networks.[32]

Decreased earnings keep communities with high rates of violence poorer, while weaker social bonds inhibit efforts to reduce violence. This keeps these communities more socially isolated and continues the cycle of violent offending and victimization.

The Indirectly Affected

For every victim or offender in these communities, there are dozens of people who are not directly involved in the violence. Their actual interaction with the violence varies in degree, from general fear to the kinds of turmoil that 2X's daughter and grandchildren endured.

Heaven, 2X's 26-year-old daughter, says she remembers that day in 2018 like it was yesterday. She first heard a series of loud bangs. Those bangs quickly sounded closer. Ironically, or perhaps as fate would have it, Heaven had recently completed training for an active shooting at work. Instinctively, she grabbed her kids, and they all lay flat on the floor as bullets ripped into their home.

She and the kids stayed on the floor until they heard police sirens. Slowly, they got up and saw the damage done to their home. They gradually made their way outside, as did their neighbors. Thankfully no one was hit, but that moment instantly changed Heaven's perception of her surroundings.

She'll tell you she felt less safe after the trauma of that day. Why did this come to her door? Why her? Why the kids? She found herself sitting up in bed late at night, knowing they weren't safe. If it happened once, it could happen again. How do you move on knowing it could happen again?

She sought professional help for herself and her kids. Her oldest son, who had never had behavioral problems in school before, began acting out. Her other children had night terrors and had to leave their neighborhood entirely when they wanted to play outside. They, too, no longer felt safe in their immediate surroundings.

Fortunately, Heaven and her children have a strong support system and have been able to navigate the trauma of that day. Thankfully, because of that same support system, they were able to move out of their home temporarily. Many are not so fortunate.

Fear, Isolation, Attitudes, and Academic Performance. Violence need not come as close to home as it did for Heaven and her children to make residents in these communities regularly fear for their safety. Central to James Q. Wilson and George L. Kelling's "broken windows" thesis was the idea that neighborhood violence and disorder create fear.[33] That fear leads to changes in behavior and weakens informal social controls in neighborhoods. This in turn produces more crime.

Perception of neighborhood disorder is strongly associated with fear of crime.[34] Black Americans are also significantly more fearful of crime than white Americans are.[35] This may help explain the results of a Gallup poll taken in summer 2020, in the midst of civil unrest and social movements to "defund the police": 81 percent of black respondents said they wanted the same amount of or a greater police presence in their neighborhoods.[36] Twenty percent said they wanted police to spend more time in their neighborhood, compared to 17 percent of white respondents.

Living in a neighborhood with high rates of violence can also lead to increased social isolation. In 2018, a team of researchers conducted in-person interviews with 504 adults in Chicago's South Side and West Side communities.[37] They found that "prior exposure to community violence was associated with a 3.3-point reduction (on a 100-point scale) in the frequency of interaction with network confidantes, a 7.3-point reduction in perceived social support from friends, and a 7.8-point increase in loneliness."[38] Social isolation can also result in adverse health effects ranging from cognitive decline to depression.

This exposure to community violence can have immediate deleterious effects on kids in terms of behavior and academic performance. An examination of an ethnically diverse sample of 4,458 children living in urban Chicago neighborhoods found that exposure to community violence had a significant effect on increasing aggressive behaviors and normative beliefs about aggression in first through sixth graders.[39]

Separately, exposure to community violence has been found to impede a child's academic performance. Exposure to community violence at age 5 is negatively associated with academic performance at age 9.[40] In fact, that negative association is far greater than the negative association between academic performance and having experienced physical abuse.[41] This impact is also swift. Living in the immediate vicinity of a homicide lowers standardized reading and vocabulary scores within a matter of days.[42]

Exposure to high rates of community violence leads to higher levels of fear in residents, increased social isolation among those residents, and poorer behavioral and academic outcomes in children. But community violence also leaves neighborhoods poorer and hinders opportunities for economic advancement for those within them.

Economic Opportunity and Poverty in "High Crime" Neighborhoods.
It is well-known that high rates of poverty and violence coincide in many neighborhoods in US cities. There is a robust, diverse body of literature examining the impact that high rates of poverty can have on community violence and crime more broadly.[43] What is sometimes less appreciated, though robustly documented, is the negative effect that community violence can have on upward mobility, business growth and employment, and property values in neighborhoods.

Community violence contributes to keeping our poorest residents poor. One study found that the level of violent crime in a county impedes the level of upward economic mobility among individuals raised in families at the 25th percentile of the income distribution.[44] Importantly, those authors found that a decline in violent crime experienced during age 14–17 increases a teen's expected income rank in adulthood. The inverse was also true. Increased exposure to violent crime in the teenage years was associated with a reduction in expected income rank in adulthood.

This decline in economic mobility among residents in communities with higher rates of violence may be due in part to the negative impact community violence has on private business. "Surges" in violence have been negatively associated with business activity, resulting in downsizing and discouraging new business from entering the marketplace.[45]

One large analysis looked at the impact of gun violence on the economic health of neighborhoods in six cities: Baton Rouge, Louisiana; Minneapolis, Minnesota; Oakland, California; Rochester, New York; San Francisco, California; and Washington, DC.[46] The findings were remarkably consistent. An increase in gun violence in a census tract reduced the growth rate of new retail and service establishments by 4 percent in Minneapolis, Oakland, San Francisco, and Washington, DC.[47] In Minneapolis, each additional gun homicide in a census tract in a given year was associated with 80 fewer jobs the next year; in Oakland, a gun homicide was associated with 10 fewer jobs the next year.[48]

That same analysis found that increases in gun violence hurt property values. Each additional gun homicide resulted in a $22,000 decrease in average home values in Minneapolis census tracts and a $24,621 decrease in Oakland census tracts.[49] This is consistent with other research findings:

Increases in violent crime in a neighborhood in a given year result in decreases in property values in that neighborhood the following year.[50]

Taken together, elevated levels of violent crime in a neighborhood reduce economic opportunities by harming private businesses and reducing home values. This leads to continued poverty and less economic mobility among young adults. These data suggest that reducing violent crime in neighborhoods not only will improve social outcomes for children in terms of aggression and academic achievement; it also is a necessary precondition to sustainable poverty alleviation in the most dangerous neighborhoods in American cities.

Righting the Ship

In the United States, the protection of public safety and the preservation of public order are largely the responsibility of local police departments enforcing state laws. That means that many solutions to the problem of community violence will come from state and local governments. However, the federal government has an important role to play.

Thankfully, there is a straightforward way to improve public safety and restore public order in cities. For as long as there have been cities, there has been community violence, and through trial, error, and evaluation, we have a good sense of what works and what doesn't. By focusing resources—criminal justice and otherwise—on problem actors and places with high crime, cities can meaningfully reduce street violence and improve the environments in which millions of children grow up. Doing so requires both the financial resources and the political will to do the right thing by constituencies that hold little political power, but it would mean safer neighborhoods, more prosperous communities, and better social and economic outcomes for disadvantaged kids.

Policing. Police are the element of the criminal justice system most visible to the public and the arm with which citizens are most likely to interact. As criminologist Gary Potter put it, "The American system of criminal justice is predicated on an assumption of effective policing. After all, in order to deter criminals and punish the evil-doers you have to catch them."[51]

This is more than theoretical. Research on policing and crime has repeatedly found that having more well-managed police officers leads to less crime. A 2018 study looked at police and crime data from 1960 through 2010 and concluded that every dollar spent on policing generates about $1.63 in social benefits, mostly through reductions in homicides.[52] An examination of data from 122 cities around the US from 1975 to 1995 found that increased police numbers brought down violent crime by 12 percent.[53] In the midst of efforts to "defund the police," it behooves local policymakers to adequately fund their police departments.

Local policymakers shouldn't have to do this alone, though. Since the 1990s, there have been two major injections of federal dollars into local policing.

On September 13, 1994, President Bill Clinton signed the Violent Crime Control and Law Enforcement Act,[54] which—along with many other provisions—established the Office of Community Oriented Policing Services (COPS) inside the Department of Justice. The aim of this provision of the law was to infuse federal dollars into state and local policing with the goal of hiring 100,000 new officers. It authorized $8.8 billion in spending between 1994 and 2000.

The funding of new officers was distributed through the new Community Oriented Policing Services Universal Hiring Program (CHP), which covered 75 percent of the cost of each new police hire. These CHP grants typically lasted for three years. CHP funding exceeded $1 billion from 1995 through 1999 but dropped considerably in the early 2000s. Less than $200 million was allocated for the program in both 2003 and 2004, and less than $20 million was allocated in each year from 2005 to 2008.

In the wake of the 2008 recession, President Barack Obama signed the American Recovery and Reinvestment Act,[55] which increased funding for the COPS hiring program, bringing it back up to $1 billion. This increase is often referred to as COPS 2.0. The COPS grants awarded between fiscal years 2009 and 2011 covered 100 percent of the hiring costs of new officers rather than the previous 75 percent.

Both programs have been extensively evaluated, and those evaluations have routinely found meaningful reductions in violence and other crimes. A 2007 study evaluating the first injection of COPS money in more than 2,000 cities with populations greater than 10,000 found that additional police hired with COPS funding resulted in statistically significant reductions in aggravated assaults, robberies, burglaries, and auto thefts.[56] Additionally, a 2019 study analyzing COPS 2.0 found that departments that received COPS grant money saw a 3.2 percent increase in police staffing and a 3.5 percent reduction in crime as compared to similar departments that did not receive the grant money.[57]

Simply increasing the number of police would be a step in a positive direction, but strategy matters; what those police do can be the difference between moderate and significant reductions in violence. The gold standard of policing strategies for meaningfully reducing violence is focused deterrence policing, sometimes known as Group Violence Intervention. Pioneered in Boston in the 1990s, focused deterrence strategies rely first and foremost on the assumption that violence is concentrated among a small group of active offenders and, second, that those offenders' undesirable behaviors can be deterred, not just prosecuted and punished.[58] The strategy was the result of the efforts of the Boston Gun Project Working Group, a collaborative effort among law enforcement, academics, social service providers, and community partners.[59]

The group first set out to identify the most active and dangerous individuals and gangs operating in the city. Once it identified those groups and individuals, the working group delivered messages simultaneously warning of consequences if violent behaviors continued and expressing a desire to see these young men live. The organization provided resources to those who wanted to change their lifestyle, while law enforcement communicated a set of meaningful, predictable consequences for any groups that continued to engage in violence. After a homicide, those consequences were swiftly carried out.

The results were remarkable. Boston saw a 63 percent reduction in youth homicides, a 25 percent reduction in gun assaults, a 32 percent reduction in shots-fired calls for service, and a 44 percent reduction in youth gun assaults in one high-risk district.[60] The team then took the strategy to other cities.

As of 2011, more than 60 cities across the country have implemented some form of focused deterrence policing practices. While they have not been universally successful,[61] many evaluations found statistically significant reductions in gang-related violence in areas implementing the approach. A 2019 meta-analysis found that focused deterrence strategies are associated with a moderate reduction in crime.[62]

A focused deterrence strategy in Cincinnati, Ohio, resulted in a 37.7 percent reduction in group-member-involved homicide after 24 months and a 58.6 percent decline after 42 months—a 41.4 percent reduction three and a half years after implementation.[63] Similarly, in Indianapolis, Indiana, the 27-month post-intervention evaluation period of a focused deterrence strategy saw a 34 percent reduction in total homicides.[64] In Stockton, California, over a 65-month post-intervention period, there was a 42 percent reduction in gun homicide due to a focused deterrence strategy,[65] while in Lowell, Massachusetts, over the 39-month post-intervention period, there was a 44 percent reduction in gun assault incidents.[66]

Focused deterrence strategies have even been successful in reducing homicides in some of the nation's most violent environments. Over the 12-month evaluation period, a focused deterrence strategy in New Orleans, Louisiana, resulted in a 23 percent reduction in total homicides.[67]

Cities should work to adopt these strategies as swiftly and efficiently as they can. This is another area where federal dollars could be leveraged effectively. Federal grants to police departments can be structured to incentivize the adoption of these kinds of strategies by local law enforcement.

If cities can adequately fund policing and optimally allocate law enforcement resources, they can expect meaningful reductions in violence—reductions that would improve the opportunities for children and the lives of all community residents.

State Laws, Criminal Sentencing, and Federal Partnerships. Lowering crime reduces the need for punishment, but it is important that the small minority striking fear into their communities is held accountable. Holding criminals accountable will also further reduce crime. Most commonly, this means sentencing convicted criminals to sufficiently punitive, proportional prison terms. A 2004 study of the crime decline from 1991 to 2001 found that about a third of that decline resulted from increased prison populations.[68] This is because imprisonment plays two important roles in crime reduction: incapacitation and deterrence.

When criminals are removed from the streets, they are incapacitated and prevented from committing further crimes because they are in prison. Professor Alfred Blumstein observed that "incapacitation through imprisonment is probably the only effective means of restraining the violent crimes committed by some individuals otherwise out of social control."[69] Incapacitation in some cases has the additional benefit of criminals aging out of their prime crime-committing years while incarcerated, further reducing crime.

Doing so may directly benefit kids, too, even if their parent ends up incarcerated. While having an incarcerated parent is undoubtedly tough for a child, for certain populations, children of single mothers have lower dropout rates than children with a mother and a crime-committing father. For all populations, it appears children of single mothers do no worse than children who live with a mother and a crime-committing father.[70]

Equally important is the deterrent effect of criminal sanctions. Deterrence theory has its roots in the work of classical criminologist Cesare Beccaria,[71] who argued that individuals seek to maximize pleasure and minimize pain. Government policy that alters costs and benefits can change behavior. Several centuries later, economist Gary Becker would posit that crime was a rational act and forge the way for modern deterrence theory. He argued that criminals, like all humans, are rational, and crimes occur when the perceived benefits outweigh the perceived costs.[72] Those perceived costs are heightened if meaningful punishment is a real and perceived possibility.

But imprisonment comes with its own costs. The average cost to incarcerate an inmate in the United States for a year in 2015 was $33,274. In New York, the state with the highest annual per-inmate cost, it was $69,355.[73] There are also social costs to incarceration. As we have already observed, convicted felons who serve time in prison have significantly reduced lifetime earnings, and communities with high rates of parent-aged men who have served time have weaker social bonds and institutions.

These costs mean that prison sentences, especially long ones, ought to be reserved for the most problematic actors. In the context of community violence in American cities, this policy should focus on gangs through narrowly tailored "sentence enhancements"—enhanced punishments if certain specific conditions are met—and greater collaboration between local and federal law enforcement.

This approach does not mean criminalizing someone for being in a gang or excessively punishing someone who commits a crime simply because they are in a gang. Instead, these narrowly tailored policies specifically address gang-*motivated* crimes, such as retaliatory violence and disputes over turf, organized drug dealing, and in some cases human trafficking. As already noted, gang members disproportionately commit acts of violence and crimes generally. By focusing sentencing enhancement on gang-motivated activities, prison resources can more effectively be deployed where they are needed. Several sentence-enhancement structures have been evaluated and have been found to have deterred both a targeted population (prior felons) and specific types of offenses (gun-use crimes).[74] These enhancements can also be meaningfully used as a part of the focused deterrence policing strategies discussed earlier.

These laws should also clearly define what a criminal street gang is, and the definitions should be in line with federal ones. This consistency can allow greater collaboration among local, state, and federal law enforcement on gang-related suppression efforts. Federal law enforcement can be an essential partner in these kinds of joint efforts and provide needed tools like wiretaps. The existing Project Safe Neighborhoods program in the Department of Justice can be reworked to better foster such increased collaboration.

Built Environment and Physical Disorder. A city's built environment is its man-made environment: its buildings, streets, sidewalks, and open spaces. These features can be a point of great pride for a neighborhood, but they can also fall into disorder. Physical disorder includes a wide array of problems, such as abandoned and dilapidated properties, litter, graffiti, and inadequate street lighting. While this physical disorder can have significant "criminogenic"—or crime-promoting—effects in a neighborhood, restoring order can significantly reduce crime in those same neighborhoods without the deployment of law enforcement or corrections resources.

Unfortunately, abandoned buildings and vacant lots have become a regular part of urban life, especially in low-income communities. These properties can have a significant criminogenic impact on a neighborhood, especially when they are easily accessible. In Austin, Texas, a study found that blocks with open abandoned buildings had twice the crime rate of control blocks that did not have such buildings.[75] Researchers also found that 83 percent of abandoned buildings surveyed showed evidence of illegal use. Unkempt vacant lots likewise attract crime and reduce community perceptions of safety.[76]

Addressing these properties can reduce crime. Simply structurally shoring up these buildings can meaningfully influence serious offending. One study in Philadelphia, Pennsylvania, found that enforcement of a city code that required abandoned houses to have working windows and doors reduced assaults by 20 percent and firearm assaults by 39 percent.[77] Tearing down abandoned properties can also reduce crime in the surrounding area. In Detroit, Michigan, destroying five abandoned buildings in a block group reduced firearm assaults in the next 14 months by 11 percent.[78] Crucially, these studies did not find any evidence that firearm assaults were displaced to other locations.

Similar results have been found following efforts to "clean, green, and maintain" vacant lots. Another program in Philadelphia, run by the Pennsylvania Horticultural Society, cleans, greens, and maintains vacant lots. In a quasi-experimental analysis of those efforts from 1999 to 2008, researchers found that they resulted in a 10 percent reduction in total assaults and an 8 percent reduction in firearm assaults per square mile in the treated areas.[79]

Inadequate street lighting also increases community fear of crime. To most people, there is a basic relationship between crime and lighting: The better the lighting, the less crime.[80] With respect to urban disorder and crime, journalist Jane Jacobs theorized in her 1961 book, *The Death and Life of Great American Cities*:

> The value of bright streetlights for dispirited gray areas rises from the reassurance they offer to some people who need to go out on the sidewalk, or would like to, but lacking the good light would not do so. Thus, the lights induce these people to contribute their own eyes to the upkeep of the street. Moreover, as is obvious, good lighting augments every pair of eyes,

makes the eyes count for more because their range is greater. Each additional pair of eyes, and every increase in their range, is that much to the good for dull gray areas. But unless eyes are there, and unless in the brains behind those eyes is the almost unconscious reassurance of general street support in upholding civilization, lights can do no good.[81]

Additional lighting, according to Jacobs, not only provides needed light but—by making people feel safer—also contributes more feet on the pavement and eyes on the street, deterring crime.

Modern research suggests that Jacobs's assessment may be right. A randomized controlled trial of nearly 40 public housing developments in New York City was conducted in which half the developments received new lights while half did not. Before the experiment, all the housing developments had above-average levels of index crime: homicide, rape, robbery, burglary, aggravated assault, larceny over $50, motor vehicle theft, and arson. The study concluded that increased levels of lighting led to a "36% reduction in index crimes—including murder, robbery, and aggravated assault, as well as certain property crimes—that took place outdoors at night."[82]

By reducing physical disorder, policymakers can reduce both fear and violence in communities without having to expend additional criminal justice resources.

Victim Services. In 1981, President Ronald Reagan proclaimed the first National Crime Victims' Rights Week. In issuing his proclamation, Reagan said,

> We need a renewed emphasis on, and an enhanced sensitivity to, the rights of victims. These rights should be a central concern of those who participate in the criminal justice system, and it is time all of us paid greater heed to the plight of victims.[83]

The criminal justice system often overlooks the plight of crime victims, especially the surviving family members of homicide victims. Inadequate assistance to this population can lead to additional crime through retaliatory violence, as retaliatory violence is a common feature of gang life.[84] However, one does not need to be a member of a criminal street gang to experience the desire for revenge and retaliation.

The desire for justice and retribution for perceived injustice—not only the homicide or shooting but also the end result of a criminal investigation—can be a powerful driver in the desire for revenge. Researchers have noted that while "revenge does not undo the harm . . . it can restore the balance of suffering between the victim and the transgressor."[85] This is exacerbated, according to additional research, when the outcome of a criminal investigation is another perceived injustice to the survivor, as survivors often have a "fear that no rescuer can be trusted" when this happens.[86]

Simple policy changes can ease these fears and help prevent retaliatory violence. While one of the major policy victories of the victims' rights movement of the 1980s was the addition of victims' advocates to prosecutors' offices, this has turned out to be insufficient. The reason is that there must be an arrest made for a case to make it to a prosecutor's office. In 2020, the national clearance rate—that is, the percentage of cases that result in arrest—for murder was 54.4 percent.[87] This means nearly half of all murder victims' families would not have the opportunity to take advantage of victim services offered by a prosecutor's office. Placing these kinds of advocates and resources in police departments is a straightforward way to fix this problem and fill this gap.

Police-based victim services should be the cornerstone of any effort in this space, but other efforts—such as simply ensuring that victims have the right to be heard through victim-impact statements and that victims are kept informed as the case progresses—can make a difference. In addition, resources for victims displaced by violence occurring in or outside their home can provide much-needed stability for an already difficult healing process. Adequate support for violent-crime survivors can not only provide better outcomes for those families but also reduce violence.

Conclusion

The unfortunate truth is that too many children find themselves exposed to community violence, in fear for their safety, and in disordered neighborhoods. There are plenty of good reasons to want to reduce community violence, but in addition to reducing the pain and suffering that come with violent crime, ensuring a minimum level of public safety is a crucial precondition to prosperity.

Not only do children do worse behaviorally and academically in communities with high rates of violence, but elevated levels of crime also stifle business and reduce upward mobility in adulthood. The status quo is failing the children in these circumstances.

Fortunately, while not easy, restoring public order and improving public safety are straightforward. We know what works. It is now about having the courage and moral clarity to do it. By adequately funding law enforcement and getting the strategy right, and by building cases against the most serious offenders and putting them in prison to let the majority of the community thrive, we can address those criminals driving the violence. By improving the built environment of a community, we can reduce opportunities for serious offending and reduce fear in law-abiding citizens. And by improving the treatment of crime victims, we can help break the cycle of violence and improve police-community relations.

All of this would then mean less crime and healthier communities for kids to grow up in. For the 3.5 million children living in communities deemed unsafe by their own parents, it would mean opportunities they otherwise may never have and life trajectories shifted upward.

Notes

1. Marcus Green and Travis Ragsdale, "2020 in Louisville: Violent Crime Up, Property Crime Down," WDRB Media, October 1, 2020, https://www.wdrb.com/in-depth/2020-in-louisville-violent-crime-up-property-crime-down/article_c7a21294-e31f-11ea-8e6e-7bd4e8170138.html.

2. Annie E. Casey Foundation, Kids Count Data Center, Children Who Live in Unsafe Communities, May 2021, https://datacenter.kidscount.org/data/tables/9708-children-who-live-in-unsafe-communities?loc=1&loct=1#detailed/1/any/false/1696,1648,1603/any/18953,18954.

3. Jack Kelly, "Remote Workers Point to Violence, Crime and a Decrepit Mass Transit System as Reasons Not to Return to New York City Offices," *Forbes*, July 7, 2021, https://www.forbes.com/sites/jackkelly/2021/07/07/fear-of-violence-crime-homelessness-and-a-dirty-decrepit-mass-transit-system-may-cause-workers-to-stop-commuting-into-new-york-city.

4. Kelly C. Bishop and Alvin D. Murphy, "Estimating the Willingness to Pay to Avoid Violent Crime: A Dynamic Approach," *American Economic Review* 101, no. 3 (May 2011): 625–29, https://www.aeaweb.org/articles?id=10.1257/aer.101.3.625.

5. Barry Latzer, *The Rise and Fall of Violent Crime in America* (New York: Encounter Books, 2016).

6. Federal Bureau of Investigation, *Rate of Violent Crime Offenses by Population*, https://crime-data-explorer.fr.cloud.gov/pages/explorer/crime/crime-trend; and Nathan James, *Recent Violent Crime Trends in the United States*, Congressional Research Service, June 20, 2018, https://sgp.fas.org/crs/misc/R45236.pdf.

7. Michael Friedson and Patrick Sharkey, "Violence and Neighborhood Disadvantage After the Crime Decline," *ANNALS of the American Academy of Political and Social Science* 660, no. 1 (June 9, 2015): 341–58, https://journals.sagepub.com/doi/10.1177/0002716215579825.

8. Anthony A. Braga, Andrew V. Papachristos, and David M. Hureau, "The Concentration and Stability of Gun Violence at Micro Places in Boston, 1980–2008," *Journal of Quantitative Criminology* 26, no. 1 (December 31, 2009): 33–53, https://link.springer.com/article/10.1007/s10940-009-9082-x.

9. David Weisburd, "The Law of Crime Concentration and the Criminology of Place," *Criminology* 53, no. 2 (May 6, 2015): 133–57, https://onlinelibrary.wiley.com/doi/10.1111/1745-9125.12070.

10. Weisburd, "The Law of Crime Concentration and the Criminology of Place."

11. James Burnham, *Suicide of the West: An Essay on the Meaning and Destiny of Liberalism* (New York: Encounter Books, 2014).

12. Alexia Cooper and Erica L. Smith, "Homicide Trends in the United States, 1980–2008: Annual Rates for 2009 and 2010," US Department of Justice, Office of Justice Programs, Bureau of Justice Statistics, November 2011, https://bjs.ojp.gov/content/pub/pdf/htus8008.pdf.

13. Matthew Redelings, Loren Lieb, and Frank Sorvillo, "Years off Your Life? The Effects of Homicide on Life Expectancy by Neighborhood and Race/Ethnicity in Los Angeles County," *Journal of Urban Health* 87 (June 17, 2010): 670–76, https://link.springer.com/article/10.1007/s11524-010-9470-4.

14. Redelings, Lieb, and Sorvillo, "Years off Your Life?"

15. Patrick Sharkey and Michael Friedson, "The Impact of the Homicide Decline on Life Expectancy of African American Males," *Demography* 56, no. 2 (2019): 645–63, https://read.dukeupress.edu/demography/article-abstract/56/2/645/167974/The-Impact-of-the-Homicide-Decline-on-Life.

16. Lula M. Redmond, *Surviving: When Someone You Love Was Murdered: A Professional's Guide to Group Grief Therapy for Families and Friends of Murder Victims* (Psychological Consultation and Educational Services, 1989).

17. Kathryn E. McCollister, Michael T. French, and Hai Fang, "The Cost of Crime to Society: New Crime-Specific Estimates for Policy and Program Evaluation," *Drug and Alcohol Dependence* 108, nos. 1–2 (April 2010): 98–109, https://www.sciencedirect.com/science/article/abs/pii/S0376871609004220; and Paul Heaton, "Hidden in Plain Sight: What Cost-of-Crime Research Can Tell Us About Investing in Police," RAND Corporation, 2010, https://www.rand.org/pubs/occasional_papers/OP279.html.

18. Matt DeLisi et al., "Murder by Numbers: Monetary Costs Imposed by a Sample of Homicide Offenders," *Journal of Forensic Psychiatry & Psychology* 21, no. 4 (February 12, 2010): 501–13, https://www.tandfonline.com/doi/abs/10.1080/14789940903564388.

19. DeLisi et al., "Murder by Numbers."

20. James C. Howell, "Youth Gangs," US Department of Justice, Office of Justice Programs, Office of Juvenile Justice and Delinquency Prevention, December 1997, https://www.ojp.gov/pdffiles/fs-9772.pdf.

21. David C. Pyrooz and Gary Sweeten, "Gang Membership Between Ages 5 and 17 Years in the United States," *Journal of Adolescent Health* 56, no. 4 (February 11, 2015): 414–19, https://www.jahonline.org/article/S1054-139X(14)00756-3/fulltext.

22. Scott H. Decker and Barrik van Winkle, *Life in the Gang: Family, Friends, and Violence* (Cambridge, UK: Cambridge University Press, 1996).

23. Decker and van Winkle, *Life in the Gang.*

24. Dana Peterson, Terrance J. Taylor, and Finn-Aage Esbensen, "Gang Membership and Violent Victimization," *Justice Quarterly* 21, no. 4 (2004): 793–815, https://www.tandfonline.com/doi/abs/10.1080/07418820400095991.

25. Peterson, Taylor, and Esbensen, "Gang Membership and Violent Victimization."

26. Sara R. Battin et al., "The Contribution of Gang Membership to Delinquency Beyond Delinquent Friends," *Criminology* 36, no. 1 (February 1998): 93–116, https://onlinelibrary.wiley.com/doi/10.1111/j.1745-9125.1998.tb01241.x; and G. David Curry, "Self-Reported Gang Involvement and Officially Recorded Delinquency," *Criminology* 38, no. 4 (November 2000): 1253–74, https://onlinelibrary.wiley.com/doi/10.1111/j.1745-9125.2000.tb01422.x.

27. Federal Bureau of Investigation, "2011 National Gang Threat Assessment," 2011, https://www.fbi.gov/stats-services/publications/2011-national-gang-threat-assessment.

28. C. Ronald Huff, "Criminal Behavior of Gang Members and At-Risk Youths," US Department of Justice, Office of Justice Programs, National Institute of Justice, March 1998, https://www.ojp.gov/pdffiles/fs000190.pdf.

29. Huff, "Criminal Behavior of Gang Members and At-Risk Youths."

30. Terry-Ann Craigie, Ames Grawert, and Cameron Kimble, *Conviction, Imprisonment, and Lost Earnings: How Involvement with the Criminal Justice System Deepens Inequality,* New York University School of Law, Brennan Center for Justice, September 15, 2020, https://www.brennancenter.org/our-work/research-reports/conviction-imprisonment-and-lost-earnings-how-involvement-criminal.

31. Craigie, Grawert, and Kimble, *Conviction, Imprisonment, and Lost Earnings.*

32. Todd R. Clear, "The Effects of High Imprisonment Rates on Communities," *Crime and Justice* 37, no. 1 (2008): 97–132, https://www.journals.uchicago.edu/doi/10.1086/522360.

33. George L. Kelling and James Q. Wilson, "Broken Windows: The Police and Neighborhood Safety," *The Atlantic*, March 1982, https://www.theatlantic.com/magazine/archive/1982/03/broken-windows/304465.

34. Brittney K. Scarborough et al., "Assessing the Relationship Between Individual Characteristics, Neighborhood Context, and Fear of Crime," *Journal of Criminal Justice* 38, no. 4 (July–August 2010): 819–26, https://www.sciencedirect.com/science/article/abs/pii/S0047235210001224.

35. Scarborough et al., "Assessing the Relationship Between Individual Characteristics, Neighborhood Context, and Fear of Crime."

36. Lydia Saad, "Black Americans Want Police to Retain Local Presence," Gallup, August 5, 2020, https://news.gallup.com/poll/316571/black-americans-police-retain-local-presence.aspx.

37. Elizabeth L. Tung et al., "Social Isolation, Loneliness, and Violence Exposure in Urban Adults," *Health Affairs* 38, no. 10 (October 2019): 1670–78, https://www.healthaffairs.org/doi/10.1377/hlthaff.2019.00563.

38. Tung et al., "Social Isolation, Loneliness, and Violence Exposure in Urban Adults."

39. Nancy G. Guerra, L. Rowell Huesmann, and Anja Spindler, "Community Violence Exposure, Social Cognition, and Aggression Among Urban Elementary School Children," *Child Development* 74, no. 5 (October 2003): 1561–76, https://srcd.onlinelibrary.wiley.com/doi/10.1111/1467-8624.00623.

40. Samantha Schneider, "Associations Between Childhood Exposure to Community Violence, Child Maltreatment and School Outcomes," *Child Abuse & Neglect* 104 (June 2020): 104473, https://www.sciencedirect.com/science/article/abs/pii/S0145213420301289.

41. Schneider, "Associations Between Childhood Exposure to Community Violence, Child Maltreatment and School Outcomes."

42. Patrick Sharkey, "The Acute Effect of Local Homicides on Children's Cognitive Performance," *Proceedings of the National Academy of Sciences* 107, no. 26 (June 14, 2010): 11733–38, https://www.pnas.org/doi/full/10.1073/pnas.1000690107.

43. Ching-Chi Hsieh and M. D. Pugh, "Poverty, Income Inequality, and Violent Crime: A Meta-Analysis of Recent Aggregate Data Studies," *Criminal Justice Review* 18, no. 2 (September 1, 1993): 182–202, https://journals.sagepub.com/doi/10.1177/073401689301800203; and Morgan Kelly, "Inequality and Crime," *Review of Economics and Statistics* 82, no. 4 (November 2000): 530–39, https://direct.mit.edu/rest/article-abstract/82/4/530/57217/Inequality-and-Crime.

44. Patrick Sharkey and Gerard Torrats-Espinosa, "The Effect of Violent Crime on Economic Mobility," *Journal of Urban Economics* 102 (November 2017): 22–33, https://www.sciencedirect.com/science/article/abs/pii/S009411901730058X.

45. Robert T. Greenbaum and George E. Tita, "The Impact of Violence Surges on Neighbourhood Business Activity," *Urban Studies* 41, no. 13 (December 1, 2004): 2495–514, https://journals.sagepub.com/doi/10.1080/0042098042000294538.

46. Yasemin Irvin-Erickson et al., *A Neighborhood-Level Analysis of the Economic Impact of Gun Violence*, Urban Institute, June 2017, https://www.urban.org/research/publication/neighborhood-level-analysis-economic-impact-gun-violence. The authors

of this study looked specifically at gun violence and excluded non-gun assaults, murders, and so forth.

47. Irvin-Erickson et al., *A Neighborhood-Level Analysis of the Economic Impact of Gun Violence.*

48. Irvin-Erickson et al., *A Neighborhood-Level Analysis of the Economic Impact of Gun Violence.*

49. Irvin-Erickson et al., *A Neighborhood-Level Analysis of the Economic Impact of Gun Violence.*

50. John R. Hipp, George E. Tita, and Robert T. Greenbaum, "Drive-Bys and Trade-Ups: Examining the Directionality of the Crime and Residential Instability Relationship," *Social Forces* 87, no. 4 (June 2009): 1778–812, https://journals.sagepub.com/doi/10.1080/0042098042000294538.

51. Gary Potter, "The Police and Crime Control," Eastern Kentucky University Online, October 1, 2013, https://ekuonline.eku.edu/blog/police-studies/the-police-and-crime-control.

52. Aaron Chalfin and Justin McCrary, "Are U.S. Cities Underpoliced? Theory and Evidence," *Review of Economics and Statistics* 100, no. 1 (March 2018): 167–86, https://direct.mit.edu/rest/article-abstract/100/1/167/58429/Are-U-S-Cities-Underpoliced-Theory-and-Evidence.

53. Steven D. Levitt, "Understanding Why Crime Fell in the 1990s: Four Factors That Explain the Decline and Six That Do Not," *Journal of Economic Perspectives* 18, no. 1 (Winter 2004): 163–90, https://www.aeaweb.org/articles?id=10.1257/089533004773563485.

54. Violent Crime Control and Law Enforcement Act of 1994, 42 U.S.C. § 13701 (1994).

55. American Recovery and Reinvestment Act of 2009, 26 U.S.C. § 1 (2009).

56. William N. Evans and Emily G. Owens, "COPS and Crime," *Journal of Public Economics* 91, no. 1–2 (February 2007): 181–201, https://www.sciencedirect.com/science/article/abs/pii/S0047272706000831.

57. Steven Mello, "More COPS, Less Crime," *Journal of Public Economics* 172 (April 2019): 174–200, https://www.sciencedirect.com/science/article/abs/pii/S0047272718302305.

58. Anthony A. Braga et al., "Problem-Oriented Policing, Deterrence, and Youth Violence: An Evaluation of Boston's Operation Ceasefire," *Journal of Research in Crime and Delinquency* 38, no. 3 (August 1, 2001): 195–225, https://journals.sagepub.com/doi/10.1177/0022427801038003001.

59. David M. Kennedy, *Don't Shoot: One Man, a Street Fellowship, and the End of Violence in Inner-City America* (New York: Bloomsbury USA, 2011).

60. Braga et al., "Problem-Oriented Policing, Deterrence, and Youth Violence."

61. Kennedy, *Don't Shoot.*

62. Anthony A. Braga, David Weisburd, and Brandon Turchan, "Focused Deterrence Strategies Effects on Crime: A Systematic Review," *Campbell Systematic Reviews* 15, no. 3 (September 9, 2019), https://onlinelibrary.wiley.com/doi/10.1002/cl2.1051.

63. Robin S. Engel, Marie Skubak Tillyer, and Nicholas Corsaro, "Reducing Gang Violence Using Focused Deterrence: Evaluating the Cincinnati Initiative to Reduce

Violence (CIRV)," *Justice Quarterly* 30, no. 3 (2013): 403–39, https://www.tandfonline.com/doi/full/10.1080/07418825.2011.619559.

64. Nicholas Corsaro and Edmund F. McGarrell, "Reducing Homicide Risk in Indianapolis Between 1997 and 2000," *Journal of Urban Health* 87, no. 5 (August 20, 2010): 851–64, https://link.springer.com/article/10.1007/s11524-010-9459-z.

65. Anthony A. Braga, "Pulling Levers Focused Deterrence Strategies and the Prevention of Gun Homicide," *Journal of Criminal Justice* 36, no. 4 (August 2008): 332–43, https://www.sciencedirect.com/science/article/abs/pii/S004723520800069X.

66. Anthony A. Braga et al., "The Strategic Prevention of Gun Violence Among Gang-Involved Offenders," *Justice Quarterly* 25, no. 1 (March 19, 2008): 132–62, https://www.tandfonline.com/doi/abs/10.1080/07418820801954613.

67. Nicholas Corsaro and Robin S. Engel, "Most Challenging of Contexts," *Criminology & Public Policy* 14, no. 3 (August 2015): 471–505, https://onlinelibrary.wiley.com/doi/10.1111/1745-9133.12142.

68. Levitt, "Understanding Why Crime Fell in the 1990s."

69. Alfred Blumstein, "Prisons: A Policy Challenge," in *Crime: Public Policies for Crime Control*, ed. James Q. Wilson and Joan Petersilia (Washington, DC: ICS Press, 2002), 451–82.

70. Keith Finlay and David Neumark, "Is Marriage Always Good for Children? Evidence from Families Affected by Incarceration," *Journal of Human Resources* 45, no. 4 (Fall 2010): 1046–88, https://muse.jhu.edu/article/466916.

71. Cesare Beccaria and Voltaire, *An Essay on Crimes and Punishments* (Albany, NY: W. C. Little and Company, 1872), https://oll.libertyfund.org/title/voltaire-an-essay-on-crimes-and-punishments.

72. Gary S. Becker, "Crime and Punishment: An Economic Approach," *Journal of Political Economy* 76, no. 2 (March–April 1968): 169–217, https://www.journals.uchicago.edu/doi/10.1086/259394.

73. Chris Mai and Ram Subramanian, *The Price of Prisons: Examining State Spending Trends, 2010–2015*, May 2017, https://www.vera.org/publications/price-of-prisons-2015-state-spending-trends.

74. Daniel Kessler and Steven D. Levitt, "Using Sentence Enhancements to Distinguish Between Deterrence and Incapacitation," *Journal of Law and Economics* 42, no. S1 (April 1999): 343–64, https://www.jstor.org/stable/10.1086/467428; and David S. Abrams, "Estimating the Deterrent Effect of Incarceration Using Sentencing Enhancements," *American Economic Journal: Applied Economics* 4, no. 4 (October 2012): 32–56, https://www.aeaweb.org/articles?id=10.1257/app.4.4.32.

75. William Spelman, "Abandoned Buildings: Magnets for Crime?," *Journal of Criminal Justice* 21, no. 5 (1993): 481–95, https://www.sciencedirect.com/science/article/abs/pii/004723529390033J.

76. Eugenia Garvin et al., "More Than Just an Eyesore: Local Insights and Solutions on Vacant Land and Urban Health," *Journal of Urban Health* 90, no. 3 (November 28, 2012): 412–26, https://link.springer.com/article/10.1007/s11524-012-9782-7.

77. Michelle C. Kondo et al., "A Difference-in-Differences Study of the Effects of a New Abandoned Building Remediation Strategy on Safety," *PLoS ONE* 10, no. 8 (July 8, 2015): 1–14, https://journals.plos.org/plosone/article?id=10.1371/journal.pone.0129582.

78. Jonathan Jay et al., "Urban Building Demolitions, Firearm Violence and Drug Crime," *Journal of Behavioral Medicine* 42 (August 1, 2019): 626–34, https://link.springer.com/article/10.1007/s10865-019-00031-6.

79. Charles C. Branas et al., "A Difference-in-Differences Analysis of Health, Safety, and Greening Vacant Urban Space," *American Journal of Epidemiology* 174, no. 11 (December 1, 2011): 1296–306, https://academic.oup.com/aje/article/174/11/1296/111352.

80. Ronald V. Clarke, *Improving Street Lighting to Reduce Crime in Residential Areas*, US Department of Justice, Office of Community Oriented Policing Services, December 2008, https://cops.usdoj.gov/ric/Publications/cops-p156-pub.pdf.

81. Jane Jacobs, *The Death and Life of Great American Cities* (New York: Vintage Books, 1992).

82. Aaron Chalfin et al., *Reducing Crime Through Environmental Design: Evidence from a Randomized Experiment of Street Lighting in New York City*, Crime Lab New York, April 24, 2019, https://urbanlabs.uchicago.edu/attachments/e95d751f7d91d0bcfeb209ddf6adcb4296868c12/store/cca92342e666b1ffb1c15be63b484e9b9687b57249dce44ad55ea92b1ec0/lights_04242016.pdf.

83. Ronald Reagan, "Proclamation 4831—Victims Rights Weeks, 1981," Ronald Reagan Presidential Library and Museum, April 8, 1981, https://www.reaganlibrary.gov/archives/speech/proclamation-4831-victims-rights-weeks-1981.

84. Bruce A. Jacobs and Richard Wright, *Street Justice: Retaliation in the Criminal Underworld* (New York: Cambridge University Press, 2006).

85. Karina Schumann and Michael Ross, "The Benefits, Costs, and Paradox of Revenge," *Social and Personality Psychology Compass* 4, no. 12 (December 2010): 1193–205, https://compass.onlinelibrary.wiley.com/doi/abs/10.1111/j.1751-9004.2010.00322.x.

86. Mardi J. Horowitz, "Understanding and Ameliorating Revenge Fantasies in Psychotherapy," *American Journal of Psychiatry* 164, no. 1 (January 2007): 24–27, https://ajp.psychiatryonline.org/doi/10.1176/ajp.2007.164.1.24.

87. Statista Research Department, Crime Clearance Rate in the United States in 2020, by Type, September 29, 2021, https://www.statista.com/statistics/194213/crime-clearance-rate-by-type-in-the-us.

About the Authors

Beth Akers is a senior fellow at the American Enterprise Institute, where she focuses on the economics of higher education.

Preston Cooper is a senior fellow in higher education policy at the Foundation for Research on Equal Opportunity.

Joshua Crawford is the director of criminal justice initiatives at the Georgia Center for Opportunity.

Chester E. Finn Jr. is a distinguished senior fellow and president emeritus at the Thomas B. Fordham Institute and a Volker Senior Fellow at Stanford University's Hoover Institution.

Robert Lerman is an institute fellow at the Urban Institute and a professor emeritus of economics at American University.

John W. Lettieri is a cofounder of the Economic Innovation Group and serves as its president and CEO.

Yuval Levin is the director of Social, Cultural, and Constitutional Studies at the American Enterprise Institute, where he also holds the Beth and Ravenel Curry Chair in Public Policy. The founder and editor of *National Affairs*, he is also a senior editor at the *New Atlantis*, a contributing editor at *National Review*, and a contributing opinion writer at the *New York Times*.

Michael Q. McShane is an adjunct fellow in education policy studies at the American Enterprise Institute and director of national research at EdChoice.

Angela Rachidi is a senior fellow and Rowe Scholar in the Center on Opportunity and Social Mobility at the American Enterprise Institute, where she studies poverty and the effects of federal safety-net programs on low-income people in America.

Ryan Streeter is executive director of the Civitas Institute. Previously, he was the State Farm James Q. Wilson Scholar and director of Domestic Policy Studies at the American Enterprise Institute, where he facilitated research in education, technology, housing, urban policy, poverty studies, workforce development, and public opinion.

Matt Weidinger is a senior fellow and Rowe Scholar in the Center on Opportunity and Social Mobility at the American Enterprise Institute, where his work is focused on safety-net policies, including cash welfare, unemployment insurance, and related programs.

Brad Wilcox is a professor of sociology and director of the National Marriage Project at the University of Virginia and a nonresident senior fellow at the American Enterprise Institute.

Scott Winship is a senior fellow and the director of the Center on Opportunity and Social Mobility at the American Enterprise Institute, where he researches social mobility and the causes and effects of poverty. He also focuses on economic insecurity and inequality, among other poverty issues.

RESEARCH STAFF

SAMUEL J. ABRAMS
Nonresident Senior Fellow

BETH AKERS
Senior Fellow

J. JOEL ALICEA
Nonresident Fellow

JOSEPH ANTOS
Senior Fellow Emeritus

LEON ARON
Senior Fellow

KIRSTEN AXELSEN
Nonresident Fellow

JOHN BAILEY
Nonresident Senior Fellow

KYLE BALZER
Jeane Kirkpatrick Fellow

CLAUDE BARFIELD
Senior Fellow

MICHAEL BARONE
Senior Fellow Emeritus

MICHAEL BECKLEY
Nonresident Senior Fellow

ERIC J. BELASCO
Nonresident Senior Fellow

ANDREW G. BIGGS
Senior Fellow

MASON M. BISHOP
Nonresident Fellow

DAN BLUMENTHAL
Senior Fellow

KARLYN BOWMAN
*Distinguished Senior
Fellow Emeritus*

HAL BRANDS
Senior Fellow

ALEX BRILL
Senior Fellow

ARTHUR C. BROOKS
President Emeritus

RICHARD BURKHAUSER
Nonresident Senior Fellow

CLAY CALVERT
Nonresident Senior Fellow

JAMES C. CAPRETTA
Senior Fellow; Milton Friedman Chair

TIMOTHY P. CARNEY
Senior Fellow

AMITABH CHANDRA
Nonresident Fellow

LYNNE V. CHENEY
Distinguished Senior Fellow

JAMES W. COLEMAN
Nonresident Senior Fellow

ZACK COOPER
Senior Fellow

KEVIN CORINTH
*Senior Fellow; Deputy Director, Center
on Opportunity and Social Mobility*

JAY COST
*Gerald R. Ford Nonresident
Senior Fellow*

DANIEL A. COX
*Senior Fellow; Director, Survey
Center on American Life*

SADANAND DHUME
Senior Fellow

GISELLE DONNELLY
Senior Fellow

ROSS DOUTHAT
Nonresident Fellow

COLIN DUECK
Nonresident Senior Fellow

MACKENZIE EAGLEN
Senior Fellow

NICHOLAS EBERSTADT
*Henry Wendt Chair in
Political Economy*

MAX EDEN
Senior Fellow

JEFFREY EISENACH
Nonresident Senior Fellow

ANDREW FERGUSON
Nonresident Fellow

JESÚS FERNÁNDEZ-
VILLAVERDE
John H. Makin Visiting Scholar

JOHN G. FERRARI
Nonresident Senior Fellow

JOHN C. FORTIER
Senior Fellow

AARON FRIEDBERG
Nonresident Senior Fellow

JOSEPH B. FULLER
Nonresident Senior Fellow

SCOTT GANZ
Research Fellow

R. RICHARD GEDDES
Nonresident Senior Fellow

ROBERT P. GEORGE
Nonresident Senior Fellow

EDWARD L. GLAESER
Nonresident Senior Fellow

JOSEPH W. GLAUBER
Nonresident Senior Fellow

JONAH GOLDBERG
*Senior Fellow; Asness Chair
in Applied Liberty*

JACK LANDMAN GOLDSMITH
Nonresident Senior Fellow

BARRY K. GOODWIN
Nonresident Senior Fellow

SCOTT GOTTLIEB, MD
Senior Fellow

PHIL GRAMM
Nonresident Senior Fellow

WILLIAM C. GREENWALT
Nonresident Senior Fellow

JIM HARPER
Nonresident Senior Fellow

TODD HARRISON
Senior Fellow

WILLIAM HAUN
Nonresident Fellow

FREDERICK M. HESS
*Senior Fellow; Director,
Education Policy Studies*

CAROLE HOOVEN
Nonresident Senior Fellow

BRONWYN HOWELL
Nonresident Senior Fellow

R. GLENN HUBBARD
Nonresident Senior Fellow

HOWARD HUSOCK
Senior Fellow

DAVID HYMAN
Nonresident Senior Fellow

BENEDIC N. IPPOLITO
Senior Fellow

MARK JAMISON
Nonresident Senior Fellow

FREDERICK W. KAGAN
*Senior Fellow; Director,
Critical Threats Project*

STEVEN B. KAMIN
Senior Fellow

LEON R. KASS, MD
Senior Fellow Emeritus

JOSHUA T. KATZ
Senior Fellow

L. LYNNE KIESLING
Nonresident Senior Fellow

KLON KITCHEN
Nonresident Senior Fellow

KEVIN R. KOSAR
Senior Fellow

ROBERT KULICK
Visiting Fellow

PAUL H. KUPIEC
Senior Fellow